Painting a W... ... ... Fl...
...re, The ... of the Earth

Painting a Wall: 'A hard witty play ... will certainly soon be recognised as a major talent.' *Time Out*

Red Earth: 'This superbly-crafted piece fuses a history of South Africa with a marvellously textured story: Joshua, a black worker, decides to leave his job in the docks and seek his family in Transkei. Like the gold Joshua once mined, this play has been laboured over with much pain and despair but it is rare, strong and very beautiful.' *Time Out*

Flight: 'Touches on such engrossing issues as the opposition of one generation to its predecessor, the demands of blood ties and, above all, the great paradox of Jewishness: the geographical rootlessness and the unwavering solid cultural foundation.' *Financial Times*

Desire: 'The sensation of peering directly into Africa's heart; of seeing it lit for the first time with a shadowy enlightenment as the power of the spirit world hovers over the traumatic events in a Zimbabwean village after independence in 1980; of sensing the metaphors that are being conjured from the past to absolve the traumas of revolution; of guessing that the whole fantastic spectacle is an allegory for our own troubled times.' *Sunday Correspondent*

The Ends of the Earth: 'It hits at the heart of everything that concerns everybody. A wonderfully rich and complex play. Like a rough road through the mountains strewn with moral questions, it's very exhilarating. I really enjoyed the ride.' *Kaleidoscope*

David Lan was born in Cape Town where he trained as an actor before moving to London in 1972. Early plays include *Painting a Wall* (Almost Free Theatre, 1974), *Bird Child* (Theatre Upstairs, 1974), *The Winter Dancers* (Theatre Upstairs, 1977), *Red Earth* (ICA, 1978) and *Sergeant Ola* (Royal Court, 1979). In 1985 he published what is regarded as a classic of modern social anthropology *Guns and Rain: Guerrillas and Spirit Mediums in Zimbabwe*. He has written a number of prize-winning films for BBC TV set in various African countries including *The Sunday Judge* – Mozambique (1985), *Dark City* – South Africa (1990) and *Welcome Home Comrades* – Namibia (1990). Later plays include *Flight* (RSC, 1986), *A Mouthful of Birds* (with Caryl Churchill, Joint Stock/Royal Court, 1986), *Desire* (Almeida, 1990), *Charlie Tango* (BBC Radio, 1995) and *The Ends of the Earth* (Royal National Theatre, 1996). In 1995 and 1996 he was writer-in-residence at the Royal Court theatre. He has written opera libretti as well as English versions of plays by Euripides, Chekhov and Verga. He has produced and directed television documentaries and recently began to direct for the theatre.

DAVID LAN

Plays: 1

Painting a Wall
Red Earth
Flight
Desire
The Ends of the Earth

*introduced by Stephen Daldry
with a preface by the author*

Methuen Drama

METHUEN CONTEMPORARY DRAMATISTS

1 3 5 7 9 10 8 6 4 2

This collection first published in Great Britain in 1999
by Methuen Publishing Limited
215 Vauxhall Bridge Road, London SW1V 1EJ

Reribo (Fiji) Ltd, 58 Beaumont Road, Mount Kuring-Gai,
NSW 2080, Australia, ACN 002 273 761
(For Australia and New Zealand)

Painting a Wall first published in Great Britain in 1979,
by Pluto Press Ltd
Copyright © 1979 by David Lan
Red Earth first published in Great Britain in 1999, by Methuen Publishing Ltd
Copyright © 1999 by David Lan
Flight first published in Great Britain in 1987, by Methuen London Ltd
Copyright © 1987 by David Lan
Desire first published in Great Britain in 1990 by Faber and Faber
Copyright © 1990 by David Lan
The Ends of the Earth first published in Great Britain in 1996 by Faber and Faber
and revised in this edition, Copyright © 1996, 1999 by David Lan
This collection and Preface copyright © 1999 by David Lan
Introduction copyright © 1999 by Stephen Daldry

The right of David Lan to be identified as the author of this work has been asserted by
him in accordance with the Copyright, Designs and Patents Act, 1988

ISBN 0 413 73680 6

Methuen Publishing UK Limited Reg. No. 3543167

A CIP catalogue record for this book is available from the British Library

Typeset by Deltatype, Birkenhead, Merseyside
Printed and bound in Great Britain by
Cox & Wyman Ltd, Reading, Berkshire

Contents

David Lan
Chronology

Plays

1974   *Painting a Wall*, one-act, at the Almost Free Theatre.
        Bird Child at the Royal Court Theatre Upstairs.
1975   *Paradise* at the Royal Court Theatre Upstairs.
        Homage to Bean Soup, one-act, at the Royal Court
        Theatre Upstairs.
1977   *The Winter Dancers* at the Royal Court Theatre
        Upstairs.
1978   *Red Earth*, one-act, at the Institute of Contemporary
        Arts.
1979   *Sergeant Ola* at the Royal Court Theatre.
1986   *Flight* at the Royal Shakespeare Company.
        A Mouthful of Birds (with Caryl Churchill), Joint
        Stock Theatre Company and the Royal Court
        Theatre.
1990   *Desire* at the Almeida Theatre.
1995   *Charlie Tango*, BBC Radio 4 and World Service.
1996   *The Ends of the Earth* at the Royal National Theatre.

English versions

1989   *Ghetto*, by Joshua Sobol, at the Royal National
        Theatre.
1991   *Hippolytos*, by Euripides, at the Almeida Theatre.
1993/4 *Ion*, by Euripides, at the Royal National Theatre
        Studio, then at the Royal Shakespeare Company.
1995   *La Lupa*, by Giovanni Verga, at the Glasgow
        Citizens' Theatre.
1998   *Uncle Vanya*, by Anton Chekhov, at the Royal
        Shakespeare Company/Young Vic.

Television films

1985   *The Sunday Judge*, BBC Global Report.
1988   *The Crossing*, BBC Schools' TV.
1990   *Dark City*, BBC Screen One special.
        Welcome Home Comrades, BBC Under the Sun special.

Preface

'Why don't you write plays set in England?'

Well, I try. But whenever I do, the characters at once pack their bags and go abroad. I suppose it's because that's where I'm from.

Between the ages of fourteen and sixteen, I spent holidays from my school in Cape Town working in the paint shop of the local theatre. The scene painter would mark out the design and do all the difficult sections. A group of four or five 'coloured' men would fill in the broad expanses of horizon or mountain or tower block. I'd help them. I loved it. The smell of paint size is for me the smell of the theatre.

When I came to London aged twenty, I lived in Hammersmith by the river and had nothing to do except rifle through the collections of Marx and Freud belonging to George who lived upstairs. I wrote a play. Those paint shop assistants turned up in it. At once I planned a cycle of further plays: 'Walking a Tightrope' and 'Drinking a Glass Water'. *Painting a Wall* was the only one that got written.

Purely literary projects have never got anywhere. I spent a year or so writing a major work about Cecil Rhodes, It all ended up in the dustbin except for two minor characters who had materialized out of memories of the Cape Town docks: going to wave goodbye to friends sailing away on ocean liners and catching sight of dazzlingly strong and light-footed Zulu or Xhosa navvies loading or unloading treasure from, or destined for, foreign parts. After all the heavy-duty labour on my 'great work', *Red Earth* was scribbled out in three days.

The Rhodes play had another spin-off too. Some scenes concerned a family who travelled all over southern Africa in search of wealth and a place to put down roots. They were drawn in pretty broad strokes. Over a number of years, the strokes were refined and refined again. By the time I'd finished, I found I'd drawn on the particular history of my own family – grandparents from the Baltics, parents born in Africa, children scattered back to Europe and the USA.

The story was transposed to Rhodesia/Zimbabwe but it drew on my parents' generations' (to a child, only dimly understood) engagement with and/or resistance to the classic socialist activist politics of the 1950s and 60s. Add to this my own (as it turned out very brief) conscription into the South African Army and you get *Flight*.

Between 1980 and 1982 I lived in a tiny village in the Zambezi Valley studying the religious dimension to the guerrilla war that had been waged there over the previous fifteen years. The central events of *Desire* happened within shouting distance of my hut. Every day brought the basis for a novel, sometimes by Dostoevsky, sometimes by Mark Twain. I didn't consciously choose Rosemary's story to turn into a play but the process began in my head while I was still in the valley. It was ten years before it was finished and staged. It follows the actual events pretty closely. Even so, at the first run through of the first production, I was astonished – and embarrassed – to discover that I had written another more or less autobiographical play.

When I had set out for the Zambezi Valley for the first time, the guerrilla war was so recently over that no research council would agree to subsidise the work I wanted to do. I went on a recce to gather proof that it was safe for a post-graduate social anthropologist to live there in peace. Almost at once I was 'arrested' by a bunch of extremely disaffected ex-guerrillas (they were supporters of a party that had not done well in the recent elections), accused of being a spy and held under armed guard in a disused military camp. 'Radio the police,' I told them, 'they know who I am'. The answer came back: 'We've never heard of him'. It's hard, under such circumstances, not to spend one's days (only four, in the event) wondering: 'What on earth is my life all about?'

Years later, while working with a director in Paris, I was told a story, said to have happened on Mount Athos in Greece. A father takes his sick child to a wise man. Can he cure her? 'Who knows,' says the wise man, 'but I see you smoke rather a lot. Do you think you could give it up?' Moral and physical ambush came together. I wrote *The Ends of the Earth* and set it in 'the Balkans'.

A year later the war in Bosnia began. My play is not about that war. But it is about war, the war with oneself, out of which one can make life, death, beauty, silence, revenge and – another word for all these things – plays.

David Lan
January 1999

Thanks to Andrei Serban, Howard Davies, Tessa Marwick, John Burgess; actors; composers; designers, especially Richard Hudson; stage crews; Pedr James, Jonathan Kent, Ian McDiarmid, Richard Eyre, Trevor Nunn; Colin Chambers, Giles Croft; Peggy Butcher, Michael Earley, Walter Donahue and, above all, Nicholas Wright.

Introduction

The 1990s saw an explosion of new writing for the theatre. A new generation of young writers burst onto the stage with a force not witnessed for generations. Gone were the *Guardian* obituaries mourning the death of new writing. In their place, critics scrambled around trying, as always, to pigeon-hole a new wave of writers who deliberately eschewed the 'political' and 'sexual/gender' labels of the 1970s and 80s

Rather than holding back plays for months – or years – waiting for a 'slot' in the financially strapped Theatre Upstairs, we at the Royal Court experimented with producing seasons of short runs Upstairs or, more daringly, introducing young writers directly onto the main stage. It was a period of unbelievable productivity. At times we were opening a new play every ten days.

For two years David Lan, as our writer-in-residence, worked closely with many of these new playwrights. In our debates about which plays to programme, his counsel was pivotal. His commitment to the intense – and often arduous – process of working with young writers on successive drafts of their plays established new models. Many of the Court's successes in those years owe a debt of gratitude to his dramaturgical skills.

As a young writer having his own first plays performed in the Theatre Upstairs in the 1970s, David was never part of the dominant ethos which suggested that a playwright's responsibility was to depict and analyse contemporary life in, say, Brixton or Moss Side. Like many of our new generation, whom he embraced, his plays reach for a wider poetical/theatrical resonance. Rereading his early plays, I have often thought of the impact they would make were they to appear for the first time in today's theatrical landscape.

Painting a Wall, written when he was twenty-two, and *Red Earth*, written when he was twenty-six, are both set in his native South Africa. They are hugely effective, deeply emotional attacks on a political system. What is surprising about them is that they make their arguments in purely theatrical terms.

In the first, all that 'happens' is that a wall gets painted. In the time this takes, we learn a certain amount about the lives of the painters – their response to their economic and political exploitation, their frustrations and so on. But at the end of the play the wall has been painted. It is this brute fact – in effect, this theatrical trick – that gives the play its meaning and its power.

Red Earth expands this exploration of theatrical forms and points the way forward. Here the forces that prevent exploited people from resisting are presented as 'demons'. The unquiet spirit of one of the politicians historically responsible for apartheid has to be exorcised before the central character of the play can become free.

Unlike any other playwright of his time, David has written a good deal about religious experience. *Desire*, set in a village in Zimbabwe, is a unique and remarkable play not just because of its subject matter but also because, by means of some theatrical sleight-of-hand, the audience seems to experience the story directly as though we are members of the society from which the story comes. It seems to me to express a deep yearning for spiritual and political redemption. Watching or even reading it is a liberating experience

As in so many of the new plays of the 1990s, the key struggle of these characters is to understand and to take control of their lives. But none of the plays in this book are 'slice-of-life' naturalistic representations of human behaviour. In *Flight*, the past, the present and the distant past all seem to vie for space on the stage. It's an epic, I suppose partly autobiographical, play which is funny, revealing and moving. David's most recent work, *The Ends of the Earth*, takes his attempt to make the form of a play express its subject to its furthest extent. Its daring lies in the number of contradictory social (and theatrical) realities it places side by side. The crisis in the play, is the crisis in the country where it takes place, is the crisis in the central charcter's head. It's a shocking, almost-but-not-quite despairing, fable which contains the most emotionally passionate writing of any of these plays.

These five plays – perhaps half of David's output to date – utilise almost every aspect of modern theatrical language. Coming to them at the end of the 1990s, you'll be surprised by how fresh they seem to this age of dissonance. For the uninitiated, this volume offers an introduction to a writer whose time has come.

Stephen Daldry
Director, Royal Court Theatre, London 1999

Painting a Wall

for Tessa Marwick

Characters

Willy, *a painter*
Samson, *a painter*
Henry, *an old painter*
Peter, *a young painter*

Painting a Wall was first performed at the Almost Free Theatre by the Ambiance Lunch-Hour Theatre Club on 25 April 1974, with the following cast:

Willy	Saul Reichlin
Samson	Tony Osler
Henry	David Haynes
Peter	Grenville Ries

Directed by Tessa Marwick
Designed by Chris Speyer and Kathy Ukleja

The play takes place in a street in Cape Town, South Africa, in the 1970s.

All the characters in this play are so-called 'Coloured' people.

Glossary:
  Ja – yes
  Cherry – girlfriend
  Peop-all – generalized obscenity e.g. fart face
  Oukie – bloke
  Constantia – a wealthy suburb of Cape Town

Light on the wall. Sunlight. **Willy** *enters in a hurry. Sees no one is there. Lights a cigarette. Waits.*

Samson *enters. Then* **Peter**, *carrying a ladder.*

Willy   Where've you all been? It's late, man.

Samson   We got delayed. We was held up. Things happen.

Willy   Where's Henry?

Samson   Give us a chance, man.

Willy   A chance for what?

Samson   Ugh, man, we's only just got here and already you grabs every word I say like a mincing machine. Give us a chance. I'll tell you everything. Only give us the opportunity.

Willy   Well?

Samson   Henry's daughter died.

Willy   Henry's daughter? Died of what?

Samson   Of sickness.

Willy   What kind of sickness?

Samson   Ugh, man, for god's sake, I don't know. Sickness. Pains and aches. Things in the blood and bones. Sickness. You know what sickness is?

Willy   So Henry's not working today, then?

Samson   Yes, he's coming, but give him time. He's sad.

Willy   What's he sad for? No reason. Someone dies – forgetting time arrives.

Samson   It's easy to say when it's not your child what's gone. You don't even have none.

Willy   So they'll never make me sad.

Samson   You're a hard man, Willy.

Willy   A hard man in hard times, hey Peter?

Samson   Ugh what does he know from nothing? He never says a sentence.

Willy   Never?

Samson   I doesn't hear him speak. I doesn't know if he can even.

Willy   I've heard.

Samson   It's so fascinating you listen?

Willy   Talking isn't trouble to a dumb man at the right time. He's got no problem making his tongue jump when he wants his pay or food. His mother never sits nursing her ears in silence when he's at home, of that you can be sure for free. And he talks to his cherry, hey Peter? He talks to his cherry all right, not so?

Peter   Yes.

Willy   See? You hear? He talks. He's a human being like us.

Samson   Shit, it's almost quarter past nine. Time passes – we stand still. Peter, where's the utensils?

Peter *goes off to fetch the paint.*

Willy   You wants to start before Henry comes?

Samson   Ja man. One hour for the job or half pay. We's got to get going man. We's got the hurries.

Willy   You're so stupid as the wall itself. It's quicker to wait.

Samson   How come?

Willy   Simple arithmetic. Three men paint faster than two, right?

Samson   Ja.

Willy   Well, what we paint before Henry arrives we could paint faster if he was painting with us. So it's quicker to wait. Logical.

Samson Shit, Willy, your talk would fertilise a field. Peter can paint till Henry arrives. He'll only be a minute.

Willy What? No. Never. He's got to mix the paint and clean the brushes.

Samson This is a wall we're painting you know not a portrait of Jesus Christ and all the saviours.

Willy He doesn't paint. He's got first to learn the trade by observing professionals.

Samson I'm stupid but you bloody mad, man. There's no boss watching us.

Willy A mad man in mad times. He doesn't paint.

Henry *enters.*

Willy Here's Henry. Hullo Henry.

Samson Look, Henry, we's sorry to hear about your daughter. You doesn't have to work today if you doesn't want to. Peter can paint instead of you. They'll have to understand for once in their merry lives.

Willy You can't make decisions like that.

Henry No – working is – you know. It helps. I must work today. So much gone today – you know. I must make new things.

Willy (*not interrupting*) Ugh shit.

Henry The boy?

Samson He's fetching the paint.

Willy Ugh shit man, that's pure shit what he said. Let him go home.

Samson Willy, he's old man.

Willy Old shit.

Peter *comes back with a box containing paint, brushes, a spare overall, etc.*

Samson   Leave him. Come open the tins. They's all new ones.

Willy *remains standing.* **Peter** *and* **Samson** *open the tins.*

Samson   No, man.

Willy   What's wrong?

Samson   They's given us the wrong colour. He said it must be white.

Willy   Then why they give us green?

Samson   Is this all the paint they gave you?

Peter   Yes.

Willy   Who told you white?

Samson   The boss.

Willy   So what do we do now in this predicament?

Samson   We can't paint it the wrong colour.

Willy   So we must sit on our arses till they come and get no pay?

Samson   If we paints it green we'll have to do it over tomorrow.

Willy   More work more pay. They can't blame us if they give the wrong colour.

Samson   It's so much wasting time, man.

Willy   There's no market for sore arses.

Samson   Ja. Okay. But it's too stupid for words, man.

Willy   So? What's new in the world?

They start to paint.

Peter *has mixed some paint to the required texture.*

Throughout the play he mixes paint when necessary, fills the painters' buckets, etc.

They paint awhile in silence.

Willy Samson, I was almost late myself just now. I got here just before you so I had no excuses to be cross like I was. I'm sorry if I was cross but I had such a time on the bus. Fuck man, it gets worse and worse. There's no way out, I tell you.

This morning there I was in the queue waiting for the twenty-seven like every morning same as usual. Always there's too many people in the queue for the bus to take and people gets left behind but I always make it on. You don't have such problems being picked up by the lorry. Or you. But I always make it so there's no problem. Except this morning.

Shit man, I had one foot on the platform and this bloody conductor with eyes like they's popping out for a drink pushes it off and says 'full up'. Right in my face. No, I say, I must get on. If I don't I'll be late. 'Full up' he says so I'm left standing.

So I run after the bus. I've got to get on I shout. I'll be late then I'll get the sack and have no money. 'Full up' he says.

And he's a coloured.

And the bus goes faster than my legs so I have to go back to the bus-stop and I try to go to the front of the queue where I was but the people there won't let me stand by the pole. 'But I was here' I say. 'Fuck off' they say. 'I'm here now' says a man so big you'd think he'd fill a whole bus by his self. I'm not scared of no human beings but I'm not having a fight with the empire state building for a bus ride. So I go to the back.

What's the odds? I'm going to be late so the more late the less difference it makes. So I wait. So I got here late. But you were later even.

So.

Samson The lorry was held up 'cause we waited for Henry.

Willy   And then when I'm on the bus there's no seats for brown bums only for white ones. So I must stand all the way.

And the white seats is empty same as usual.

So I sit down on one of the white seats until the conductor comes and he says they're for whites only, so I say 'Ugh man, my bum's as white as anyone's. It's not my bum that's black it's my heart.' 'No' he says 'I can see your skin's black. Man you think I'm a fool?'

This time the conductor's a whitey.

'Yes' I say 'all my skin's black except my bum. That's white and if you don't believe me I'll show you.'

Samson   What did he say?

Willy   He's flabbergasted 'cause he's never heard of anyone who's black and white striped like a zebra before.

Parts of me is white and parts black I tell him. I'm a multi-racial society all by myself. My face and hands just happens to be black but my bum's as white as yours so I can sit here.

'Show me' he says. 'Here?' I say. 'Now?' 'Show me your white bum then you can sit on a white man's seat' he says.

'All right' I say and in front of all the white ladies I undoes my belt and takes off my trousers and sticks out my bum so he can see it's white.

'Okay' he says 'you can sit there on your white bum.'

So I pull up my trousers and sit next to all the white ladies and have a nice ride.

But then I say to the conductor 'Hey mister you better check that some of these white ladies haven't got black bums. You can't tell just by looking at their faces. Some of them must be sitting in the wrong seats and you don't know so you'll lose your job.'

Samson   No man, you didn't say that.

Willy Ja I did. So he tells all the ladies on the bus to take down their panties and show him their bums so he can find out if they's in the right seats. And they do and both of us inspect their bums and there were three that had black ones and had to stand.

Samson Ugh no man, you lie.

Willy Ja I do.

Samson How much?

Willy All.

Samson All about the bums?

Willy Ja.

Samson I knew. God man you crazy. (*He laughs.*) White women wouldn't show their bums on a bus. They'd be put in jail. No man.

They both laugh. The laughter grows – until they can't paint. Then it dies.
They paint awhile in silence.

Tell me if anything at all was done.

Willy What?

Samson Hey?

Willy What you say?

Samson Nothing.

Willy I heard you say something.

Samson I said – tell me if anything at all was done.

Willy I can't understand you.

Samson It doesn't mean nothing.

Willy Why you say it then?

Samson I heard someone say it once.

Willy Who?

Samson I don't know. Maybe I read it somewhere. I can't remember.

They paint.

(Sings.)
   You are my sunshine, my only sunshine
   You make me happy when skies are grey.

Willy *and* **Samson**
   You'll never know, dear, how much I love you
   So please don't take my sunshine away.

Willy *(making it up)*
   You are my peop-all, my only peop-all
What comes now?
   You make me happy . . .

Samson *(making it up)*
   And have nice tits.

Willy *and* **Samson**
   You'll never know, dear, how much I love you . . .

Willy What rhymes with tits?

Samson Fits.

Willy *(making it up)*
   So we'll be happy so long as it fits.

Willy *and* **Samson**
   You are my peop-all my only peop-all
   You make me happy and have nice tits
   You'll never know dear how much I love you
   So we'll be happy so long as it fits.

Samson I like to sing, man. Always when I's at home I's singing all the time. New songs, old songs going through my head like a built-in juke-box. When the right song is playing to fit the mood I'm in, it just comes out by itself and I start singing without even knowing it.
(Sings.)
   Moon river, wider than a mile
   I'm crossing you in style, some day.

Willy He thinks he's Danny Williams 'cause he's got a brown skin.

Samson
Whereafter the da – da da da
Waiting round the bend.

Willy Okay.

Samson
My huckleberry friend.

Willy Stop it, man.

Samson
Moon river and –

Willy Shut up!

Samson What's the matter with you?

Willy Nothing. It's you acting peculiar.

Samson I'm only singing. There's nothing peculiar in that.

Willy There is when you do.

Samson You was singing just now.

Willy Ugh man. Don't try and act such a big for your boots. Just paint.

They paint.

Samson Tell me if anything at all was done.

Willy No, nothing.

They paint.

Be careful, man. You splashing paint all over like a walrus having a tooth out. Paint gently. Gently like a Bentley.

Samson You keep getting in the way.

Willy I'm getting in your way?

Samson I's trying to paint this part.

Willy   Why you change the system all of a sudden without telling anyone? You always done the middle part.

Samson   This is the middle.

Willy   Talk shit.

Samson   It is. It's the left-hand part of the middle.

Willy   You can just go paint the right-hand part of the middle 'cause at the present moment I happens to be painting the right-hand part of the left-hand part. Don't come at me with that razzmatazz, Jamima.

Samson   Henry's over there.

Willy   Do the top then.

Samson   Now?

Willy   You got objections? Is there regulations to stop you doing the top-hand section of the middle before the bottom? You's expert of middles.

Samson   All right. Peter, bring the ladder.

He climbs the ladder and paints the top of the wall. They all use the ladder when necessary.

I'm sorry, man. You doesn't have to be so sarcastic like a school teacher. I'll do the top. I doesn't want to make things more complicated than they already is. I mean I doesn't want to be difficult, you understand. I mean you can paint where you likes. I'll paint wherever you says just so long as I'll be out of the way and painting my own area what has been set aside for me by the – for me to paint I mean. Fuck. I don't even know what I'm talking.

Willy   Shut up then.

Samson   I just doesn't want to be difficult.

Willy   Just paint and hold your mouth shut.

Samson   I only wants to oblige.

They paint.

Willy   My daughter also died. Her mother also. Together.

Samson *kicks him.*

Willy   What the fuck you do that for?

Samson   You'll upset him.

Willy   So? He upset me.

Samson   Shame. Don't talk about it now that's all.
Forget it.

Willy   I also had a family. I'm not sad though. Not like
him.

Samson   Ugh, Willy man.

Willy   All right. Hold your horses, man. He's more tough
than you think. People are tough, man. They don't break.
Men people. Women break easier and children snap like
twigs on a tree. But men don't break so easy.

Samson   Okay professor.

Willy   Fuck you.

They paint.

Are you sure it's the wrong colour?

Samson   He told me white. All public walls facing a road
get painted white. New regulations.

Willy   Maybe they changed their minds.

Samson   They never do.

They paint awhile in silence.

Willy *stops painting and puts his brush down.*

Willy   No, man. I'm not doing more.

Samson   You tired already? What you get up to last
night, hey my boy?

Willy   No, I's not tired.

Samson   You feel sick?

Willy   No.

Samson   What then? Come on, Willy. They'll be here in a minute and if it's not finish –

Willy   What's the time?

Samson   Twenty-five past nine.

Willy   So we got thirty-five minutes. How's thirty-five minutes one minute all of a sudden? How come?

Samson   I was only figuring speeches, man.

Willy   I'm not painting no more walls.

Samson (*quietly*)   Ja. I know.

Willy   Why must I paint walls? Me paint walls? It makes no sense. I've got better things to do with my time. I've got too much brains to paint walls.

Samson   What better things?

Willy   Lots of things. Why must I spend my life painting walls, for the love of God?

Samson (*painting*)   You can paint other things. It's not all the same. Painting a house isn't like painting a wall. You've painted houses already. Having a roof makes a difference. You must be careful if there's a roof. That's interesting. You get variety.

Willy   It's like painting lots of walls, man. Rubbish. I'm not going to paint anything. I don't see what this wall's got to be painted for anyway. It was all right like it was. I thought it was all right. I never complained. I never heard no one else complain. I don't know why they can't just leave things like they is. If they wants to change them they can do it without me 'cause I'm finished with all this nonsense. Shit man, there's lots of interesting things to do. And it's my time now.

Samson *continues painting.*

Samson   You going to sit there all the time? Me and Henry'll have to do it ourselves then.

Willy   Or you can stop.

Samson   Talk sense man.

Willy   I am talking sense, man. Can't you see a simple thing? They don't need the wall painted – they just make you do it so you can't do other things.

Samson   No one's making me do it. I does it 'cause I wants the pay. If I doesn't want to paint the wall I doesn't have to.

Willy   It's more complicated than that.

Samson   You keep talking about other things but you never say *what* other things. Peter, take Willy's brush and come paint. I need the pennies even if he's got so rich he can throw them into the trees.

Willy   Peter's not painting. I told you.

Samson   If you're not, someone must. We can't all starve for your cleverness.

Willy   Peter mixes the paint and looks after the brushes and that's all.

Samson   You deserted your job, why must he do his? At least what I's asking him will be useful to people outside his own self.

Willy   Listen, you stupid – you've got to get to a point where you stop – you've got to stop somewhere. You must say I won't waste my life. I haven't even got a proper life, Samson. You've got a family. The only life I see is paint and brushes and bricks and that's not enough and that's why I'm saying stop. Let's see what happens, man. Let's give it a try. What'll they do to us? Nothing.

Samson   You know how many people are wanting your job?

Willy   It's my life – job – ugh shit man – I can't think any more. Schools! Fuck man, I don't know the words to tell you what I mean. I've just had enough, can you see? Enough.

Samson You do what you like with your life and your words. I's not got time for words. I's got more than me to think of.

Willy So I'm luckier than you.

Samson Lucky lucky lucky – oh you lucky man – all alone. Get a wife and you'll understand. Then you won't think you're such a lucky.

Willy It's for your wife too I'm talking.

Samson Peter, take the brush.

Willy Take the fucking thing. You can eat it and piss paint.

Peter *takes up the painting where* **Willy** *left off. They paint.* **Willy** *walks about.*

Willy Here give me that. You're fucking the whole thing up. Can't you do anything?

Willy *takes his brush back. They paint.* **Peter** *mixes paint.*

Henry A man must keep finding things to do, you know. No man can just sit under a tree all day. A man is full of energies, you know, and they don't all get used up in his work, you know, and if they get stored up inside too long they explode. That's not good.

Willy For who?

Henry I found things, you know. Painting pictures of my home, my wife, my children. Those paintings are real, you know, so I paint other things easily, even walls because you can use the time well, you know. Practise to hold your hand still, drawing lines straight – all those are useful. I'm not a losing man.

Willy Ugh man. Leave me alone.

They paint.

You don't understand Henry. You too old. I don't want to do any kind of painting. I want to do all the other things now. I've done painting. I *want* to sit under a tree.

Henry   There are no other things, you know.

Willy   Of course! There is!

They paint.

Oh fuck – all right look – I'll do a painting.

The others stop and watch him.

Samson   What's that?

Willy   Wait and see.

Samson   Is it modern art?

Willy   Shut up, barbarian.

Samson   You's just wasting time. You can't paint for jelly babies.

Willy   Don't you want me to use up my energies?

Henry *is in the way.*

Willy   Mind, Henry.

Samson   What is it?

Willy   Can't you see? Man, you're so blind as a pig's arse.

Samson   I can't see what isn't there. That's a man. What's this in his hand?

Willy   A whip, for god's sake. Oh I forgot to draw the thing at the end. There. And that's us there painting the wall. It's a picture of us.

Samson   Which one is me?

Willy   The one with the small head.

Samson   Let me do one now.

Willy   You're too stupid. You got to finish the wall.

Samson　It won't take long.

Samson *does a painting.*

Willy　Ugh man, that's terrible. I can't even see what it is. Is it a face?

Samson　Of course. What do you think?

Willy　Who is it?

Samson　It's me. It's a self portrait.

Willy　It looks like a baboon.

Samson　It's got more art than your nonsense.

Willy　There – now it's a baboon with ears.

Samson　You've spoilt it. Jesus – can't you leave nothing alone.

Willy　We've got to paint over them anyways. What difference does it make?

Samson　It's the principle of the matter. What's mine is mine and belongs to me.

Willy　It's on their wall. Henry's doing us a painting.

Henry *has done a beautiful painting.*

Samson　It's shameful to have to cover that up. It's beautiful. I wish I could paint like that, hey.

Willy　We each ought to paint over our own paintings, then we won't be so sad about losing them.

Samson　They'll always be underneath. And mine will be even underneath what you did to spoil it.

Willy　Oh shit – you talk such rubbish I'm surprised you aren't Minister of Coloured Affairs. What about all the writing people do on walls every day? They don't come and moan like you.

Samson　They doesn't know and they doesn't care. That isn't art.

Willy   Of course they care. They wouldn't write things if they didn't care. Some of the things I've seen on walls is the most personal I've ever read and that gets covered up.

Samson   Too bad. My heart pumps eau de cologne for all those words and cocks and things on walls. They ought to be painted over for decency.

Willy   What's wrong with cocks? You haven't got one so you's jealous.

Samson   You talk like a child. There's nothing wrong with cocks in the right place. But not on walls where anyone can see them walking past. Even children.

Willy   So? It doesn't hurt them. They must know about things like that.

Samson   How many children have you got that you know so much what children must know?

Willy   I was a child myself once.

Samson   You're a child now, man. You're still a child from all the things you say. You haven't learnt nothing even from all what's happened.

Willy   You paint the wall and shut up.

Samson   Just like a child.

They fight abruptly and with skill. They are too equally matched for either to win. When they realize this they stop. They watch each other then slowly pick up their brushes and paint.

They paint awhile in silence.

Peter, go fill the bucket with water.

Willy   What you want water for?

Samson   Was I speaking to you?

Willy   You can't just sent him about on useless jobs for your own devices. You want the water to drink? Or for what? To wash? You can bloody drown yourself.

Peter *goes.*

They paint.

Peter *returns with the bucket full of water.*

Samson *comes off the ladder, takes the bucket up the ladder and continues painting.*

Willy   What's the water for man?

Samson   Me.

They paint.

Henry   Peter bring me the cloth.

As **Peter** *passes,* **Samson** *empties the water over him.*

Peter   Hey.

Willy   What are you doing?

Samson   I don't know.

Willy   He's wet man. You've wet him. All his clothes is wet. What for? You mad man?

Samson   No.

Willy (*to* **Peter**)   Can't you say nothing?

Peter   I'm wet.

Willy   He's wet man. You hear? He's wet now. All over. Why you pour the bucket on him? Come down.

Samson   I'm busy.

Willy   Come down here. You can't do things like that to your friends and fellow workers. I mean he's only young. Tell him sorry.

Samson   No.

Willy   Ugh man, you bloody crazy.

Peter   Doesn't matter.

Samson   I just wanted to so I did.

Willy Ugh man, where will we be if even friends you can't trust now to leave you happy and contented when you're young. Come, Peter. Don't stand there like a bathing beauty. Take your clothes off.

Peter I can't take them off here.

Willy Who you afraid of? There isn't ladies here.

He gets the spare overall.

Put this on. Come on. You'll die from shivering.

Peter I'm not cold. It's hot.

Willy Don't argue. Here.

*He gives **Peter** the overall.*

He paints.

Peter *undresses. He puts on the overall.*

Willy That's better. Put your clothes there in the sun to dry.

Peter *does so.*

Willy You do that to me, you crazy like a cuckoo bird gone mad, you won't get off so light as a feather.

Samson Tell me if anything at all was done.

Willy Ugh shut up, you nonsense.

They paint a long while in silence. **Henry** *puts down his brush and sits.*

Samson You just sit down Henry, man. That's all right. Just sit and relax yourself. When they come I'll tell them all what happened to – to you and you can go home and look after them all. Peter, come on since you dressed for the part.

Willy Jesus Christ man.

Samson The wall man – just think of the wall for a minute. We's running out of time with all this carry-on here.

Peter *paints.*

Willy   Fuck the wall. Fuck the fucking fucked up fucking wall.

They paint in silence.

After a while **Henry** *picks up a tin of paint and starts drinking it. He splutters and retches but remains calm.* **Peter** *sees him and makes* **Samson** *look.*

Samson   Henry *no* man!

He dashes to him and takes the tin from him.

Willy   What's he doing?

Samson   Drinking the paint. Hold him! Henry you'll die. You mustn't drink that stuff. It's poison. Spit it out – all of it. It's got lead. It'll clog your veins. I'll get you water if you thirsty. Peter get me that cloth. Hurry man. Willy take this away in case he gets thirsty again.

Willy   He's not thirsty.

Samson   You bloody mad, Henry.

Willy   His sadness drove him mad.

Samson   How much you swallow? Any? Did you swallow any paint? Answer me, man.

Willy   He's unconscious.

Samson   We better get a doctor quick.

Willy   No, he's all right. His eyes is moving.

Samson   Henry – how much did you drink?

Willy   This one was half full.

Samson   Henry, talk to me man. Did you drink all this paint.

Willy   He'd be dead if he drank all that.

Samson Why doesn't he talk? Lift him up. Henry. We have to get a doctor or he'll die. Peter, go knock at that house and tell them there's a man here sick and they must call an ambulance. Go on man! What you waiting for? Official confirmation?

Peter *goes.*

Willy Someone must give him the kiss of life. Can you do it?

Samson That's only for drowning.

Willy Maybe he's drowned from the paint. It's like water.

Samson He can't have swallowed much. It's too thick.

Willy The tin's empty.

Samson It's all over his overall and the ground. His sickness is in his mind not his stomach. That's why he won't talk.

Peter *comes back.*

Peter There's no one there.

Samson Go somewhere else then.

Willy No, look he's moving now. He's all right. His eyes is open.

Samson Henry. Can you hear me? Are you all right?

Henry Yes. I'm all right, you know. I fell down. I'm all right, you know.

Samson Can you stand up?

Henry Leave me. There. I can stand.

He stands, walks from them, collapses again.

Samson Ugh no man, Henry, it's wet, man. You're making such a mess.

Willy Leave him. It doesn't matter. He's very sad. Just sit and forget and go to sleep. When they come we'll take you to a doctor and see if you all right.

Samson Jesus Christ, he's better painted than the wall. What a day. Peter go on!

They paint.

You all right, Henry?

Henry All right. Tired you know. I'm fifty-two.

After a while **Peter** *makes sure he's not seen, takes his clothes and leaves.*

Willy Where's Peter?

Samson Gone off.

They paint awhile.

Samson It's hot.

They paint.

Willy Peter! Where the fuck is he? He's not allowed to go off just like that. He's got to ask.

Samson He's gone to piss somewhere. You're painting well now.

Willy It's hot ja.

They paint awhile.

No. He's gone. Away. Look. He's taken his clothes.

Samson *goes off to look for him – shouts his name – comes back.*

Samson He's gone.

Willy You mean gone?

Samson Ja.

Willy Fucking hell.

They paint.

He did right.

Samson Who? Peter? With Henry sick?

Willy   We can manage.

Samson   That's not justice, man. He gets paid same as us.

Willy   Not to paint.

Samson   He can't just go off like a – a old tomato.

Willy   He's still young man. This isn't life.

Samson   He could of told us.

Willy   Why must he care for us?

They stand awhile.

Henry *stares away.*

They paint.

From this point **Willy** *takes over* **Peter***'s jobs – mixing paint, moving the ladder, etc.*

Samson   Tell me if anything at all –

They paint.

The sun gets brighter.

Willy   You know I been thinking about the way we talk.

Samson   Ugh man, everybody's got some kind of accent.

Willy   No, not that. All the words. We use so few words and some of them don't even mean nothing anymore.

Samson   Words mean something. Of course! If they didn't mean something they wouldn't be words.

Willy   No shut up, man. Let me tell you first.

Samson   Okay professor.

Willy   No man, don't be like that. What made me think was your name.

Samson   What's wrong with my name?

Willy   What does it mean?

Samson   Samson's from the bible. He's the oukie with the hair. You knows the story, man.

Willy   Ja but you not like Samson. So why's you got his name? You not strong like him even.

Samson   I have to be called something so people knows who I is. Samson's not my proper name. It's the name I got in school.

Willy   But it's what you's called now. It's not just your name. It's all names. I'm Willy. What does Willy mean? It's just a word.

Samson   It means you.

Willy   But it doesn't tell you who I *is* at all. Look, when we talk we say 'man', you know. We say 'man'. We say I'm very hungry, man. What does that 'man' mean?

Samson   It doesn't mean nothing.

Willy   Why say it then? It's stupid. Like ol' Henry says 'you know' all the time. 'I just fell down, you know.' 'I drank up all the paint you know.' 'You don't know what I know, you know.' It's nonsense, man.

Samson   So what? It doesn't matter what people say.

Willy   It matters. Ja. It matters. Words is like – words is like cages, you know. Cages.

Samson   You said it now. 'You know, cages.'

Willy   Ugh shit man. This is important. You're too stupid to know something serious if it was shoved right up your nose. What I'm saying is that we don't have our own words what means our own things.

Even in the English language, even in Afrikaans the words don't belong to us. We can't make them mean anything. Look we say shit. I say it all the time. And I'm not really talking about shit. I never talk about shit. But I always say shit. The only words I know are shit and fuck and I don't mean to talk about fucking either. They's just words that come out but they don't mean nothing so when they's out they's like bars around me – bars what keeps me doing the same things – thinking the same things – not letting me out to grow – to learn new words. Some people speak beautifully. They know lots of words and they's free men. More free than us. I can't go and talk to anyone 'cause all I can say is fuck and shit. That's not enough.

Samson   You talking to me.

Willy   Ugh man. You only know two words also and one of them I don't even think you can do.

I want to learn new things, man. I want to have new words. Like I said, the only words I know are paint, brushes and bricks. And fuck and shit. Fucking paint, fucking brush, fucking bricks. Paint shit, brush shit, brick shit. The end of all my information and words.

It's terrible man. I could do anything if I knew the words. Change this country – build a new world. I could. If I could say the right words in the right way so people would understand about me and my life and all that and you and Henry and his daughter and all of us. If I could use the right words they'd understand, man.

But when they ask me I can't answer them. They say 'Why are you late today?' And I must make a joke 'cause how can I tell them all what happens in the place where I stay, on the bus, why I'm late, what I did – I can't.

So I joke and they think I'm rude.

But that's not what I want. I want them to understand. Fuck man. It's not difficult. Lots of people can talk. Why not me? Why not, hey? Where can I learn? How can I learn if I have to paint this fucking wall all day? Shit man. I'm sick of it. I've had enough. I'm not doing more. This time I'm not. Fuck. I'm not. I'm leaving too. It's not too late. Fuck, I'm going. I'm not painting this wall anymore. This fucking bloody shit covered load of rubbish. Fucking shit I hate it. I'm not staying – fuck – fuck shit the fucking thing to hell – fuck it – !

He can't go. He throws himself at the wall as he shouts the last words, pounding his body at the bricks. His speech dries up altogether before he is physically exhausted.

When he is exhausted he falls to the ground and lies there.

Samson *watches.*

Henry *stares away.*

Eventually **Willy** *recovers, stands, picks up his brush, paints over the marks he's made.*

Samson   Man, you know something. People are funny. I don't understand.

You know, my younger sister Gertie? She's twenty-four now. Well, she was a serving girl in a house in Constantia for two years. She's just an ordinary girl. No pretences, no fancies, nice, not very pretty, a bit fat and she doesn't always know what she's doing with her elbows or where's her feet. Falling over things what isn't there and cutting her knees. Clumsy, you know?

Well, at her madam's place she broke things. Glasses and cups and plates. Not expensive ones always but often when she was washing up. And her madam used to shout at her and she'd cry, Gertie my sister. And her madam would take money off her wages to pay for it and Christ knows she didn't get a fortune every week and she was always going to leave but she got good food there and she liked the madam's children what she looked after. Anyways, one day. You see, this madam's husband was in the diplomatic corps and he was always travelling to countries like Ghana you know and also Swaziland and all those places where black people run their own governments.

Well, one day one of the cabinet ministers from Swaziland comes to Cape Town and he goes to visit Gertie's madam and master to eat. They's black but they's important and they come from another country so they can go and the police don't say nothing.

Well, the point of the story is that with him he also brings his secretary who's a coloured man from Cape Town but he's important now 'cause he's got a good job with this minister in Swaziland and he sees Gertie in this house dressed up in her little white apron and cap and her slippers with the bobbles on and he falls in love with her and they get married. In a hurry.

We think they's been playing around and gone too far but Gertie says no.

So there's Gertie living in a big house in Swaziland and she's no more a second-class citizen. She's invited to all the cocktail parties and all that and she's a big lady now and a madam herself. And she dresses in fancy clothes and she gets fatter and she has children four boys.

Anyways one day she comes back to see us. She comes to our house in a car. Grand, you know?

So we talking and I says 'How's life in the big city living like the white peoples?' And she says 'There's no comparison because we's not living like the white peoples but like all the black peoples ought to be living.'

And we talk and laugh about the old times. And then she says this thing what I wants to tell you.

She says the only real problem is with the servants she has. 'Servants?' I say. 'You got servants?' 'Yes' she says. 'You got to have servants to run a big house. I got three. Three servants.'

'White or black' I ask, with a look of amazement on my face. 'Two black, one coloured' she says. Gertie my sister has a coloured person as a servant.

But she says they's so much trouble you must always be watching them. 'Why?' I say. 'Do they steal?' 'No' she says. 'They break things. They're always breaking things. They's so much trouble 'cause they break all my things.'

That's what she said. True. It's a funny world.

Samson *finishes painting the wall.*

Willy *puts the brushes in one tin and the lids on the others.*

Samson *looks at his watch.*

Just nice time.

Willy   Where to now?

Samson   Dunno.

Willy *goes off with the box.*

Samson *goes to* **Henry**, *helps him to stand, starts him off.*

Come on, Henry. We's going now.

Samson *takes the ladder.*

They leave.

The wall stands wet and bright in the hot sun. It stands awhile, then fades away.

Red Earth

for Maurice Bloch

Characters

Moses Kotane, *General Secretary of the Communist Party of South Africa.*
Joshua Mudakwa, *thirty years old.*
George Madidi, *thirty years old.*
Lord Alfred Milner, *British High Commissioner and Governor of the Cape Province of South Africa 1897–1905.*
Herbert Cibuwe, *a dentist.*
Selina Sinaba, *a visionary.*

The play takes place in South Africa – Cape Town and the Transkei – in the mid 1970s.

Red Earth was first performed at the Institute of Contemporary Arts, London on 25 October 1977, with the following cast:

Moses	Molephi Pheto
Joshua	Victor Lindsay
George	Frederick Brobby
Milner	Christopher Godwin
Herbert	Doyle Richmond
Selina	Nadia Cattouse

Directed by John Burgess
Designed by Doreen Watkinson

A number of wooden crates standing on a quay. Each has a sign which includes one of the following clearly legible words: London, Leeds, Manchester, Birmingham, Crewe, Cardiff etc.

Some suggestion of — not too far away — the sky, the sea. Faint sounds of lapping waves and seagulls.

Moses Kotane *sits on a plain chair with a sheaf of notes in his hand.*

Kotane's *manner is at first benign and relaxed. As the interruptions follow each other he becomes progressively more boisterous and desperate. His concern is always to make the content of his speech as clear as possible. He never gives up until every hope of getting his message through is gone. The last speech is delivered in a manner similar to the first but shows evidence of the struggle he has been through.*

Three oranges are lying on the stage.

Joshua *crosses at top speed, pushing a trolley with a crate on it. The crate's label reads: Montevideo. He wears street clothes. He goes off.*
The crates are always carted to their dock from right to left.

A loud crash off and six oranges cascade on to the stage and mingle with the ones already there

George (*off*) Who in the world pays out cash for this?

George *comes on at no great speed, pushing his trolley with a crate which is labelled: Hamburg. He wears overalls. He scoops up the oranges, throws them into the crate and knocks the lid into place with a mallet. He pushes the crate off.*

Joshua (*off*) But where is this Montevideo?

George (*off*) Way along the quay.

Joshua (*off*) I looked and looked.

George (*off*) Of which country is Montevideo the capital?

Joshua (*off*) Oh, capitals. Montevideo. . . . (*Thinks.*)

George (*off*) Uraguay.

Joshua (*off*)   Oh Uraguay. Dock nineteen?

George (*off*)   Have you forgotten everything I taught you?
Twenty-three.

George *crosses casually with his empty trolley and off.*

The stage is empty.

Moses Kotane *comes forward.*

Kotane   Ladies and gentlemen, comrades, friends. I am Moses Kotane. Since the year 1938 I have been General Secretary of the Communist Party of South Africa. Today I wish to speak to you about the history of the organized black resistance in South Africa from 1902 until the present day. I choose 1902 as a starting point because in that year the Treaty of Vereeniging was signed. Why was this done? To end the Anglo-Boer war. The British promised the defeated Boers that they would get their independence from the crown. But when they signed that sheet they signed the black man's voting rights away. This Treaty is the earth on which our people's blood is shed. In 1910 the Union of South Africa was signed. Still the British waved it through. 'No Votes for Blacks.' But hardly had the ink on that unhappy document run dry than the African National Congress was begun – the famous ANC of which I was, for many years, a leading member. Then in 1921 the Communist Party of South Africa began, only four years after the inspiring events of 1917. The CP and the ANC face the struggle hand in hand. We in the CP base our analysis on the divisions caused by the privileges of class. The ANC prefer to see the heart-rending oppression caused by the bigots of race. Both have one end in view: to build a democratic independent nation where now a reactionary violent gang of European bandits force a proud, and once so mighty, people to submit to an arrogant regime. We've had over sixty years of struggle. We may have many more. Until our rulers blocked off every other path, our struggle was a peaceful one. But 'Freedom, Freedom' is our cry. 'Set the people free –'

Meanwhile:

During the last part of this speech the following events occur:

Joshua *pushes his trolley on at top speed, in front of* **Kotane**, *and stops.*
George *pushes his trolley on bearing a crate labelled: London.*

George   Did you find it?

Joshua   In the end.

George   Tomorrow I won't be here to lend a hand. You've had all week to learn the trade. I'm giving you my job. A precious gift. So keep it well.

Joshua   It's in the bag. (*Taps his head.*)

George   You get one shipment wrong, chaos throughout the civilized lands. Starvation. Civil war. This world's a very fragile place. It's on your shoulders now.

Kotane *expresses no disapproval of* **Joshua** *and* **George**. *He simply measures up the force of their competition and when he considers himself outclassed he gives up and sits down. As now.*

Joshua   Where did it come from?

George   What?

Joshua   This Uraguay.

George   Dock twenty-three.

Joshua   No, in real life.

George   Oh. Overseas.

Joshua   But where?

George   Far. Far, far.

Joshua   Then we should place it in a dock that's far, far far along the quay. Close countries close and far ones far. Systematic.

George   You're not apprenticed from today. You must learn to hold the knowledge in your head.

A helicopter passes quickly overhead. They watch it go. **Joshua** *sits.*

Worn out?

Joshua *nods.*

George   You go too fast.

Joshua   We must.

George   I didn't hear that word.

Joshua   We must go fast.

George   Says who? An even, measured lollop does the job.

Joshua   A lollop?

George   Technical term. It's like a trot. See? (*He demonstrates.*) Nice and easy. Keep the stirrups loose and strut. Strut. You've got all afternoon to watch me still. Don't be too proud to learn. This passing knowledge on. My father told me –

Joshua   What was his job?

George   My father? He never left his home. He was diviner of the village. Very wise.

Joshua   Where did he come from?

George   From Transkei, of course. From Port St Johns, beside the Indian Sea.

Joshua   That where you're heading for?

George   Indeed. Tonight.

Joshua   My father went for the mines. Like me. My father was a fool. Again like me. We must work. Hard. He said to me: the more we work, the more we make, the more there is for us to share.

George   You believe that?

Joshua   Can't you see I do?

A bell rings briefly but loudly – more a doorbell than an alarm.

Joshua *leaps to his trolley and wheels it off.* **George** *tries to shift the crate from his trolley. It is too heavy. He struggles with it, groans and sweats.*

Meanwhile:

Lord Milner *rises out of a crate. He holds a bottle of whisky and a glass, which he proceeds to fill.*

Milner
    Stacked wooden crates on a windswept quay. A sight
    Sublime as Big Ben on a summer's night.
    I'm Lord Milner. Alfred to my friends. I'm sure
    You're friends. Sea air, sunshine, rest. The perfect cure
    For all unease. South Africa's warm, humane clime
    Will make you twice yourself in half the time
    And not only in health but wealth. Who's not impressed
    By the dividends paid, whatever you invest
    In this gold land, this setting, as it were,
    For our jewel, England. Long life, good health to her.
    When I came out – in 1898 I think –
    As High Commissioner, we trembled on the brink
    Of the Boer War, then crossed into her bed and fought
    And won – now there's the thing As boys we're taught
    The thing's to fight well. Yes. But the make or break
    Is victory – as we had here – if you're to take
    Advantage of the reason man was made:
    To turn the vulture war into the pigeon trade.
    Ah, how I loved this country. Oh it was a thing
    So beautiful, some nights you'd hear an angel sing.

As **Milner** *finishes,* **George** *gives up his struggle with the crate.*

Milner *sips his whisky while the scene proceeds. After a minute he sinks back into his crate.*

Joshua *comes on with a crate labelled: Montevideo.*

Joshua   Another one for Uraguay. (*Reads.*) Tinned fruits.

George   Dock twenty-three.

Joshua   I know, I know.

George   A test then, if you know so much. Get set. Go. France?

Joshua   Seventeen.

George   Spain?

Joshua   Number twelve.

George   Germany?

Joshua   I know them. Fifteen, sixteen.

George   The U and S of A?

Joshua   Eighteen, nineteen, twenty, twenty-one.

George   Nigeria?

Joshua   That's eight.

George   And Pakistan?

Joshua   Thirty-one. You see?

George   Great Britain?

Joshua   Just right here.

George   Not bad.

Joshua   I'll feed the world.

George *takes a half-bottle of brandy out of his pocket.*

George   Have a hit to celebrate my going home.

Joshua *looks about carefully and takes a quick swig. He screws the top back on, hands the bottle back to* **George** *and goes back to the trolley.*

George   Wait for the bell, my darling. Your manhood's not in question. Did you know?

George *drinks.* **Joshua** *starts to wheel his trolley out.*

George   Sit, you jackass. Rest while you can.

Joshua   I can't. I can't, George. Believe me, brother. I can't.

The violence of this surprises **George**.

George Are you jealous of us Xhosa people, having our own home? Is that it? Yours is on the cards. You Zulus will get one too.

Joshua No Zulu would give up his rights to this land.

George Rights? What rights? I can't give up what I never held down. It's law. I'm citizen of the Transkei now. That's all the rights I've got. Come set this straight.

Together they edge the crate off **George**'*s trolley and put it with the others. While they do this:*

Where did you ever learn to work like that?

Joshua *shows* **George** *his hands.*

George Whew! From what?

Joshua The mines. A wall falls in. A drill explodes. You move like hell.

George I would never work down there. Not if they made me king of Timbuktu.

Joshua *lifts the lid off the crate.*

George I just put that back on.

Joshua *waves the lid and climbs onto a crate to see what's in the lidless one.*

George The bell will go. You're caught in mid-air. Then? How long were you down the mines?

Joshua *gestures the irrelevance of the question.*

George Was it gold or diamonds?

Joshua *takes an orange out of the crate, which is clearly packed to the brim.*

Joshua It was gold.

He throws it to **George**.

George No! Put it back. (*He throws it back.*) I won't have any stealing on my quay.

George   No stealing? Right.

He laughs and throws the orange back to **George**. **George** *lets it sail past him.*

George   Can you see me? Can you? I'm still here. Until I leave you give me your respect. You'll lose my job.

Joshua   The way I work? (*He roars with laughter and takes a second orange from the crate.*) This job! I'll study all the countries, where they are. Close, close. Far, far. This job! (*He slowly peels his orange as he talks.*) Down there, there was no light. Here – look, the sun. (*The orange.*) You see a gold band on a lady's arm. The light is dancing. In the earth, no. Dark. I never could say which is gold, which stone. Some miners could see through the dark. Like moles. (*He laughs.*) A line of moles. Sleep in a line, eat in a line, squeeze your shit out in that damn line. The baas said: 'Oh you men can see just like a mole? Then teach the others to be moles as well and I can turn the lights off underground.' We were always seeking for that spark of light. Since I've been working here – one, two, three, four, five days – sometimes I forget the mines. But then I think, how can a man forget a thing like that? Thirteen years can't disappear so fast. So I believe someone put his hand inside my mind, slipped his finger in behind my ear and tore the memory out. Whose hand? Whose hand? (*He laughs.*) I'm going so high in the world, some mornings I can see the sun before it starts to shine. This job! (*He laughs.*) It's almost like a dream. (*He is about to put a segment of orange into his mouth.*)

The bell rings.

They gather up the oranges and peel, throw them into the crate, replace the lid and hurriedly push their trollies out, **Joshua** *noticeably faster than* **George**.

Kotane *sees no one is about and comes forward. As he speaks the seaside sounds fade and end. The light becomes harder and brighter.*

Kotane   The problem that has given us most suffering has been the distribution of the land. As far back as 1913

the Native Land Act threw thousands of people off their
traditional homes. They wandered, abandoned, across the
broad uncultivated wastes. They may not settle anywhere
for fear of punishment. By 1927 we had caught our
master's eye. He increased by half the territory we native
people had the right to own. Three-quarters of the people
in our land were allocated twelve per cent of the most
valuable resource the country has.

A hen cackles and flies on.
Kotane *stops, then continues.*

In 1936 our masters saw our sufferings had not come to an
end. They raised the total of our land by one further per
cent. And this land is the worst our country has. Dry and
barren as a bone and underneath the stony soil is rock.

The hen flies across the stage and out. **Herbert***, carrying a box,
runs on after the hen.*

Rock on top of rock on top of –

Kotane *gives up and sits down.*

Herbert   Haai! Haai! Sweetpea! Haai! Sweetpea!

*He chases her off. The hen is scuttling round in a large circle, only a
short section of which traverses the stage.*

*A strong wind blows and in the distance the sound of a mbira (finger
piano).*

George *comes on wearing a heavy coat and a woollen balaclava
cap. He sits. The wind blows.*

The hen flies on again. **Herbert** *chasing and yelling. They vanish.*
George *watches them go. He takes a half-bottle of brandy from his
pocket and drinks. The wind blows. He turns up his collar and pulls
down his cap.*

A loud thump off. Followed by **Herbert***'s whoop of victory.*
George *takes another quick slug and puts the bottle away.*

Herbert *comes on holding Sweetpea by her feet.*

Herbert   Windy morning! Haai! The feathers ripple in my Sweetpea's tail and oh she'd give her heart to be a bird. Resting?

George *nods.*

Herbert   Walking long?

George *nods.*

Herbert   How far from here to Kimberley?

George   On foot or bus?

Herbert   On what God leaves to him with nothing left?

George *offers* **Herbert** *a knife.*

George   Slit her throat – two days. Otherwise a week.

Herbert   She's food and friendship. You are George Madidi.

George   So? And you?

Herbert   I'm Herbert.

George   Herbert?

Herbert   Martha's boy. You sold my ma a cow.

George   How did I know the foolish beast would die? I gave no guarantee. Tell Martha she can't ask for money back. I'm empty. That cow, I loved her like a son.

Herbert   I didn't say she's dead.

George   She didn't die?

Herbert   She gave a calf each year and one year two.

George   I sold her to your ma dirt cheap. I'm owed one calf at least.

Herbert   There's none left. All sold out.

George   But whose cow was she in the first place? Good, my brother. My children will not starve now that our land is free. (*He takes a mouthful of brandy.*)

Herbert Your wife is Winny Madidi?

George You know her? Is she well? I must admit it's three years since I'm home – not once since independence came – to see my wife and kids. (*He hands* **Herbert** *the brandy.*)

Herbert *drinks.*

George I have six kids. My eldest girl is twelve, the youngest almost three. And then I must confess the last letter I wrote fell in the box a good two years ago. No, don't describe a single item. I'll be home in one and one half days. Then I can see my dear wife and my kids with my own eyes and that will be too sweet.

Herbert Come, Sweetpea.

Sweetpea has been strutting up and down, tied to a string. **Herbert** *hands the bottle back and puts Sweetpea in a box.*

George Madidi, good to see you, sir. I'm on my way.

George No, don't you go yet, Herbert. Your eyes are far too sad. Another hit. Like Moses woke the skies with joyful song when the promised paradise lay just beyond the hill after – how long was it?

Herbert Forty years.

George That's it exactly – in the desert waste. That's how I feel. My heart is overflowing all its banks. I'll drown us all. My dear, I think I'm going to sing. Drink. Drink. Give her some too. Come little hen – chick, chick.

Sings.

> Does it matter?
> No no no.
> Does it matter?
> No.
> But outside is rain and snow.
> And I'm no fatter.

I'm overjoyed with pleasure, son. I am almost home.

Herbert I am a dentist.

George *roars with laughter at* **Herbert***'s toothless gums.*

George You!

Herbert Qualified in dentistry. University College Hospital, London. June 1975. Second class. I came here to work. But there is none for me.

George *roars with laughter again.*

George No people with sore teeth?

Herbert There's no facilities. They told me: this Transkei will be your country. Independent. No apartheid, no Afrikaans, none of that shit. Join the United Nations, join the world. Rubbish. Pig piss. Every word.

George No, no. You break my heart to talk like that.

Herbert I saved up all my cash. I studied like a dog. I need a surgery. A chair. A drill – old fashioned, I don't care. Gas cylinders and half a dozen mirrors, different sizes. There's no facilities for a professional. What must I do, sir? Tell me. Sit the patient on an orange box and draw his teeth with this? (*He shows a pair of pliers.*) Any raw black trash can do that trick. I ask you sir, what must I do? I practice on myself. (*He shows a tin box, rattles it, opens it and displays the contents.*) An upper molar I extracted from my jaw. It hardly hurt at all. Incisor. Canine. Molar number two. Perfect specimens all, as you can see. But now no one will let me in their mouth. I have too many missing teeth myself.

George *laughs and laughs till* **Herbert** *is forced to join in.*

George Herbert.

Herbert George Madidi?

George What a stinking waste.

Herbert Of what?

George Yourself. Your hard-won skill. Th[...]
thousand people, children too, crying out in [...]
could set them free.

Herbert But I am London trained. Where are they?

George Who?

Herbert These crying people?

George Man, the world is full.

Herbert I cried. I cried to drown the sea. I'm going for the mines.

George You what? You're mad to go down there. Believe me, son. This is our place, however few facilities. Stay. Build. Who heard of miracles that sprouted up like weeds? The soil is watered with our tears. Now is the time to plough and sow, not run off to the trading store for a tin of beans. It's slow work, progress. I had a job, quite good. I gave it up. Come with me, Herbert. I'll give you my teeth to fix and all my children's too. That will keep you occupied. My home is Port St Johns beside the Indian Sea.

Sings.

> Does it matter?
> No no no.
> Does it matter?
> No.
> But outside is rain and snow
> And I'm no fatter.

Herbert *follows* **George** *out.*

Kotane *sees no one is about and comes forward.*

Kotane The year 1939 saw a significant occurrence on the international scene – fascism in Germany. Our great white father General Jan Christian Smuts told us: 'All native men must fight.' We said: 'Fight who?' The answer came; 'The fascist enemy.' Our people asked him: 'Will you arm us if we fight for you?' And Smuts cried: 'Yes, we'll arm you as you always have been armed – with

ears and knives and nobkerries.' The people answered:
'You, sir, are our enemy.' But then the tyrant Hitler
marched on Russia. Could we let the one true workers'
state be crushed? Some of my brothers faced a tank attack
with nothing in their hands but sticks and stones. And yet
they fought. Against an enemy and on the enemy side.
Twice only in our history – twice – could all our suffering
have come easily to an end. One – if the British didn't
sign our voting rights away. Two – in 1944 Jan Smuts
believed the Japanese were planning to invade our land. All
his troops were fighting in North Africa. He gave black
workers' guns. And when the war was done, he asked and
got them back. What foolishness! 'Moses, give back the
weapon of your liberation. Put it on that pile.' 'Yes, my
baas. Yes, my baas. Yes, my baas.'

Meanwhile:

*During the second half of this speech singing is heard offstage. It
gradually increases in volume.*

Singers
Don ya knock, don ya knock
Don ya knock, don ya knock
Don ya knock Christ's bicycle down

*A banner is magically unfurled and raised. It bears, in one long line,
the legend: 'The East Grinstead Natural Baptismal Congregational
Church of Christ in Zion of Black Africa South – Cape Town
Division'.*

As the singing swells, **Selina Sinaba** *appears and sings so loudly
she drowns out* **Kotane***'s speech. He sits.*

Selina *sings.*
Oh listen ye white drivers to my song
(yea listen well)
In your Cadillac the road of life you're travelling along
(yea listen well)
Then you hear a soft crack like the snap of a spring
    chicken's neck
(O yea white man)

You veer into a tree and your Cadillac's a write off, a
   wreck
(O yea white man)
You crawl onto the road and stagger 'bout a half mile
   back
(yea listen well)
And there's sweet Jesus' body in a pool of blood across
   the track
(O yea white man
O yea white man
O listen listen listen
yea white man
yea white man)

Don ya knock Christ's bicycle down
Don ya knock Christ's bicycle down
Hear me heathen, hear my plea
Don ya knock Christ's bicycle down
Don ya knock (don ya knock)
Don ya knock (don ya knock)
Don ya knock Christ's bicycle down

Towards the end of this chorus **Selina** *starts to speak.*

Selina   O Lord! We are your children! We bear hatred
against no man, nor white nor brown nor black as devil's
hoof.

Singers   O no, o no, we don't!

Selina   God prised apart my feeble mind and stuck the
knowledge in. Clouds swill about the dark, dark, dark red
sky. Is it cream pouring down a dish of stewing prunes?

Singers   O no, o no, it isn't!

Selina   It's the white, white, white of the Lamb of God
swimming strong against the tide. Christ spilled a tide of
blood but we will spill no drop. Our lives are spent packed
back to back and top to toe – green apples in a box – but
soon we say:

Singers   Yea, soon we say:

Selina We were hungry and did you feed us? We were naked and did you clothe us? You fearful and you unbelieving, you abominable, you murderers, you whore-mongers, scorcerers, idolaters and liars! Leviticus 9 verse 18. All you liars and you policemen and native commissioners and you pass-book inspectors, you labour supervisors and Prime Ministers and parliamentary candidates and all you wretched thieves and savage slaughterers, all you who robbed our fathers of their years – all, '*All* of you shall have your place in the lake which burneth with fire and brimstone' and pitch and tar and mud and wet cement – slime, cow dung, pig shit, dog vomit, horse piss. Revelations 21 verse 8. 'The silver is mine and the gold is mine, saith the Lord of Hosts.' Haggai 2 verse 7. And I your prophet add: I'll take the diamonds too. Your time is up. The honey comb has now run dry. The dried-out husk will soon be swept away. Our earth is set to loose a bowel and pour his dribbling filth into the air. For I have had a dream.

Singers A dream! A dream!

Selina A vision, yes. As sharp as horseflesh, clear as ice. White men – beware!

Singers Beware! Beware!

Selina Your days, your days, you child of shallow dreams, are numbered on the knuckles of my thumb. Cry Halleluja!

Singers Halleluja!

Selina Halleluja!

Singers Halleluja!

Joshua *has come slowly in pushing his empty trolley which he now leaves.*

Joshua My name is Joshua Mudakwa.

Selina Sit and speak.

Joshua Joshua Mudakwa.

Selina   True, my brother. I am yours to use.

Joshua   I am not my own man anymore.

Selina   Who is? Speak to the point.

Joshua   I have another man here in my head.

Selina   What type of man is this?

Joshua   A ghostly type, as thin as sleet.

Selina   Describe the apparition.

Joshua   It can not be done.

Selina   God puts his mouth against my lips and pumps me full of generosity. He gave me for your use.

Joshua   He has – a white face.

Selina   More.

Joshua   A black moustache.

Selina   And then?

Joshua   I never see his back.

Selina   What else?

Joshua   His face is high above me. Like the moon. I look – he's lying at the root of my palm.

Selina   A fearful sound. Show him to me.

Joshua   But, woman. I can't make him come. He chooses his own time. I was a worker in the mines. Each time I turn my face to wipe the sweat I see him. Such an anger in his eye I turn back to the rock and work again. I work until I fall. Each time I stop he comes. Two shifts in a row – some bad days, three. I leave one team that's pouring from the shaft and join up with another streaming in. I have to leave that place or I am dead. Now I'm in a fine job at the dock. For some good time after I started there he never came. Till now. If I keep moving he stays gone. I stop – he's back. Advise me, please. What can I do to save my soul?

Selina   Oh brother in our suffering, show me this tyrant ghost.

Joshua   I can not make him come!

Selina   But are you working now? Your body is at rest. Is he not there? Or do you lie?

Silence.

Joshua   I do not lie.

Selina   Then show him.

Silence.

Sometimes a foreigner may do some deed here in our land which he comes to regret. He may commit some act so filthy cruel, his soul cries out from deep within his grave to set the record straight. His spirit stalks the lonely earth until he finds a body he feels comfortable inside. Perhaps he chose you, brother.

Joshua   He is there.

Selina   He is.

Joshua   He stands behind my neck.

Selina   So turn and see.

Joshua *turns quickly, sees nothing.*

Selina   So turn again.

Joshua *turns quickly.*

Selina   Catch him?

Joshua   He's there.

Selina   Tell me your spirit's name.

Joshua   I feel – he's there – he's there.

Selina   Cry it aloud – your spirit's name!

Joshua   Whisky.

Lord Milner *rises from his crate.*

Selina His name! His name!

Joshua Whisky! Whisky!

Selina Cry out your spirit's name!

Joshua Whisky! I want – want – give me whisky!

Milner

I won't deny I do have one regret.
When the Boer War ended the terms we set
Were these: blacks will not have the vote until
White self-government's introduced. That pill
Proved far too bitter for the Boers and so
(Don't tell me it was wrong. It was. I know.)
The clause was changed to let the Boers debate
After self-government achieved a peaceful state
If the blacks might vote or not. I signed my name.
Shortsighted? Naïve? Yes. But can you blame
Us? Surely not. We'd almost lost our pants
And there they stood, those crude recalcitrants
Sticking to this one clause and underneath their feet
Lay fields of diamonds, copper, gold – repeat,
Vast seams of gold ran deep and rich and red.
They might have gone to Germany instead
I do regret I wrote that clause. What could we do?
Pray such an odd enigma never tortures you.

He takes a bottle of whisky out of the crate and pours himself a glass.

Joshua *is lying back exhausted.*

Selina This one is far too strong.

Singers Too strong. He's far too strong.

Joshua Get him out.

Selina We used to give assistance with the sly African devil. But no more. Archbishop Juice of Salisbury, Rhodesia told us: give the struggle up. To fight those boys is far too big a fuss. It gives them credibility when in his private view they don't even exist. So my advice to you is: Work hard. He'll be still.

Joshua   Oh get him out of me!

Selina   Alternatively, try this one: find out what evil he has done and make it good.

Joshua   Then tell me what it is.

Selina   I only see the future not the past. I'll pray for you, my brother. You will be well in time, there is no doubt.

Singers   She'll pray for you.

Selina   We must all work, work, work until we die. The freedom time will come. I know. Believe it will. Till then draw strength from me. Cry Halleluja!

Singers   Halleluja!

Selina   Halleluja!

Singers   Halleluja!

Selina   Two and three:

Singers   Don ya knock etc.

Selina *disappears. The banner magically furls up and vanishes.*

Joshua *is left lying on the floor.*
Milner *pouds another glass of whisky.*

Sound of helicopter passing overhead.
A tug hoots and seagulls cry.
Milner *sinks into his crate.*
Joshua *stands. He is still a moment, then he bursts into action and pushes his trolley off at top speed.*

Kotane *sees there is no one about and comes forward.*

Kotane   1948. The Nationalist Party came to power and the sentiment of separate development became a creed. The homelands – that is, the land black men can buy – will be made independent states. Democracy is guaranteed, but only in your own group area. 1950. The Communist

Party is banned. It dissolves and forms again but
underground. 1952. The ANC launch a great defiance
campaign. We pledge to use every peaceful means available
to bring the government to its good sense. Strikes, boycotts,
speeches – no avail.

Kotane *looks off and sees someone approaching. He talks on but
keeps looking off. He talks faster to finish in time but eventually the
weight of feeling expressed by the approaching people becomes too great.*

So many of our leaders are arrested, charged with the
violence they've sworn never to commit, found guilty,
jailed. Oh what a time it was! Trials lasting many months
and worse to come –

He sits down.

Silence a moment.
Wind.

George *and* **Herbert**, *carrying Sweetpea in her box, come on.*

George So they knock houses down, but trees! And
fields!

Herbert Gone.

George Gone.

Herbert Gone.

George Where?

Herbert Some here, some there. They come with trucks,
bulldozers, guns. They sweep the village flat.

George But who are they to sweep our homeland flat?

Herbert All around is ours. Except this town. Not Port
St Johns.

George This is where my people live.

Herbert They've gone, Mr Madidi. Can't you see this
fact? They've gone.

George You kept it from me. Why? Why, why?

Herbert   Each man must face his own destruction for himself.

George   Destruction? Me? They'll sink the mountain first.

Herbert   A port smack by the sea. Too valuable to put in kaffirs' hands. Can they export their goods if our black arms control the waves?

George   Let them pay us. We need the cash. We won't refuse.

Herbert   Pay kaffirs? They can take it all for free.

George   I'll find my people.

Herbert   No lists, no records. Black on black and white on white. How will you live?

George   I'll work.

Herbert   There is no work here, Mr Madidi. Throughout the whole Transkei who has a job is called a lucky man. I'm going for the mines.

George   I made those children. We must make work.

Herbert   With what? Ten times too many people on this land. They promise us one day the British will construct their factories out here. Then there'll be plenty work. Till that good day, off for the mines.

George *scoops a stone off the ground.*

George   Look. What's this? What's this?

Herbert   A stone, Mr Madidi.

George   No! Oh yes but no. Look here. What does it say?

Herbert   W. N.

George   M. M. – W. M. I carved that in. Winny Madidi. I put it for my wife to hold the washing in the wind. (*He holds it to his cheek.*) Ah, Winny, Jojo, Constance, Petie, Dickie, Martha, Bob. Your husband and your father has come home. But where are you?

Herbert My brother used to tell me:
Hope is heaven
Despair is hell
Travel with a smile
And all will be well.

George Hope is dead.

Herbert That's what you said about my mother's cow.
I'm quite a lucky one. In dentist school they taught me
how to use a dentist drill, how to dig out bits of hidden
tooth. I just adapt that skill. Big man – small tooth. Small
man – a hill of gold. A change of scale, that's all. I heard
in Kimberley there's mines so deep some men climb down
and never see the light of day again.

George Herbert, we've all got trouble. I'll do you a turn.
But in exchange for one. OK?

Herbert What is it?

George What I want or what you get?

Herbert Both sides of the bargain.

George You're full of answers. I've lived deep in shit six
years. Take my advice.

Herbert OK, Mr Madidi.

George My half first.

Herbert What is it?

George Sweetpea.

Herbert She's food and friendship to me.

George I gave you friendship. (*He gives* **Herbert** *the
bottle.*) My wife and kids will need the food. (*He picks up the
box.*)

Herbert *drinks*.

Herbert And my half?

George   Come here. Here, right here. Lay your head on the ground. I'll teach you a secret of the cities.

Herbert   I've been five years in London, George Madidi.

George   Bend down. You hear the buzzing?

Herbert   No.

George   Then clean your ears. You hear it now?

Herbert   I know this trick. I've been five years. (*He stands.*)

George *forces him down.*

George   That's the deep soul of the earth you hear. That's the heart of every secret. Hear it?

Herbert   No.

George *gives* **Herbert***'s head a sharp kick.*

George   That's your half. A lesson. In this life you get nothing in exchange for what you give.

Herbert *stands, more in sorrow than in anger.*

George   Kimberley, that way.

Herbert *throws the bottle of brandy down. He takes a pair of pliers out of his pocket and puts them in his mouth.*

The wind picks up.

George   Father! You promised you would teach me all you knew. You entered the cave of death. Where did it go? I came back full of joy. You dying men. The times are too, too bad. You think your knowledge of the world too weak to do us good. Not true! Not true! We need it now. We're sand. Blow wind. We're gone.

Herbert *has pulled out a tooth. His mouth fills with blood. He spits it onto the earth. He puts the tooth into his box, shakes it and runs out.*

The wind blows strongly. In the distance the mbira.

George *is still a moment. Then he takes a mouthful of brandy. He opens the box and lets Sweetpea run away. Then he lunges at her. She bites him.*

Haai! Yes, fight back, sister. Don't let them cut you down.

He stalks her again and pounces. She escapes.

Smart girl. Now here I come. Look out!

He chases her off.

Kotane *sees no one is about and comes forward.*

Kotane In 1961 the military wing of the ANC known as Umkonte we Sizwe, the Spear of the Nation, performed the first acts of sabotage. Not one of these was aimed against a human life but only property. But the ANC had little knowledge of techniques of secrecy. Our policy had always been to act quite openly. To let the people see. When had we anything to hide? Our military leaders were arrested, tried, condemned to life-long sentences which some are serving even to this day.

Meanwhile:

Milner *has risen in his crate and is clearing his throat.* **Kotane** *raises his voice.*

It could not be denied that our policy to achieve a racially integrated state by non-violent means had achieved nothing. All our peaceful demands had been crushed by merciless force.

Milner *starts speaking through a microphone he has taken out of his crate.*

Milner Testing. Testing. One, two, three, four. Testing. Testing.

Kotane We still hoped to avoid a full-scale civil war. We have always sought our liberation without shedding blood. But what more could we do? Give up the struggle? This is unthinkable. It was no time for words. But action. Action on the street. And blood, if it must fall, falls back to earth to nourish it. It was no time for words –

Kotane *shouts above the noise. He gives up and throws his notes into the air and is silent.*

Milner
    Just one question more: Could *you* debate with coons
    Who dine on crocodile and worship moons?
    Is there a neat solution? Simply: no.
    Progress moves like an ice drift – hard, clean, slow.

Distant sounds of the sea.

Joshua *enters with a crate, labelled: Tel Aviv, at top speed. He is wearing the overalls* **George** *wore at the start of the play. He stops, sweeps up* **Kotane**'s *pieces of paper, puts them on the trolley. The bell rings.*
He pushes the trolley off.
Milner *is pouring himself a glass of whisky.*
Kotane *has not moved.*

Kotane   My life has been a struggle to unite the two
streams of our movement. Socialism. Nationalism. The CP
and the ANC. Some people in the ANC, they say: 'This
socialism – foreign. Imported. Nothing for us there.' I ask:
'But does it help or hinder? Does it cure or kill?' This
thing I know: Until we free the black man from the white
we cannot hope to free the white man from his foul
imagination. So I am first an African and only then a
Communist. But who has given us the helping hand? The
so-called free world? Or the dictators of the East? Who
puts a weapon in our hands? Who ties our hands behind
our backs? How long can we wait? What are we waiting
for?

Joshua *enters, pushing the empty trolley at top speed, across and off.*

Milner *sinks back into his crate leaving the half-full bottle of whisky visible.*

Kotane *sits.*

George *comes on.*
Police motor boat sirens in the distance. **George** *climbs on a crate to watch them pass. He takes off his jacket and shirt.*

Joshua *enters, with a crate labelled: Peking, at top speed. He sees* **George***'s back and stops.* **George** *turns. The bell rings.* **Joshua** *pushes the trolley on very fast.*

George *leaps off the crate and stands in* **Joshua***'s path.*

George   New destination.

Joshua   Dock forty-two. We signed a trade agreement.

George   We? (*Laughs weakly.*) We? And what else did we sign?

The bell rings.
Joshua *tries to push past.*
George *holds his ground.*

I need the job back.

Joshua   But there's a waiting list of fifty-four.

George   I worked here six years, man. I lost my everything.

Joshua   It's different now. Near, near. Far, far. New system. Mine.

George   This is my overall. This dampness – it's my sweat. (*He kicks his shoes off.*) Please, Joshua. It's all I know.

Joshua   And me? Where do I go?

George   Back to the mine?

Joshua (*quietly*)   No way.

George   No bread has passed my lips for three whole days.

Joshua   Back to the Transkei, friend. We don't want Xhosas here.

He starts pushing his trolley off.
George *tries to take the handles of the trolley from* **Joshua***.*
Joshua *shoves him aside and starts pushing the trolley off.*
George *tries again and succeeds.* **Joshua** *is pushed over. He stands.*

Joshua   I've got to work. There's no two ways.

George   Who's got the trolley? Hey? Who's got the job?
(**George** *starts pushing the trolley off.*)

Sings:

> Does it matter?
> No no no.
> Does it matter?
> No.

Joshua *whips up the half-full bottle of whisky and is about to bring it down on* **George**'s *head.* **George** *turns and for a split second they stare each other in the face.*
And in a flash **Joshua** *is exorcised of the ghost of* **Milner**. *His arms fly up in the air and he seems to be dragged upward. The whisky pours out of the bottle. He cries out:*

Joshua   Come back Africa!

He drops the bottle.
He pushes over the crates. They do not break or spill.

George (*in anguish*)   No, man! No, man! No!

Joshua *whips up the mallet and smashes it into the crate that held* **Milner**. *The crate comes apart and oranges pour out drowning the floor in gold.*

George *watches, his agony passing.*

Joshua *is still a moment. Then he scoops up an orange, tears off the peel and stuffs it into his mouth.*

The bell rings.

Joshua *peels a second orange and eats more carefully.*

George *picks up an orange and slowly peels and eats it.*

The bell rings again.

Kotane *comes forward to speak. He takes a new set of notes out of the inside pocket of his suit.*

George *and* **Joshua** *are eating the oranges.*

Kotane *makes a gesture and opens his mouth to speak.*

The lights come up sharply.
Tableau.

Songs to be sung before the play – not after.

Oweh weh weh weh weh
Uncle Job had many fields
Two for Peter, three for Paul
Earth so dry but millet made his beer
See Uncle Job so drunk he has to crawl
Government say – we need the wilderness
Ho ho!
Move your land, farmer – move your land
An export crop is better than a pot of beer
Give your land, farmer – give your land

Oweh weh weh weh weh
Uncle – he cry
But me
My feet are in the air
And I kick my heels
I put my feet up high

Oweh weh weh weh weh
Uncle Job had many cows
Four for Peter, more for Paul
Skin and bone but oh they bought him wives
And Uncle Job he loved them one and all
Government say – we like our women fat
Ho ho!
Kill your cow, farmer, kill your cow
One fat woman is better than a skinny herd
Kill your cow, farmer, kill your cow

Oweh weh weh weh weh
Uncle – he cry
But me
My feet are in the air
And I kick my heels
I put my feet up high

* * *

I want to tell you 'bout Gertie
She was a sweet little girlie from Zululand
All the boys were crazy for Gertie
But it was me, just me, who held her by the hand
She had brown eyes like a melting stone
She had skin soft as the wild sea foam
She was an angel floating down from the skies
She was my wish, my dream and to my surprise
She dreamed of me
That's Gertie

So now let me tell you 'bout Gertie
She was a maid for a madam in a ten room flat
All the boys can tell you 'bout Gertie
You got a pain to eat, you lie down on your back
She had pale eyes like there's no one at home
She was thin as her broomstick, all skin and bone
She worked all month long for one week's pay
She had no one to love her all night and day
So she dreamed of me
That's Gertie

Gertie – join the party
Gertie – join the party
Gertie – join the party
Gertie – join the party

* * *

The police commissioner's brow
Has furrows so deep
You could lose a sheep.
Someone steals your hoe or your cow
He says – 'Don't waste my time
The land is thick with crime
I've spent seventeen nights without sleep.'

But I say – 'What evil does a murderer do
That isn't done worse by a famine or two?
If they arrest every person who breaks a law
The government will only go and pass some more.'
So I'm happy
I don't interfere
And there's balance
In the social sphere
I say – 'After every night comes day
So leave the sleeping dog that way.'

One day Henry Shabalala grew sick.
The sister said –
'Spend the day in bed'
But his conscience went to his prick.
He said – 'Look, I got V.D.'
The nurse said – 'What you need
Is penicillin but there's none.' So he's dead.
But I say – 'What evil does a sickness do
That can't be done by a murderer or two?
If we solve every problem we stumble upon
The government will only put its thinking cap on.'
Why I'm happy
You don't need to guess
Nothing changes
And that's progress ·
I say – 'After every day comes night
So leave the growling dog to bite.'

Flight

in memory of Golda Lan

Characters

Isaac Levine, *at first (aged forty) a book-keeper in Salisbury, Rhodesia, and then (aged twenty) in Kovna, Lithuania.*

Hannah Levine, *Isaac's wife, of the same age, a dressmaker, first in Salisbury, then in Kovna.*

Lily Tabor, *Hannah's sister, a year or two older. At first a teacher in Salisbury, then a labour organiser in Kovna.*

Mike Levine, *Isaac and Hannah's son. At first a shop assistant (aged twenty) in Salisbury, then the owner of a jewellery store and then (aged forty-five) of a chain of such stores.*

Rose Kossew, *at first (aged twenty) the daughter of a failed farmer, then Mike's wife (aged forty-five).*

Albert Hamadziripi, *at first a young Shona pupil of Lily's (aged twenty), then the manager of one of Mike's stores (aged forty-five).*

Gideon Sachs, *a political leader in Kovna (aged thirty).*

Paul Levine, *Mike and Rose's son, a soldier (aged twenty).*

The play takes place in Harare, Zimbabwe (then known as Salisbury, Rhodesia), between the years 1952 and 1980, and also in Kannas, Lithuania in 1930.

Flight was first presented by the Royal Shakespeare Company at The Other Place, Stratford-upon-Avon, on 2 April 1986 and subsequently in the Pit at the Barbican, London, with the following cast:

Isaac Levine	Joe Melia
Hannah Levine	Dinah Stabb
Lily Tabor	Gillian Barge
Gideon Sachs	Peter Guinness
Mike Levine	Nicholas Woodeson
Rose Kossew	Geraldine Fitzgerald
Albert Hamadziripi	Joseph Mydell
Paul Levine	Max Gold

Directed by Howard Davies
Set designed by Bob Crowley
Costumes designed by Alan Watkins
Lighting by Chris Parry
Sound by John A Leonard and Chris Johns

Part One

Scene One

1952. The front room of a house in Salisbury.

Isaac, *dressed in sports shirt and trousers, is sitting at the table drinking and playing Patience.*

Hannah, *wearing a dressing gown, is polishing cutlery and laying places.*

Isaac   I'm waiting. Name one Jew and I'm happy. One Jew who made money in business.

Hannah   Weinberg!

Isaac   Six on the seven. Hoi! Which Weinberg?

Hannah   Pinkie.

Isaac   Pinkie Weinberg? Ladies' hats and accessories?

Hannah   Now *he's* done well.

Isaac   Machullah. Bankrupt. Finish and done. Three on the four. Hoi!

Hannah   Pinkie! Since when?

Isaac   Five on the six. Hoi! Two months, maybe three months. Weinberg? Pinkie? So many debts he had to send out his boy for red ink twice in one afternoon.

Hannah   For each one that fails one succeeds.

Isaac   You can prove this? No. The lord our god is an honest man. But his book-keeper? A shvindler. By me, that's lesson number one.

Hannah (*to herself*)   But how can it be?

Isaac   Five on the six, five on the six . . .

Hannah   A dozen forks, a dozen knives went walking?

The phone rings.

Hannah   Oy! Isaac. Isaac, the phone. Isaac!

Isaac   What is it? The phone makes such a racket I can't hear what you say.

Hannah *answers the phone.*

Hannah   Yes? Oh, Hilda. (*To* **Isaac**.) Now Hilda won't come. (*Into phone.*) So late? . . . With the food sitting waiting in the oven?

Isaac   She don't like to come to my house? Stay away.

Hannah (*to* **Isaac**)   We don't got a proper service! (*Into phone.*) You *know* what kind service we got here. Hebrew, Yiddish, Jewish . . .

Isaac *grabs the phone from her.*

Isaac   Tell Jacob from his brother Isaac . . . listen to me, sweetheart . . . I'm *trying* to be reasonable . . . I wouldn't welcome you? I'd set my dog on you . . . well, I'd buy a dog and then set him on you . . . *I'm* rude? Half past five passover evening? (*He gives the phone to* **Hannah**.) I don't wish to upset her. I'm going to shul. Where's my tallis?

Hannah   In the bread bin.

Isaac *unwraps his prayer shawl from a loaf of bread.*

Isaac   My hat?

Hannah   By the vegetables. (*Into phone.*) Me? Upset? . . . no, darling, I'm busy tomorrow, washing up, putting away – you know how it is when the whole family comes round . . .

Isaac *takes his hat from a basket, removes from it two melons and brushes the dirt off it.*

Hannah   . . . and the day after . . . all next week . . . and to your loved ones also. (*She puts down the phone.*) Six chickens waiting in the oven – everyone's going to Jacob . . .

Isaac *embraces her.*

Isaac   Hilda's father was who? Uncle Pincus, the fool who didn't know even to come out the woods to escape from the Cossacks. You're weeping for Hilda?

He puts on his coat.

Hannah   Wait for Mikey. He'll be home in two twos.

The doorbell rings.

Isaac   Bolt the door. We don't need from anyone. We'll eat, dance, sing. Laugh! Will we laugh? Hm? The pair of us. Sweetheart?

Lily comes in.

Hannah   Lily!

Isaac   What for you came here? Everyone's going by Jacob.

Lily   That's why I came here. (*To* **Hannah**.) Everyone?

Hannah   Millie, Able, Jackie, Morris, Ezra, the children –

Isaac   The whole world!

Hannah   Josie, Miriam . . . Now Hilda.

Isaac   What a party he's kicking up. What a giant! What a sage! He wins ten thousand pounds in the state lottery –

Lily   I heard fifteen.

Isaac   Ten! In one leap – hoi! – head of the family. This is Jacob the pisher I'm talking. A family of good honest working people line up to polish his tochus. A gambler! Lily, explain to me.

Lily   Something for nothing. People respect it.

Isaac   But is it right or is it wrong?

Lily   I don't care a fig for the whole world. I care for you.

Lily *hands* **Hannah** *a box she has taken from her bag.* **Hannah** *opens the box.*

Hannah   You shouldn't.

Lily   Why shouldn't I?

Isaac   How much does she care?

Hannah   Apfelkuchen.

Isaac   She cares!

Isaac *takes a cake and eats it.* **Hannah** *kisses* **Lily** *then looks at her closely.*

Hannah   She got teaching. She got charity work. But her baking . . .

Isaac   Nah, you're right and I'm wrong. God is just. He makes an idiot like Jacob, he looks after him. What right I got to complain?

Isaac *takes another cake and goes out.*

Hannah   Your eyes!

Lily *breaks away and takes things from her bag.*

Lily   Here's the pattern for the blouse, the yarn for the stockings.

Hannah   So red, so sore.

Lily   I work day and night. So?

Hannah   This isn't working. It's weeping.

Lily   Why shouldn't I remember him? On Passover, once a year? A man like he was, that's too often?

Hannah   Don't be angry. Or miserable. Darling. Not today when the family – his family – deserted me. You're my strength.

Lily   And you're mine. What is it? Ask me.

Hannah   I didn't lend *you* my pesach knives, forks?

Lily   How you even know you lost them?

Hannah Ach, old jokes. You neat, me untidy. Ask where's anything. Ask me.

Lily The whisky.

Hannah By the toothpaste.

Lily *laughs, gets up and starts to go out. Then she stops.*

Lily And the toothpaste?

Hannah By the food for the ducks.

Lily *laughs again, takes a bottle of whisky out of a box and pours drinks for herself and* **Hannah**.

Hannah But the knives and forks? No one touched them since last year. (*She goes to the table.*) Only four. And such a big table.

Lily We'll be plenty. My number-one pupil is coming. I told you?

Hannah He wants to? By us? Marvellous. I can kiss him. (*She is on the verge of tears. She holds up a dress.*) What you think?

Lily (*sleepy*) Beautiful. Really

Hannah One thing I *can* do is sew, am I right?

Lily Like feathers, like clouds.

Hannah It's for Dora Kaplinsky. Two pound ten. Cheap. She won't mind if I wear it?

Lily Slip it on.

Hannah *bursts into tears.*

Hannah Everything just how *they* like it. Tsimmis. Dumplings. Herring. Not the way *our* mother made it. *His* family taste. Sweet, sweet, sweet. Wait. There should be six chairs in this room. One, two, three . . . Knives and forks! Chairs! Where's everything gone in this house?

She hurries out. **Lily** *drinks, then drinks* **Hannah**'s. *Then she sits, looks at her face in a powder compact she takes from her bag, fixes* *her face with powder and lipstick, then brushes her hair, deep in thought.*

Mike *comes in through the front door. He stands and watches* **Lily**.

Mike Where's ma?

Lily *starts in surprise.*

Lily Mikey! Your mama's a little bit everywhere. Look at me. The wild woman of Timbuctoo.

She kisses him warmly and hurries out. **Mike** *eats one of the Apfelkuchen. He is about to put a second into his mouth when* **Hannah** *comes in with a tray of plates and little bowls.*

Hannah Just in time, Mr Sneakypants.

Mike . . . hungry.

Hannah Sweet, sweet, sweet isn't hunger. It's greed. Eat an orange. So sweet, makes you sweat.

Mike *slips the cake into his pocket and takes an orange.*

Hannah Where you been? I told you – from work, straight home. Mama's got carpets to beat, tables to schlep. Pesach is when mama needs you. Lochinkop! (*She cuffs his head, then ruffles his hair.*) Don't take it personal.

Mike Rose is coming, all right?

Hannah For dinner? By us?

Mike Why you crying? It's not a wedding announcement.

Hannah *wipes a tear and turns back to laying the table.* **Mike** *starts to peel and eat the orange.*

Mike Did you go look at it?

Hannah Every year I forget something. Shank bone? I got it.

Mike Ma!

Hannah Look at what?

Mike The premises for my shop.

Hannah   I looked.

Mike   So?

Hannah   So. Very good. Boiled egg? I got it.

Mike   But?

Hannah   Bu-ut ...

Mike   But what?

Hannah   I don't say it's not good.

Mike   Good but what?

Hannah   I can't say no to you, darling. You want an honest opinion. Ask your daddy.

Mike   I know what he thinks. I'm asking you.

Isaac *comes in wearing a dressing gown.*

Hannah   You got a present for pesach. There. By your daddy's spare razor.

Isaac   What a pity. Someone came.

Hannah (*to Isaac*)   Shul – half an hour.

Mike (*opening his present*)   A vest.

Hannah   You don't need? Everybody needs vests.

Mike   I need shoes. I've got only one pair of trousers.

Isaac   Noo? You got only one pair of legs.

Mike   There's not one smart shirt in my cupboard.

Hannah   Wear the cream one. I turned the collar beautiful.

Mike   I need new ones.

Isaac   Tell Hertzveldt: put up your wages.

Mike   He won't.

Isaac   You don't deserve it?

Mike   I deserve twice what he pays. Right. I'll keep what I earn for myself.

Isaac   And Millie? She needs milk for the baby. Miriam the cripple? She can't afford even tea. Ivan with eczema? He needs fruit. On a pound a week? And you're crying for fashionable clothes.

Mike   It's my money.

Isaac   In what sense?

Hannah   Please, boys. Later. Not now.

Isaac   You're not interested, his point of view?

Mike   Uncle Jacob's got piles of cash. He can look after them.

Isaac   That schnorer cares so much (*Snaps his fingers.*) for his family.

Mike   He's caring tonight.

Hannah   Cheek isn't argument.

Mike   The problem isn't my wage. It's yours. Care for the family? How can we care without cash? You give everything away.

Isaac   My brother wins five thousand pounds. My son wants to go into business. It's a family of gamblers! Of highway men! Listen, you haven't got cash? You're in luck. Care with your mind, with your heart. He knows this. Look how he's helping his aunty. Hm? Marking her pupils' books. Teaching. (*To* **Mike**.) Am I right? (*To* **Hannah**.) He knows what I'm talking. He's not a big boy? (*To* **Mike**.) Have a drink. (*He starts to open a bottle of wine.*)

Hannah   Not the pesach wine. There's only one bottle. (*She gives him another bottle.*)

Isaac   I can kosher some more.

Mike   You can kosher wine?

Isaac   Wasn't my mama a Cohen, a priest? So, tell me what I can't kosher. Double kosher, no problem. (*Intoning.*) Baroch atah adonai, elohainu melech haolum, borai peri hagafin. (*Making passes over the bottle.*) Kosher once, twice, three times.

He opens the bottle and pours glasses of wine for all of them.

Isaac   Drown greed in generosity. Promise daddy you'll forget all your business nonsense. Promise.

Mike *says nothing.*

Hannah (*embracing* **Mike**)   What we did to make you so strong? Outside he's a lamb. Inside – a lion. He can roar.

Isaac *puts his arms round* **Hannah** *and* **Mike**.

Isaac   Let Jacob the pisher win a million pounds. Isn't so?

Lily *comes in.*

Lily   A wash, a brush. I'm back in the land of the living.

Isaac *has poured a glass of wine for* **Lily**.

Isaac   Lily?

Lily *takes the glass.*

Isaac   To us? Yes? A family of lions? Am I right?

They all drink then stand and grin at each other.

Isaac (*toasting*)   Peace!

Hannah   The family!

Lily   Freedom!

Mike   My own shop!

Mike *drinks, puts down his glass and goes out.*

Hannah   He's not happy, I'm not happy.

Isaac   He's not happy. You're not happy. What can I do? I'm happy.

Isaac *puts his arms round* **Hannah** *and starts dancing round with her. At first she tries to push him off but quickly succumbs, laughs, relaxes.*

Isaac (*dancing round with* **Hannah**)   Oh, my sweet, my honey sweet . . .

Hannah   Sweet, sweet, sweet. All the same.

Isaac   . . . my little pot of cherry jam, my silver dish of Apfelkuchen . . .

Hannah   Isaac, my pesach cutlery, my chairs – I want the truth. You lent it to Jacob?

Isaac (*finally unable to escape*)   He asked me. He's got the whole family coming round . . . You want our family should walk round the world each one carrying on his back his own chair? He asked me. I should say no?

Hannah *goes back to setting the table.*

Hannah   Salty water? I got it.

Isaac *pours a second glass of wine for* **Lily***.*

Lily   I'll fall asleep straight away.

Isaac   No one escapes from this life so easy.

He pours himself another glass. **Lily** *drinks her wine in one go.* **Isaac** *fills her glass again.*

Isaac (*to* **Lily**)   So – how's your pupils? Keep you on your toes, nice and frisky?

The doorbell rings. **Isaac** *makes for the door.*

Hannah (*harsh*)   In your dressing gown? No. What are you? A monkey? Take off *all* your clothes. Let's see what you are.

Isaac *looks at her, then goes off back to his bedroom.* **Hannah** *catches her breath, wipes her eyes, picks up her dress, presses it against her and goes out. The doorbell rings again.*

It is 1930: Kannas, Lithuania.

Gideon *comes in carrying a chair.*

Gideon   No, no, wait. If the past *is* a nightmare, how are we to wake ourselves? Please, just a moment more. If you don't mind. I think best on my feet. (*Broad smile.*) A nightmare. Good word. What does it imply? A kind of a fantasy but composed out of elements we recognise. Religion. God. Holy books. Rabbis. Demons who pass streams of silver instead of water and cash instead of – you know what I'm talking, excuse me. Composed of the drek of the soul. And especially in our nightmares: the family.

Isaac (*aged twenty*) *enters carrying a chair.*

Gideon   In my own dreams my grandmother's half-sister appears. She wears a rabbitskin coat and a fez. Ask me why. (*To* **Lily** *who is bursting to speak.*) Wait. To summarise: the centuries have shaped around us particular patterns of kinship relations which we, only partially aware of their meaning, experience as a nightmare. Good. So. Criticise.

Lily *speaks with fire. She is twenty-two years old.*

Lily   Listen. Families? I'll tell you. Day after day I say to the tailors, the crate makers, the stocking women, the soap makers, the book binders: you want better wages? Make demands! Go on strike! They say: well, but the manager is a cousin of my mother's on her uncle's side. If only that wise and holy gentleman could hear how we suffer, what he wouldn't sacrifice to help us. Huh? Isn't so? It's belief in the power of the family that keeps people back.

Hannah (*aged twenty*) *comes in. She carries a wooden stool.*

Gideon (*to* **Isaac**)   You agree with this?

Isaac   A Jew without a family? Then what is a Jew? (*Of* **Lily**.) She laughs at me. (*To* **Lily**.) Gideon doesn't laugh. (*To* **Hannah**.) What is it now?

Hannah   There's no firewood.

Isaac   Half a minute.

Hannah   I've been waiting two hours. When you chop in the dark you cut yourself, you know that.

Isaac   By me, the family is . . . (*Thinking.*) wait, wait . . . a pillow to lie on when times are hard.

Hannah *snorts derisively.*

Isaac   Please, Hannah. (*To* **Gideon**.) You want to chuck away something? Religion. Believe me, they'll sigh with relief.

Lily *clicks her tongue with impatience.*

Gideon   How to approach the Jewish worker of Europe? Announce the revolution brings with it the end of religion. But religion is his life. For him there is no warmth, light, shelter outside the arms of his God. For God's sake then, speak to him as one Jew to another.

Hannah   And oil for the lamps. You hate to sit in the dark.

Hannah *goes out taking her wooden stool with her.*

Lily (*to* **Gideon**)   What you say, I agree to this point. First understand by what knots their emotions are tied. Then start to untie them.

Isaac (*to* **Lily**)   Not possible. Didn't you hear? It's not possible.

Gideon   Another example. We call out the Jewish workers against the state. Each worker knows if it goes against, he can hide for a time in the woods. But the army will punish his family. Torture. Starve. Execute. So would they join us? And will they be right to? Don't look to me for an answer. (*Broad smile.*) It's a problem. So. Criticise.

The doorbell rings again. **Gideon** *and* **Isaac** *go out taking their chairs.*

It is 1952: Salisbury again.

Hannah *comes in with* **Rose**.

Hannah   In this house it's always a little later than we wish. What can you do? Mikey will be dressed in two twos. Your mama doesn't mind you being out on pesach?

Rose   She hates a celebration.

Hannah   No! But why?

Rose *shrugs.*

Hannah   Is she alone? Go home. Fetch her. We can find a knife and fork. Mike will go borrow a chair.

Rose   She won't come.

Hannah   Shame. A lost soul. You want give me a hand in the kitchen?

Rose *shrugs.*

Hannah   Darling, in this house we want only you should be happy. Help yourself to anything. Anything at all.

Hannah *takes the box of Apfelkuchen and goes out.* **Rose**, *immediately bored, wanders about, picking at things.* **Lily** *looks up.*

Lily   You know what was my dream? Blue sky, sunshine, birds singing. I'm strolling by a river. No classes, no pupils, no meetings. Inside my head is perfect peace, perfect quiet. You're Rose?

Rose   Mm.

Lily   I had a boyfriend once.

Rose   Only one?

Lily   He'd come into the house, straight to the kitchen table, worn out as he was, no food, no rest, up till cock crow, writing, writing. A book must be written with tears fresh in your eyes, with pain hot in your heart. A book, he would say, is a tree standing firm against the storms of history.

Rose   Is it all right if I have something to drink?

Isaac *comes in dressed in his suit.*

Isaac   Who wants to watch the fastest game of Patience in the world?

Rose   Wouldn't say no.

Isaac Lightning Patience. It's a gift straight from God. (*He takes his pack of cards.*) One, two, fire, go!

He plays Patience at amazing speed, naming each move as he makes it.

Isaac Three on the four! Six on the seven! Queen on – where the hell is it? – king! – eight on the nine! Hoi! Nine on the ten! Four on the five! – queen, king, ace – two, two, two – where you hiding, you devil? Ten on the jack! Three on the four! Hoi! – two, two? – I got him! King, king, king, there he appears! Eight on the nine! Hoi! It's coming. It's coming. Four on the five . . .

Meantime, **Hannah** *has dressed. She enters holding a necklace.*

Hannah (*to* **Isaac**) Not now. (*To* **Rose**.) With that dress, not gold, darling. This coral necklace belonged to my granny. Red like blood. You want it? Isaac!

Rose, *who has eyes only for* **Isaac**, *puts it aside as soon as* **Hannah** *turns away.* **Mike** *comes in smartly dressed.*

Hannah (*to* **Rose**) Isn't he handsome? More than the film stars. You think so? (*To* **Isaac**.) Not now.

Mike Dad, time to go.

Rose He said it's a race with his God.

Hannah Isaac!

The cards explode out of **Isaac**'s *hands and go all over the room.*

Hannah Now look what you done.

Isaac It's numbers. Only numbers. Sometimes it comes out, sometimes no. When did it harm anyone?

He sits at the table with his head in his hands. **Hannah** *starts to pick up the cards. The doorbell rings.*

Lily I'll go.

Hannah But go slowly.

Lily *goes out.* **Hannah** *picks up all the cards as quickly as she can.*

Mike (*to* **Rose**)   I look all right?

Rose   Pants a bit shiny.

Mike   You coming to shul?

Rose   I never go. Unless I lose someone's phone number.

Lily *returns with* **Albert**, *a young Shona man, dressed in a shabby suit.*

Lily   This is Mr Hamadziripi.

Albert   No, please. Albert.

Lily   My number-one pupil. Albert has been teaching Mikey and me all about the customs of his people. I want he should learn a little about ours.

Hannah   You're very welcome. A little wine?

Albert *looks round nervously.*

Hannah   We're all good friends here.

She pours wine into a silver cup.

The silver cup – special for you.

She gives the cup to **Albert**. *He drinks*

Rose   Mr Levine, I must congratulate you. My mother says your brother won twenty thousand pounds in the lottery. You must be proud and excited.

A silence falls.

Isaac   Mr Albert, you want to know why do I celebrate passover? I myself, Isaac Jahuda Levine. So I'll tell you. For the lesson it teaches from history. Many years ago, we Jews were a class of slaves in a corrupt feudal state. Egypt. What did we do? Mikey?

Mike (*bored, embarrassed*)   We analysed class relations.

Isaac   And then?

Mike   Dad!

Hannah   You can't answer? Say so.

Mike   We took appropriate action.

Isaac   Flight! We journeyed across a great desert. At last
we reached a land with no immigration restrictions, no
influx control, not one bit of legislation which the state
always imposes on those with no national home. At last we
reached – where? Who knows? Mike? The Baltic States –
Lithuania, Latvia, Estonia, even mother Russia herself. But
what did we find there? A centralised bureaucracy – the
Jews at the bottom once more. So – once again: flight! (*He
picks up objects from the table.*) This roasted shank bone is a
symbol of the sacrifices made by Jews as slaves in Egypt or
wage slaves in Europe. You're free to choose. This salt
water is tears we cried when we were arrested and tortured
by the secret police of the Pharaoh or the Tsar, as you
please. That silver goblet full of wine we place by the door
to hasten the arrival of the Prophet Elijah. When he comes
we shall see prosperity, joy, the downfall of the state, no
nations, no borders, no need to flee anywhere anymore
ever again. This is the lesson of passover. We who were
slaves had such power in our minds we could bring
crashing down in the dust the whole Egyptian state. The
spirit of the Jewish working man will always triumph over
the state. So. My brother wins five thousand pounds in the
state lottery? I must throw a dance, hire a caterer, book
the town hall? So. Who's coming to give thanks to our
God for our freedom from tyranny? Mikey? Hannah? Lily?
Mr Albert? Are we ready? Shall we go?

Scene Two

Six months later. A small jewellery shop in Salisbury.

*To one side a desk with an electric light burning. On the desk and on
the wall are a variety of clocks and watches all with price tags
attached. It is early morning. The sun shines weakly into the room.*

Rose *is asleep on a large battered armchair.*

Mike *has been working at the desk through the night. He finishes writing and lays down his pen. He shivers as he becomes aware of the morning cold. Then he goes over to* **Rose**.

Mike   Doll?

Rose   . . . mm . . .

Mike *(with a grimace of distaste)*   Your face is all pink.

Rose   . . . isn't . . . is it? . . . isn't . . .

He kisses her.

Rose   . . . kiss like a farm boy . . . lips and spit . . . lovely . . . again? . . . *(She shivers.)* Oooh, but it's cold . . .

Mike *takes his jacket off the back of his chair and drapes it over her shoulders.*

Rose   . . . love to spend the night . . . here . . . love to . . . can't . . . no good begging me . . . see? . . . you see? . . . *(She shivers again.)* . . . better take me home . . .

Mike *laughs.*

Rose   . . . laughing at me? *(She sits up.)* What time is it?

Mike *(indicating the clocks on the desk)*   Take your pick. Just after seven.

Rose   Come again?

Mike   In the morning.

Rose   You lie!

Mike   I've been working all night.

Rose   And my mother? She'll slaughter me. What are you staring at?

Mike   Take off your jersey.

Rose   You crazy?

Mike   Feel the cold on your neck, on your shoulders.

Rose Cold? I'm burning up. Feel. No! Don't touch me. (*She tries to stand.*) Now my leg's gone to sleep.

Mike *unbuttons his shirt.*

Rose What you *doing*?

Mike . . . want to feel the cold . . . my whole body . . .

Rose She'll slaughter you too.

Mike . . . your hand . . . sh! . . . closer . . .

He takes off his shirt and pulls her arms around him.

Mike . . . hold me . . . baby . . .

She pulls off her jersey, shivers with pleasure and holds him.

Mike I'm so *happy* here. Are you? Doll?

She nods.

Mike This is my kingdom. My island.

The sunlight is suddenly more intense.

Mike No, more like a tree house, you know? Where you run away, escape from your ma and your dad.

Rose I never ran away. I couldn't. My home sort of ran away from me. If my ma thinks *I've* run away all hell will break loose.

Mike Ooh. I love a good shiver. Ooh. Makes you feel so alive.

He grabs her hand and tries to pull her down into the armchair.

Come on. Make up for lost time.

Rose I'm black and blue.

Mike Lie on me.

She sprawls next to him.

Mike . . . ooh . . . doll! . . .

Rose Move your knee.

Mike   . . . ooh . . . can't I? . . .

Rose   I *said* –

Mike   . . . know what I was doing? . . .

Rose   What?

Mike   . . . planning . . .

Rose   And your elbow. Planning what?

Mike   . . . where we'll be . . . five years time . . .

Rose   Where's that?

Mike   Top of the world.

She pulls away.

Rose   Don't say that.

Mike   . . . wha? . . .

Rose   Just don't.

She gets out of the chair.

Ach, my dress is all crinkled. My grandpa used to say –
what you said. He'd climb to the top of a water tower on
our farm – fifty, sixty feet. He'd shout: here I am, oh great
Jehovah. At the t- o- th-. One time he climbed up half
drunk with a jug of my granny's home brew, finished the
lot, slipped, fell off, landed in a hole. A deep one. With a
thorn tree growing in it. His collar caught on a branch. He
hanged himself. That's why.

Mike   Ancient history.

Rose   But what a life that old man had, hey? This
country was actually wild when he came here. He tamed it.
Single-handed. Adam in Paradise.

Mike   That's how I feel. Here. Now. With you.

Rose   After my dad I loved him best. But I never once
saw him happy. So I felt bad. Why? When the tobacco
was in, he'd stroke a finger along the leaves, pulling on his

pipe. And he'd curse. Kucken and pishen! Gai kucken
ahfen yam! We'd hide behind the barn, laugh our heads
off. He'd catch us in his huge bear arms, beat the hell out
of us. Women's feelings are all kept in their breasts, you
know that? You think you want to grab them and squeeze
them just for the fun of it. In fact you're trying to pull
them off. You know why? Jealousy. And that's why men
beat up women. They've got nothing to hold their own
feelings in. They want us to lose ours. Two months after
my grandpa died, my dad got up from breakfast, climbed
on his tractor, started ploughing a field. I looked out the
window. I thought: hey, the field's bigger than I thought.
He broke through the fence, made one furrow into the
bush sixteen miles. Never saw him or the tractor again. So
we sold up, came into town. Granny, ma . . . me. Since
then I've cried myself to sleep every night of my life.

Mike   You didn't cry last night.

Rose   I didn't know I was going to sleep, did I? Idiot.

She cuffs him on the head.

Mike   I won't run away. I swear on God's teeth. You
know why? I'm where I want to be. Here, with my girl, on
my piece of the earth. I'm going to work and work –

Rose   Can't you hold me tighter than that?

Mike   . . . work, work, work . . .

Rose   . . . plough your fields . . .

Mike   . . . plough my fields? . . .

Rose   . . . plough your wife . . .

Mike   . . . plough my wife . . .

He giggles.

Rose   Ja, I'm just a farm girl. Get me my farm back.

Mike   Sorry?

Rose Make money. Buy my farm back for me. No, hold me. That farm's the only place I'll ever feel peaceful.

Mike If that's what you want.

Rose You want it too. To put up a fence. That side: let them come, let them go. This side: it's home.

Mike I'll do it.

She looks at him for a moment, then yawns.

Rose Go sit somewhere else.

Mike Don't sleep now.

Rose But I'm sleepy . . . move . . .

He gets up. She nestles down into the chair.

Rose . . . I'm trusting you, Mike. All right? . . .

Mike All right, doll. Trust me.

*She falls asleep. He watches her for a moment, rubs his crutch, sighs, picks his jacket off the floor, lays it over **Rose** and goes back to his desk. He turns off the desk light. Sunlight floods in.*

Mike *sits bathed in light. He stretches, rubs his fingers over his naked chest, beats his fists on it. He opens his ledger and turns a page. The doorbell rings.*

It is 1942.

Hannah and **Lily** *come in carrying deckchairs. They wear very light clothes, sandals and sunglasses.* **Hannah** *also carries a sewing basket. They set down the chairs and sit on them in the park by the river.*

Hannah He shouldn't lie in the sun with no hat on. I told him. Such skin. Like a woman. You wouldn't believe.

Lily A lovely boy. I love him.

Hannah You want him?

Lily He did something wrong?

Hannah Stealing sweets.

Lily No!

Hannah Breaks my heart.

Lily I'll talk with him.

Hannah Would you? To me he's a brick wall.

Lily Why he did it?

Hannah Where I got money to buy for him sweets?

Lily Hannah – sweets for the children!

Hannah Where I got it? And now ... with Isaac.

Lily Isaac?

Hannah You don't know?

Lily What?

Hannah Sh!

Lily Who?

Hannah I don't want he should hear.

Lily He's sleeping.

Hannah He got always open half an ear. Oh, oh, oh.
Oh, Lily.

Lily Tell me.

Hannah You know Mr Brightman? Fool. That fool! He
gave Isaac the sack.

Lily *sighs.*

Hannah You criticise Isaac? You?

Lily Up to his waist in dirt, he wants to breathe the
sweet air.

Hannah Business by you is dirt. OK.

Lily Business by him is fine when it brings the family
cash. But when it hurts another? No good. A philosopher
not a businessman. Book-keeping systems, abstractions, fine.

Decisions – hard, practical, me or you, one or one thousand, pink or green – ?

Hannah (*at the same time as the above*)   You earned a living wage once in your life? You break your back teaching loafers. They pay what? Monkey nuts. You criticise?

Hannah *takes a packet of sandwiches from her bag, opens it and offers it to* **Lily**. **Lily** *doesn't take it.*

Hannah   You on a diet? Why? Cream cheese, I made it nice. I don't want a fight in this family. Nothing is worth it. You hear what I'm saying? No fights!

Lily   It's true they pay me nothing. So? You were the only one who never understood. To be part of a movement. You listening to me? It's more than one person, more than two, than a family. It's history. You think I want to get up, leave this nice park, cool river, sit in a dark room, listen to arguments, half of them foolish?

Hannah   You love it.

Lily   I hate it.

Hannah   Since when?

Lily   Since my nerves.

Hannah   You're nervous?

Lily   I speak – the whole room becomes like a cave underwater, waves and shadows. I'm drowning. There's no one to leap in, pull me out.

Hannah   But you do it.

Lily   For he who isn't here. Who should be – would be . . .

She is crying.

Hannah   Sorry, sorry, darling.

Lily   I need nothing. Only my memory of him, of what he did or would have done.

Hannah   That's fine. But in the end, what we got? (*Shouting.*) You wipe up your tears, in two twos you're busy with meetings again. It's no good! (*She opens her purse.*) Look what I got. Bath plug. Pencil sharpener. Pipe cleaner. (*Of something she finds in her bag.*) What *is* this? One shilling and sevenpence. And the rent? Sh! Sleep, sleep, darling. Electricity? Mikey, you sleeping? And the telephone? No, no. Not good enough. You got to choose. Is it politics? Is it the family? Someone got to choose.

The doorbell rings.

Hannah *and* **Lily** *take their chairs and go out.*

It is 1952 again.

Mike *puts on his shirt and goes out.*

Meantime, **Isaac** *comes in dressed for synagogue.* **Mike** *follows* **Isaac** *in.*

Isaac   You coming to shul?

Mike *says nothing.*

Isaac (*of* **Rose**)   You can't afford a better watchdog? What happened? Friday night, just mama and me at the table. We waited and waited. Is that nice?

Mike   . . . working.

Isaac   Come again? On the shabbes every Jew takes a rest. He was working. Well, mama won't forgive you but God? Maybe. Put on your coat.

Mike   . . . not coming.

Isaac   Not?

Mike   . . . got to keep the shop open.

Isaac   Shop? Which shop?

Mike   My shop.

Isaac   You got a shop? Very nice.

Mike You like it?

Isaac I like it, I don't like it? Is it my shop? Nah, it's some shop, what I heard about it? Nothing. Till I'm with Solly Greenberg yesterday four o'clock in the Turkish bath. 'Mazel tov', he tells me. 'It's a pleasure, but what I achieved?' 'You? Nothing. Your son. I signed a contract to rent him my shop on the square.' My son got a shop? From a stranger I learn my son − got − (*He indicates.*)

Mike Greenberg's not a stranger.

Isaac Compared to you?

Mike Mama didn't tell you?

Isaac She tells me this, she tells me that.

Mike *thinks for a moment then looks up at* **Isaac**.

Mike I'm sorry I didn't discuss this with you.

Isaac You're sorry? Can you turn back your clocks? Bring back last week, last year? What's done for is over. So? It's not the end of the world.

He takes **Mike**'*s jacket off* **Rose** *and holds it out to him.*

Rabbi's waiting. Come.

Mike *opens a ledger and starts writing.*

Isaac OK. Never mind shul. God will enjoy if we walk in his mountains. Come.

Mike *goes on writing.*

Isaac So last night I told Greenberg you'll give notice the end of the week. That made you look up. What for we need this? People care what's the time? There's a clock on the town hall. Doo-dads. Bangles. Does that make a full life? Hertzveldt will take you back in his shop, no hard feelings. I fixed it up. Wake the girl, lock the office, come to shul.

Mike *says nothing.*

Isaac   You want a klup on the kop? I'm telling you, throw away your papers –

Mike   This is my shop.

Isaac   You had it a week. Mazel tov. Now it's Greenberg's again.

Mike   We need the money.

Isaac   I need it? Who needs it? Your mama needs it?

Mike   With this shop she can take it easy, she won't have to sew anymore.

Isaac   That's how much you understand. She loves it. Take away sewing, what will she do all day long? You didn't hear about Jacob?

Mike   I heard.

Isaac   My little brother Jacob? You don't know what happened?

Mike   Yes, I know!

Isaac   You call yourself a businessman? You don't hear what goes on in this town. Jacob – machullah. Two questions it took. Number one: can we please have some tax on your winnings ten thousand? Number two: funny thing, we can't find a file for any tax payments in the past. Hm? Hm? Hm? Nothing left, nothing, less than nothing.

Mike   A shop is not a lottery.

Isaac   But it is! You take for yourself and add what to the world? Not a baked bean! Hoi! Such a good trick, in two twos you think you're a boss. Marvellous. But who bosses you? The bigger boss. Tax inspectors, lawyers, police. The state. You're my son. I love you. I'm begging. If you stick out your head like a chicken, you end up in the soup. This we don't do. Us? A boss? No. I'm a worker. I got workers' blood in my veins.

Rose *wakes, yawns loudly and stretches.*

Rose   Ooh! I didn't snore?

Isaac   Good morning, madam. These premises are closing down. We advise a swift removal to a more natural place of repose.

Mike   He wants me to close down the shop.

Rose   Why? You won't, Mikey, will you? You can't.

Isaac   Can't is a word I can't learn in any language of the world.

Rose   Tell him! Mike!

Mike *is too upset to answer.*

Isaac   I don't want you should complain I've been pushing. Give one good reason for keeping open?

Rose   He wants to be free of you.

Mike   That's not it. Not all of it . . .

Rose   But why shouldn't you? We're grown up. We've got our own plans, our own dreams.

Isaac   You think he'll marry you? Big mistake. He's sensitive. He won't take a girl with a horse like a face.

Rose   What?

Mike   He means a face like a horse.

Rose   I know what he means!

Mike   He's upset. He doesn't want to hurt.

Isaac   I want! I want! Go home!

Rose   When you came to this country –

Isaac   1931. July 14.

Rose   You came on your own?

Isaac   On the same two feet I wear to this day.

Rose   Weren't you glad to leave your father behind?

Isaac   My father – he was a marvellous fellow.

Rose   But you were glad he wasn't with you. Tell the truth.

Isaac   Tell the truth. Listen to her. This is my son. Would I lie to him?

Rose   Of course. Why not? To get your own way.

Isaac *hits* **Rose** *with the back of his hand.* **Mike** *goes to* **Rose**.

Isaac   From where you know this shikseh? I don't want you should see her again.

Rose   Leave me. I'm used to it.

Isaac   Let's go.

Mike *takes a letter from a file and holds it out.*

Mike   Dad!

Isaac   What is it?

Mike   Read it.

Isaac *takes it and looks at it.*

Isaac   I didn't bring my glasses.

Mike   It's a letter from Greenberg. Look at the address. And the date. You didn't see him last night at the baths. Did you? You didn't tell him anything about giving notice. Did you? So she's right. No bosses, is that it? As long as the boss remains you.

Isaac *walks over to the desk and sits down.*

Isaac   So. So, so, so. So.

Isaac *plays with the papers and ledgers then gets absorbed by them.*

Rose   I'm going now. Don't try to touch me.

She puts on her coat.

Rose   Goodbye, Mr Levine.

Isaac   You interested in book-keeping?

Rose   Me?

Isaac   You.

Rose   Don't know anything about it.

Isaac   So what interests you?

Rose   Right now?

Isaac   At this precise moment.

Rose   Making money.

Isaac   Me – I'm interested in book-keeping. And I want to know what kind of book-keeping is that?

Mike *goes to the desk.*

Mike   What's wrong with it?

Isaac   I didn't say wrong. First I ask what it is.

Mike   It's a projection. Our next five years.

Isaac   Drek. What did God give you a head for? Come, sit by me. Perhaps I can teach you a little. Let me see. Profit margin twelve per cent on capital of eight hundred and fifty-two pounds. (*He concentrates then grabs his right ear lobe and jiggles it up and down.*) Nine hundred and fifty-four pounds, four shillings and eightpence. You want three years? (*He looks up at* **Mike**.) I'm sorry. I got no choice. If you're here I got to be with you. Can I sit while you struggle?

Rose   Who says he's struggling?

Isaac   You're drowning, I can't throw you a hand? Rosie, you know a lot but not yet quite everything. You think profit comes from selling? Buying and selling, out in the open, above ground, in the fresh air? One loaf of bread – one shilling. Fair trading, fair exchange. No. What is the work of the book-keeper? Atrocity. I grab an innocent figure by the hair and drag him from this red side to the black. Whole columns, villages, uprooted, set on fire, burning, burning – red – I force across the valley, into my lands where they live and work for me. The fires die down – ash, grey – black. I'm satisfied. My land is fertilised with suffering. We grow rich. You want I should do this for you? Mikey? Rosie? Well, it can be done.

Scene Three

1955. The bedroom of **Mike** *and* **Rose**'s *house in a suburb of Salisbury.*

A dressing table with a triptych of mirrors. A bed covered with a pink candlewick bedspread. Music is playing in another room. It swells and falls as the door of the bedroom is opened and closed.

Rose *is sitting at the dressing table trying to replace a false eyelash that has come off.* **Lily** *is sitting on the bed holding an infant in her arms.*

Rose   Damn! I thought I'd nailed it. It's off again.

Lily   . . . the heat, sweetheart. Even this lamb chop is sweating.

Rose   Unless Mike's ma put something in the glue.

Lily   You're so bitter against us. Why? Don't we all wish you well?

Rose   You don't think. I've had my baby only eight days. I'm weak. I need rest. (**Rose** *tears off the other eyelash.*) How do I look without?

Lily   Beautiful. Always.

Rose *surveys herself in the mirror.*

Rose   I slap on powder. The blotches show through. I'm huge. Like a sow. Nothing fits. I can't go out. Lily? I can't.

The music (light orchestral pop versions of classics) swells and falls as the door of the bedroom is opened and closed. **Hannah** *comes in and immediately takes the baby from* **Lily**.

Hannah   Did Mikey come? Rosie! You phoned up the office?

Rose   Obviously.

Hannah   He's not there?

Rose   I phoned the sports club, Mervyn's place, everywhere. No one's anywhere. Everyone's here. Except him.

Hannah   Little dumpling. Like ice.

She takes a shawl from her shoulders and wraps the child in it.

Rose   Take it off! He'll suffocate!

Hannah   Don't snap at me, Rosie.

Rose   Rose! For the umpteenth time. Rose!

Hannah   Bobch's worried sick. Isn't she, bubeleh?

Lily   But when is Mike not home late?

Rose   For his own son's bris?

Hannah   And Isaac? You saw him? He's not in the garden, on the stoep, lecturing the maid by the back door. Something's wrong between Isaac and Mikey, Isaac runs away, hides.

Lily   Anyone need me? No? Good.

Hannah (*to* **Rose**)   Did Mikey sleep?

Rose   He didn't come home.

Hannah   The whole night?

Rose   Not till three, four . . .

Hannah (*to* **Lily**)   What I told you? And Isaac? The whole night, not a wink. This bubeleh's special day they pick to fight. It's killing me.

Rose   He didn't undress, lay on the bed, went out at dawn.

Hannah   Without even fresh clothes? You let him? Oy oy oy.

Rose (*to* **Hannah**)   Give!

Hannah (*holding back the child*)   You love your husband? I want the truth.

Rose   Give my baby to me!

She snatches the child and pulls the shawl off him. It lies spread out on one end of the dressing table. **Hannah** *stands a moment.*

Hannah   And the chair for the rabbi?

Rose   I hired hundreds of chairs.

Hannah   For the rabbi, a hired chair? Oy oy oy.

Hannah *hurries out.* **Rose** *immediately gives the child to* **Lily**.

Rose   Okay, Rosie. Take a deep breath. Try again. (*She has another go at her eyelashes.*) I hate her to see me like this. If I hadn't caught a man by the time I was twenty, I'd have slashed both my wrists. So I caught him. Now I've got that little man as well. Don't jiggle him. And you know what? I don't actually remember what I wanted them *for*. You never had any of this. Is that why you're good? You're famous for being good. If your Gideon had come to Africa you wouldn't be. Or patient. Or care for anyone. You'd snap and complain and lie awake at night feeling empty and lonely like any ordinary woman. You don't like to talk about him, do you?

Lily   If I must be honest –

Rose   Make a nice change.

Lily   You don't find me honest?

Rose   Not you. You're a pal. But the rest! In this family everything has to be spelt out all the time. 'Do you love your husband?' Don't you find that rude? The number of times a week Mike asks: 'Do you love me?' 'Yes.' 'But really and truly, do you love me?' For two years, I couldn't make head or tail of it. But I've thought it out. If people don't trust you it's because they know they can't be trusted themselves.

Lily   Today I'm happy. I want to dance. I got a thousand pounds a year for my school. Guaranteed by two bishops. I got land. And today – I got the plans. (*She takes plans from her briefcase and shows them.*) Look! First floor. Second. The stairways. The cloakrooms.

The music swells and falls. **Isaac** *comes in.*

Rose   Hannah's looking for you.

Isaac   I'm in Mikey's den with the rabbi.

Lily (*to* **Isaac**)   Come look at my plans. (*She unfolds them over the bed and examines them.*)

Isaac   What a fella. What a sage. By him circumcision gives such strength, virtue, honour, I asked while he's got out his knife perhaps he would do me again. (*To* **Rose**.) I told him you'll come and apologise.

Rose   What for?

Isaac   It's your house. It's your husband keeping him waiting.

Rose *pulls off her one attached false eyelash and gets up wearily.*

Rose   All right, little man. Mommy's coming back now now. Hold his head up. I don't actually remember why I agreed to all this fun and games. I promise you, never again.

Rose *goes out.* **Isaac** *lies on the bed.*

Isaac   Oy!

Lily   The heat?

Isaac   I don't feel it.

Lily   Tired?

Isaac   I don't feel it.

Lily   So what you feel?

Isaac Nothing. I feel dead.

Lily Not by me.

Isaac Ach, Lily, go piss in the sea.

Lily You feel bad, I must feel rotten? I don't feel it.

Isaac So what's good in the world? Nah, don't tell me. Tell me.

Lily This classroom.

Isaac Oy!

Lily Lots of air, lots of light. And cheap! Time after time, you think, but I made such a pigsty of this, that, the other. Life is over and done for. You turn round – it's started again. (*To the child.*) Didn't it, darling. Yes. Yes, it did.

Isaac *gets up. Dragging the bedspread over his shoulders, he sits at the dressing table.*

Isaac He smells.

Lily Nah . . .

Isaac . . . never knew a boy for such smells. Like a pit. Like a bucket of . . . like his (*Whisper.*) mama. Don't tell me nah.

He finds something interesting on the dressing table.

So that's how it works. That I never knew.

The music swells and fades. **Hannah** *comes in.*

Hannah Quick. Tillie's booties. Take those off. Put these on. She notices nothing.

Lily For this child she's got eyes like a hawk.

Hannah Pull. Pull! No, let me. There. Tie the bow. You'll feel better, darling, in Tillie's nice booties, yes, bubeleh.

Isaac So that's how they do it? So many years I lived with old women, I didn't think once: how's it done?

Hannah Where can I hide these now?

The music swells. **Rose** *comes in.*

Rose He's here. In a terrible state. Typical. What's he done to my bed? Actually Mike's in a rage. Yes, a fury. With him. (*Indicating* **Isaac**. *To* **Hannah**, *who has the baby*.) What have you done to my man? Take them off. Now!

The music comes to an end. Applause is heard.

Hannah But it's the booties from Tillie. If Tillie don't see her booties . . .

Rose *takes the other booties from* **Hannah** *and puts them back on the child.* **Isaac** *turns around. He has stuck on* **Rose**'s *false eyelashes, rouged his cheeks and put* **Hannah**'s *shawl over his head.*

Rose You'd think I crawled out of the earth like a mole. I've got cousins, nieces, nephews, a granny as good as you. Better. My cousin gave the little man these. He'll wear them on his big day if I have to kill.

Mike *comes in. He looks exhausted.*

Rose There.

She looks up and sees **Mike**.

Mike Why're you all hiding in here?

They all watch **Mike** *as he takes off his coat, throws it on the bed, takes off jacket, shirt, vest, looks at himself in the mirror. He sees* **Isaac**. *He takes this in.* **Isaac** *shrugs his shoulders and grins at him.*

Mike *puts on a fresh vest and shirt, puts on a tie while he looks at himself in the mirror, slaps aftershave on to his face, combs his hair, puts on his jacket.*

Mike If the phone rings call me. I don't care what else is happening. Call me. Is that clear? (*To* **Lily**.) Keep my dad in here.

He takes the child from **Rose** *and goes out.* **Rose** *takes a hat with a veil from the dressing table, puts it on with a quick glance in the mirror, gives* **Hannah** *and* **Lily** *a look and goes out after* **Mike**.

Hannah I don't know what it is about her. She always leaves me feeling I don't do enough for all the poor people in the world.

Hannah *sees* **Isaac**.

Lennie!

Isaac (*in* **Rose**'s *voice*) I got cousins, I got nieces, I got a tochus like two geese in a sack.

Hannah (*laughing*) It's not a joke.

Isaac (*in* **Rose**'s *voice*) I got bright red claws like a tiger.

Hannah Quick. Clean up. They're wanting to start now.

Lily I'll do it.

Hannah Bottles, jars, boxes. But vanishing cream? Nowhere. (*To* **Isaac**.) No more monkey tricks.

Lily They need granny.

Hannah What he gets up to. Sweetheart.

Lily I'll look after him.

Hannah Oh, Lennie, Lennie.

Hannah *goes out.* **Lily** *has taken the shawl off* **Isaac** *and thrown it on to the bed. She takes a box of tissues from the dressing table.*

Lily Hold still.

She dabs at **Isaac**'s *face.*

Isaac She called me Lennie. You heard it? The first time in twenty-five years.

Lily Ach, it's got on your collar. Never mind. So. That's it. Now, what have you done?

Isaac I done something wrong by this family. (*He sniffs, wipes his nose on the bedspread, then smiles at* **Lily**.) Ah, Lily. Lily! What do I care? Truth and courage. Courage and truth can still change the world.

The phone rings. **Isaac** *leaps up, snatches the receiver.*

Isaac Yes? Who is it? Hullo?

He gestures furiously to **Lily** *to go.*

Lily I can't leave you.

Isaac (*to* **Lily**) Get out! Shut the door!

Lily *hesitates then goes.*

Isaac So? . . . Nah, he's busy. I don't care what he told you. You can talk to me . . . Isaac Jahuda Levine. (*He listens a while.*) Yes, quite clear. I will convey this message to my son.

He puts down the phone. He stands a moment and thinks. He grabs his right ear lobe and jiggles it up and down, stops, jiggles it again but he can think of no solution to his problem. He sits on the bed.

It is six months earlier.

Albert *comes in carrying a chair.*

Albert Excuse me, master. The front door was open. Did Miss Lily come home yet?

Isaac Lily? At home? I've been waiting two hours and a half. Take a seat. Join the queue.

Albert *remains standing.*

Albert Could you perhaps teach me a little more history?

Isaac You're one of her pupils?

Albert I'm Albert. Hamadziripi. I was at your house last April for pesach.

Isaac The one who stayed all night asking questions, taking notes, who went to sleep on the floor? What kind of history you want to hear?

Albert I favour the history of exploited people, sir.

Isaac That's what you favour? My Uncle Pincus was exploited. He lived outside my old city of Kovna in a beautiful forest of spruce trees. One day he was milking his goat when a Cossack – you know what's a Cossack? – rode up on a big black fiery stallion, pulled out his sabre – you know what's a sabre? – and cut off my Uncle Pincus's head. Then he tied the goat to the back of his horse and rode away.

Albert   This was the master's – uh, your uncle, sir?

Isaac   My mother's brother.

Albert   I see. Though an event may be pitiful, to be classified correctly as history it must rise above more than a purely personal significance.

Isaac   As a matter of fact, on that same day, seventy-six men and women lost their heads. Half the Jews in the province lost their goats.

Albert   Seventy-six out of how many, sir? And was goats their only or their primary source of subsistence?

Lily *comes in carrying an orange box full of exercise books.*

Lily   I'm late. Forgive me, forgive me.

Isaac   Not at all. I've been having a chat with Mr Ouspensky here.

Albert   Ha-ma-dzi-ri-pi.

Lily *takes the books out of the orange box and looks through them.*

Lily   The meeting dragged on and on. You wouldn't believe the legislation they're pushing through now. It's an evil. We fight it. Here, Albert. Maths. Science. History. Have a look. Then we discuss.

Albert *takes the orange box and sits on it as he looks through his corrected homework.*

Lily (*to* **Isaac**)   I'm putting on the kettle. Tea for us, cocoa for Albert. Or you want Russian? I got lump sugar somewhere. What is it?

Isaac I'm uneasy in my heart.

Lily Tell.

Isaac I can't work by Mikey anymore.

Lily Then don't. Get out.

Isaac 'Get out.'

Lily Then don't get out.

Isaac Do, don't. This kind advice you're giving your pupils?

Lily When Mikey makes his fortune he can give to the fund for my school.

Isaac When? He made. Did he give? You see what I'm talking?

Lily Isaac, I'm busy. Make a choice, come back, tell me what it is. OK?

Isaac *can't say anything.*

Albert Excuse me, Miss Lily. Here is a red pen I brought you.

Lily Why waste your money? I got a drawerful.

Albert There's almost no corrections in these books. So I think you want to save your red pen. Use this one. Use it up. I need many, many corrections. Take it, please.

Lily *is close to tears.*

Lily This boy – what he got? Nothing. What he chose? Life! He chose knowledge! And you? What good you done with your famous brains? I must waste time on you? No. Now is the time. Work by Mike or don't. Choose life or sit down in silence. Choose, Isaac, darling. Which way?

Mike *comes in carrying a glass of whisky. It is six months later again.*

Lily *and* **Albert** *go out taking box, chair and books.*

Isaac   I'm coming.

Isaac *gets up from behind the desk.*

Mike   It's finished. You missed it.

Isaac   So quickly?

Mike   It's a little flap of skin.

Mike *finishes the whisky, puts the glass down.*

Isaac   He cried?

Mike   He's a man.

Mike *goes to the dressing table, tries to open a drawer which is locked. He pulls on it. It won't open. He turns to face* **Isaac**.

Mike   When you kept books for Greenberg, you paid tax for him?

Isaac   Naturally.

Mike *scratches his forehead, finds it is running with sweat, looks for his handkerchief, can't find it.*

Mike   You did, huh? (*He takes off his jacket, mops his forehead with the sleeve, throws a jacket down.*) You want a drink?

Isaac *shrugs.* **Mike** *pulls on the drawer. It won't budge.*

Mike   Drawer's locked.

Isaac   You lock the drawers in your own room?

Mike   . . . the servants . . .

Isaac   Don't trust them? Keep them out. Rosie should clean up herself. Locks and keys where you sleep, make love. Ay-ay-ay!

Mike   And for Milstein? You paid for him taxes? And Mr Brightman? And Hertzveldt? You filled in returns, got them in on time?

Isaac   My responsibility.

Mike   Keep them out of trouble.

Isaac   I had a reputation.

Mike   First-class book-keeper.

Isaac   Twenty-three years. Altogether.

Mike   So why not pay taxes for me? Don't answer yet.
All right, answer. No, wait. (*He tugs on the drawer.*) Any kind
of taxes. And not only that. Not only have you not paid
my taxes – . All right. Tell me. Why?

Isaac   Mikey –

Mike   Why won't you let me talk to you about it?

Isaac   Talk to me, darling. Hold back nothing. Hurt me.

Mike   If I needed even a new pair of shoes . . . needed,
not wanted . . . mine were held together with string . . .
and the string came off a shopping bag and the shopping
bag was given free at a jumble sale. Anything of my own
. . . you made me feel I was stealing. Stealing from who?
That you didn't say.

Isaac   What you talking shoes? You got plenty. Italian.
French I never saw so many pairs shoes.

Mike   All the boys in the school had a father who
worked, made money, at the end of the year there's more
in the house than at the beginning. *You* were *interested* in –
what was it? Tell me again.

Isaac   You want my shoes? Here! Here!

He takes them off, holds them out. **Mike** *pulls at the drawer and
thumps on the table.*

Mike   I wanted to say this is ours.

Isaac   . . . what's mine is yours . . .

Mike   No, mine. Mine. Ours. For next year, for ten
years' time.

Isaac   Security? You want it?

Mike   I wanted it. Why not?

Isaac Happiness? You want it?

Mike To stop moving. To need no one. To be safe.

Isaac In this world?

Mike You got another on offer?

Isaac It's a joke. Earthquakes. Drought. Famine. War. Labour camps. Pogroms. In this world.

Mike *is in control again. He puts on his jacket.*

Mike So. All right. Number one – what exactly have you done? Number two – how do we get out of it? Walter says it's the best fraud he's seen. Subtle. Scientific. It took his boys twenty-three hours to crack it.

Isaac Walter?

Mike He says the revenue office will take maybe a week.

Isaac Walter Balinsky?

Mike You're good. But you're not that good. Yes, Balinsky. Why?

Isaac *(very angry)* He was kicked out our discussion group 1931, 1933 and twice in 1939. You talk to him before me?

Mike I've got the jewellery shop opening in the north. I've got the watch repairs opening in the east. I need to keep my cash liquid. I thought I could pull through by myself. I can't. I go to the bank for a loan. 'Sure, Mr Levine, anytime. Just bring in your books, we'll take a quick look . . .' I take a quick look myself. *(He pulls on the drawer then leaves it.)* They stink to high holy heaven. For the life of me I can't see where it's coming from.

Isaac Why not come to me?

Mike Because I needed to talk about money. About making lots of money. You won't talk to me about getting rich. Will you? Hey, Daddy? Isaac! Will you?

Isaac If you'd ask me I'd tell you. You took the wrong books.

Mike You tell me? Stories, ja. Plenty. What happened to Aunty Sofka when the Prussians moved the Polish border. But what's going on in my own business? I don't want to hear your voice tell me anything as long as you live.

Isaac grabs **Mike** *by the shoulders and shakes him.*

Isaac Listen to me, damn you! You took to the bank the wrong books!

Mike *takes this in, then he thumps on the table and wrenches the drawer. It opens. He takes out a bottle of whisky, opens it, pours himself a drink. He drinks it and pours another, holds it out to* **Isaac** *then drinks it himself and puts the bottle and glass down.*

Mike You keep two sets of books?

Isaac Two? What you talking, two? Three. I learnt it from Misha Volkov the tailor, 1924. Deduct half the turnover from the first day of business. Then deduct ten to fifteen per cent every day after that. Everyone did it, Polonsky the inspector of taxes included. By the end of the year, you can't show a profit. Not possible. But set number three shows your actual profit plus fifty per cent. Who knows? One day you're wanting to sell up, then it comes in useful. You don't ask me. What happens? You show to the bank the wrong books.

Mike So my tax has been paid?

The music, which has started again, swells as the door opens. (The music is now the Andrews Sisters: 'Bei mir bis du schein', 'Goody Goody' etc.)

Rose *comes in holding her child.*

Rose Everyone's asking: where are you? Where are you? What have you done to my table? Are you crazy? There's dozens of bottles out there.

Mike I can't come out.

Rose The key's with my hairclips. Why smash the woodwork? (*To* **Isaac**.) What you done this time?

Mike   Go away.

Isaac (*to* **Rose**)   Darling, what I need – soda water. The whisky's too strong for my inside. Even a little one. Please, sweetheart. Oh my God. (*He weeps.*)

Rose (*to* **Mike**)   You'd better tell them all to go home.

Isaac (*to* **Mike**)   Do you love me?

Rose   . . . can't bear it . . .

Mike (*to* **Rose**)   Go and dance.

Rose (*to* **Mike**)   Are you stupid?

Isaac   Do you love me?

Mike (*to* **Rose**)   It's not serious. Fetch ice cream. Make hot dogs. Go away!

Lily *comes in humming and dancing to the music. She looks quickly around, takes it all in, puts her arm around* **Rose**.

Lily   Let the boys fight it out. Then we'll come in to pick up the pieces.

Rose (*to* **Isaac**)   You spoil everything. I hate you. (*To* **Lily**.) And I hate you.

Mike *holds out his hands for the child.*

Rose (*to* **Mike**)   No, no, no. I didn't mean it.

She hands the child to **Mike** *and runs out.*

Lily   You got two minutes. Then you come out smiling. Agreed? It's the party of a lifetime. I'm waltzing. And foxtrot. And samba. Who knows when such a day comes again? Two minutes. 'Goody, goody. Goody goody.'

She dances out. The music falls. **Mike** *jiggles the child up and down.*

Mike   Anyway. Let's look on the bright side. This morning Walter said maybe he can make it look like failure to declare and not actual deceit. As soon as he knows one way or the other he'll phone. (*He grins at* **Isaac**.) No need to panic yet.

Mike *holds out the bottle to* **Isaac**. **Isaac** *takes it, pours and drinks.*

Mike   So – that's the bright side.

Isaac *drinks again.*

Isaac   Walter rang. I'm good but I'm not that good. Anymore.

Mike   So. (*Then, waking from a reverie.*) Oh, yes. Tell me why.

Isaac   In 1939 –

Mike   I don't want to hear history.

Isaac   – one thousand Jews from Czechoslovakia, Austria, Hungary –

Mike   Or geography.

Isaac   – applied to come to this country. Why? To escape Hitler. The government refused. Why? Because, so they say, in the eyes of the natives Jewish people are racially inferior to people of British descent. The Rhodesian state will rock if the native man sees the depths to which white men can fall.

Mike   And no bloody politics!

Isaac   To such people you want I should hand over our cash?

Mike   You paid for Greenberg! You paid for Mr Brightman!

Isaac   Greenberg says pay so I pay. Greenberg's money is Greenberg's. Brightman's money is Brightman's. I'm working with my son. My flesh. My blood. What's mine is yours. What's yours is mine. It's the only one law of the universe. I can't do it.

Mike   And for *that* I go to jail?

Isaac   You? A businessman? Never. Me? Maybe. I'm only a Jew.

The music swells and falls. **Hannah** *comes in. She takes the child from* **Mike**.

Mike   You know what he's done?

Hannah   I don't want to know nothing. He's your daddy. He loves you. He loves –

Mike   He's destroyed this family.

Hannah   – your son. Don't say that. (*She screws up her face and spits three times.*) I beg you. So he lost your money? So sometimes a family needs money and sometimes it don't. Give me what money you got. You're not so big your mama can't klup. I'm warning you. Give!

Mike *takes some notes from his pocket and gives them to* **Hannah**. **Hannah** *tears them up.*

Hannah   See? We don't need it. All we got in the world is each other. You understand? Mikey, say yes. Say yes, darling. Believe me, it's yes. Yes, yes, yes.

The music swells. **Lily** *comes in dancing the cha-cha-cha.*

Lily   Times up. Change partners and – one two three and one two three. One two three and one two three.

She sweeps **Mike** *into her arms and dances him round.*

Hannah wants to cha-cha-cha. And Isaac wants to cha-cha-cha. (*To* **Hannah**.) Go on! Go on! And cha-cha-cha. Leave Mike to me and cha-cha-cha.

Hannah *takes* **Isaac** *in her arms.*

Lily   Is he easy? Cha-cha-cha. And is he greasy? Cha-cha-cha. And Hannah get him out cha-cha. Get out, get out and cha-cha-cha.

Hannah *and* **Isaac** *dance round and out.*

Lily   Cha-cha-cha and cha-cha-cha. And one and two and – (*The music falls.*) – that's enough. (*She deposits* **Mike** *in a* *chair.*) I don't know how I can help you. If I can, I will. So let me know. OK? (**Lily** *turns to go.*)

Mike   Wait.

The door is still open. The music can still be heard. **Lily** *does a few steps and goes out. The music falls.* **Lily** *comes back.*

Mike   Drink?

Lily   You got glasses?

Mike *offers his.*

Lily   Never mind.

She takes the bottle and has a long pull. She shivers. **Mike** *lies on the bed.*

Mike   More?

Lily   The last time I drank twice from the same bottle, next thing the young man in question invites me to join him in a sexual practice I would have sworn was impossible. (*She drinks.*) As it turned out, it was. (*She drinks again.*) Isaac was always Isaac. The biggest heart by the Baltic Sea. Since so high. His brain works so quick, how can it also go deep? Don't feel angry. You got a lovely boy. Your health. A nice house. A good wife.

Mike   I want you to come in with me.

Lily *gets up and dances.*

Lily   'Goody goody. Goody goody.'

Mike   Did you hear me?

Lily (*dancing*)   Yes I heard you. Yes I heard you.

Mike   And?

Lily (*singing*)   You're a cuckoo. Crazy cuckoo.

Mike   We'll talk about it tomorrow.

Lily   No. Now.

Mike   Remember how we used to talk? Saturdays in your house by the river . . . with your friends . . . talking, talking into the night.

Lily   You were what I longed for. If a person got a clear view of the world, of herself . . . are you following me? . . . but no one to share it . . . You got such character. You got my character. You know that? You're a fighter. I'm a fighter.

Mike   Come in with me.

Lily   Darling, I can't.

Mike *gets up, fetches the bottle of whisky, goes back to the bed, lies, pours whisky into the glass, gives it to* **Lily** *who has sat on the bed and drinks from the bottle, emptying it.*

Mike   Isaac has committed a fraud. In a week it will be reported to the receiver of revenue, within hours to the police. I, and possibly he, will be arrested, tried . . . and possibly jailed.

Lily   Possibly. You can make an old pussy like Isaac cry with this possibly. Not an old tom-cat like me.

Mike   The truth is – . Look, you can organise people. Everyone knows it. I got two shops opening, another in April. I got nine people working for me. Every time I go out of the shop, someone puts his hand in the till. You're family. With you I can leave every damn door, window, till open wide and know the business is safe.

Lily   I said no.

Mike *looks at her for a moment.*

Mike   Actually, there's only one answer. This school of yours. You think it'll happen? People don't like it.

Lily *starts to pick up her plans lying on the bed and the floor.*

Lily   It's got nothing to do with other people.

Mike   Yes, you can close up your eyes. I live with them, work with them.

Lily   Work with who?

Mike   People! In the banks, on the town council . . . For
example – don't tell Rosie – I'm negotiating to buy back
her family's farm. The owner's a rich man, a mine owner.
You don't know him. He knows you. He asks me – have a
word with you. Remind you where you are.

Lily   I see. I pack up my work nice and quiet, you get
the farm at a good price.

Mike   Rosie wants it. It's the only place she feels at
home. Lily! I don't want to put pressure. The lease on
your land . . . Did you sign it?

Lily   Of course.

Mike   Even so, I can arrange they withdraw. You can't
only think of yourself. Listen, my father wanted to screw
me. He almost managed to do it. But what's he and my
ma going to live on in twenty years' time. What are you?
I'm the family now. Mike Levine. I'm not asking you to do
book-keeping. I want senior management. You'll pick it up
in two twos. The family needs you.

Lily   What's a Jew without a family? I heard it once,
twice, a thousand times.

Mike   You want me to beg? I'll beg. You want me at
your feet? I'll do it. When we make our fortune, I'll give
schools, libraries . . .

Lily brandishes her plans.

Lily   Where this comes from? Two bishops! From the goy!
Not from you!

Mike   That's what I'm telling you. That isn't family. This
is family I'm talking.

Lily   I'm talking my life! You want I should change it?
Why? My life is perfect. My life is what I was born for.
There are people who need me.

Mike Like who? Oh ja. I knew there was something. Your Albert, what's his name? I thought you might need a sweetener. I've taken him on. You can have him as right-hand man. He's pretty smart for a kaffer. But he should be, hey, shouldn't he, Lily? I mean to say, he's had a teacher like you.

The music swells and fades. **Hannah** *comes in. She looks at them, then goes to* **Lily**.

Hannah What is it? Tell me.

Lily I want to go home. I can't stay in this place any longer.

Hannah What is it? The heat? The cooking? Tell me, I'll fix it up.

Lily (*to* **Mike**) I sweated blood for that boy. Damn! Damn! I didn't make him for you. I want to go home.

Hannah You are home. This is home.

Lily I want to be young. I want to see him. To talk with him. Ask him what to do.

Hannah Talk with who?

Lily Gideon. Gideon!

Hannah What you done to her? Mikey? What's going on in this house?

Part Two

Scene Four

1930. A room in a wooden house in Kannas, Lithuania. The room is empty except for three suitcases which stand in the middle of the floor. **Hannah** *and* **Isaac** *(aged twenty) have just come in from the front door. They wear coats.*

Hannah What's going on in this house?

Lily *(aged twenty-two) enters from the back.*

Hannah Where is my table? My chairs?

Lily Even to *raise* your voice while they're here. Yitkin next door will hear and go running. You want that? Discipline.

Hannah Didn't I beg you? Didn't you agree?

Lily I have to hear what they say. No, don't follow. *(Appealing.)* Please, Hannah. *(Formal again.)* Wait. *(She goes, turns back.)* It's a good solid floor. It won't hurt you to sit on it.

Lily *hurries out.*

Hannah I begged her: no meetings till we've gone. Twenty-four hours, they can have all three rooms. Revolutionaries. They can't break even a habit. *(To* **Isaac**.*)* Don't try to listen.

Isaac It's about us.

Hannah Don't.

Isaac Lennie I heard. Hannah. You heard it?

Hannah What about us?

Lily *comes in.*

Lily Did you get them?

Hannah What meeting is this?

Lily You weren't here.

Isaac To the station and back – forty-three minutes.

Lily It was called half an hour ago. I asked: can you attend? But you're leaving this place. They say no.

Lily *turns to go.*

Hannah Who called this meeting?

Lily I can't tell you. They want to know: did you get the tickets?

Hannah Three tickets. One, two, three. If we're raided now they'll take them. Or us. Or both. And these? Useless. After so many years? Lily? Twenty-four hours.

Lily I can't tell you who called the meeting – I can't get the word out.

Hannah *takes this in.*

Hannah No!

Isaac Who?

Lily I'm so happy, I'm floating.

Hannah They let him go?

Isaac Who is it? Mikael? Arkady?

Lily I know I must come to the ground. I can't.

Hannah *starts towards the back room.* **Lily** *catches her, holds her back.*

Lily He's ill. No emotion. No strain.

Isaac Gideon!

Lily No! Lennie!

But **Isaac** *has dodged into the back room.*

Lily This afternoon. Three o'clock.

Hannah Why?

Lily Ask why, you put ideas in their heads. He's free. It's enough. I can't stop crying.

Hannah Let me look at you. You haven't cried at all.

Lily *pulls away.*

Hannah I'm glad. He's like a brother. But even so, Lily. Even more. For his sake also. Is there nowhere else they can meet?

Lily We've got all the cups and glasses. If you want tea – no, you'll have to wait. Show me again.

Hannah *holds up the tickets.*

Lily Thank God.

Lily *takes the tickets and goes out.* **Hannah** *is left standing for a moment.* **Isaac** *comes in.*

Isaac He's like a figure they burn on the bonfires down by the river – twigs and string. I was frightened to touch him.

Hannah What did he say?

Isaac *starts to search his pockets.*

Isaac To me? He didn't see I was there. I've lost the passes.

Hannah They weren't issued. We fetch them tomorrow.

Isaac *is still searching.*

Hannah Tomorrow! We fetch them tomorrow!

Isaac Now the tickets!

Hannah You see what they do to us? Someone's arrested, we're thrown into confusion. They bring him back, it's even worse. She's got them. She wants one for him.

Isaac *walks over to a suitcase and sits.*

Hannah Tell me again. How does it look to you?

Isaac   First of all – the sea.

Hannah   Sonya lives far from the sea. I'm sorry. Go on.

Isaac   The distance between Lithuania and the United States of America – 4,136 miles.

Hannah   But the place itself?

Isaac *thinks but says nothing.*

Hannah   I try but I can see nothing. To imagine is just like to look out a window. But the wind's blowing. It forces the shutters back. I take all my strength. I push them open. One crack. Another. All I see is Sonya sitting on a washing board. Why a washing board? And around her? Empty space. Is it there, this other country?

Lily *comes in.*

Lily   Lennie, a vest. The sweat pours off him. He needs to change every hour.

Isaac *makes for the entrance to the bedroom.*

Lily   I already took one from your cupboard. That was the last.

Isaac   The rest are packed.

Lily   He's so thin. He can't afford to lose any moisture. Give me two. With three he'll get through the night.

Isaac *turns to* **Hannah**.

Hannah   It's no problem.

She opens a suitcase and unpacks clothes on to the floor.

Lily   I can tell you what's happening. We're voting for a new leader. So far, no decision. He's a hard man to follow. Hannah . . . (*She laughs.*) How can I say this? Odd thoughts pop into my mind. Organise them! (*She laughs.*)

Hannah   You want to get him out. Why not say it?

Lily   They'll fetch him again in the morning. I know it.

Hannah   Mikael they left alone. They didn't touch him.

Lily   Mikael! He's nothing. Gideon they want to destroy. Of course they do. So we, the circle, will choose a new leader and tomorrow – . Where are the passes?

Isaac *feels in his pockets, then:*

Isaac   They weren't issued.

Lily   So. They'll be watching the trains. It makes no difference. What is life? Taking risks. Smaller or larger. He will take this one.

Hannah *gives her the vests.*

Hannah   And who stays behind?

Lily   Me. Of course.

Lily *goes out.*

Hannah   If I am strong. Now! As an ox. The rest of life will be a stroll across a field.

Hannah *opens a suitcase, takes out a tin, opens it, takes out a biscuit, eats it, takes out another, closes the tin.*

Isaac   The best thing is: take back the tickets. When we're ready, we'll buy them again. I can risk one more week.

Hannah   And if they come for you? What will you tell them? No more risks! I can't bear it.

Isaac *goes into the bedroom.* **Hannah** *eats the second biscuit. Then she takes an envelope from under her blouse, removes the letter and unfolds it.*

Hannah   'My one regret is leaving my dear mother behind. I hoped and believed she would follow soon. Now I know in my heart I will never see her again.' (*She folds up the letter. She thumps the heel of her palm on the floor.*) I won't leave her. I swear.

Isaac *comes in, goes to the suitcase from which the vests were taken, forces it closed, picks it up and starts carrying it towards his room.*

Hannah   Where are you going?

Isaac   I'll stay.

Hannah   No!

She runs to him and tries to drag the suitcase from him. They struggle. The suitcase bursts open scattering clothes and books all over the floor. **Isaac** *roars with laughter.* **Hannah** *immediately starts gathering them up.* **Lily** *comes in.*

Lily   We must have quiet.

Isaac   She won't leave you. Keep the ticket, keep the damn thing!

Hannah (*wailing*)   He's the one who can't stay. He's the one of all who has to go.

Isaac *takes off his clothes and puts on the jacket and trousers of an old suit lying among the clothes on the floor.*

Hannah   He's who I worked and worked to save, to buy, to go, to save him. He stays, he goes into the army. Two years? Four years?

Lily   So leave me.

Hannah   Break a family, it limps till the end of the world.

Lily   You have to choose.

Hannah   You're my right hand, he's my left. You're my mind, he's my heart. You tear me and tear me.

Lily *holds out two tickets.*

Lily   I'll work. I'll earn. I'll come.

Hannah (*laughing*)   You've earned nothing in five years.

Lily   I'll buy my own ticket. I'll come on my own feet.

Hannah   You'll smoke. You'll drink. You'll starve. I'll never see you again.

Lily   What did mama say? Lily will set the whole world on fire. I will. Trust me. I will.

Isaac *is now dressed in his suit.*

Isaac How do I look?

Lily Like the bear at the bar mitzvah. Now take it off.

Isaac I'm going to the Department of Mass Economic Statistics. Me, a Jew, they want. Why? I can add and subtract faster than any man, Catholic, Protestant, Jew, between the two rivers. And if I work for them, they won't call me into the army. So. I'll be fine. There's no need to worry.

Lily You don't want to do this. It is the oppression of the state that causes the masses of the people to live in their squalor and ignorance.

Hannah Shut up.

Lily To work for the state of his free will?

Hannah *slaps* **Lily**.

Hannah Free will? Who has it? He's terrified. Can't you see? All night he moans in his sleep. He's broken half the teeth in his jaw. Nothing here is good for him. A Jew in the army? They'll kill him. A Jew in the State Department? Scratching his pen for the next fifty years? With his brain? What is he to do in this life? Only one thing. Run away. He's my husband. Gideon isn't yours or you wouldn't speak as you do.

Lily We could have been married a thousand times. It means nothing to us. Or, to be frank, to you. This is merely an argument. Tasteless opportunist rhetoric. There are only two questions. For whom is it most dangerous to stay? Gideon. Who can be of most value there where we – you and you are going? (*She throws two tickets down.*) We wouldn't know why night follows day if Gideon hadn't opened our eyes.

Lily *goes out.* **Isaac** *takes off his jacket.*

Isaac In fact, she's right. This job? I can't do it. They oppress us, lock us up – . Counting is a gift from God after all. What do you want me to do?

Hannah *kneels on the floor and covers her face with her hands.*

Isaac He is a great man, there's no disputing. But after all, there, on the other side, won't there be many great men? If he's so ill, she'll finish him off moving him now. Tell her. This isn't a walk in the forest, a visit to poor Uncle Pincus. Tell her!

He puts his jacket on again. **Hannah** *is rocking backwards and forwards.* **Isaac** *takes his jacket off and flings it down. He picks it up again.*

Isaac Hannah?

Hannah *is still.*

Hannah When mama died I swore – she and I – apart? – never . . .

Isaac In whose name did you swear?

Hannah God's.

Isaac Ah well, so that's that.

He puts on his jacket and goes out the front door. **Hannah** *is alone.* **Lily** *comes in.*

Lily Where is he? Lennie!

Isaac, *who has been waiting outside the front door, comes in immediately.* **Gideon** *comes in. He walks with great difficulty.*

Lily (*to* **Isaac**) Fetch a chair.

Isaac *goes into the back room.*

Gideon Hannah.

He holds out his arms to her. **Hannah** *doesn't move.* **Isaac** *brings in a chair.* **Lily** *helps* **Gideon** *over to it.* **Hannah** *goes to* **Gideon** *and takes both his hands.*

Hannah I am very, very pleased to see you.

Gideon Of course. It is always a joy to see old friends. So, Lennie? Nothing to say? He never has words for the occasion. Why? Too much self-consciousness? Not good.

Hannah It's only with you he can't speak. Otherwise . . . (*She laughs.*)

Gideon Leonard. Come.

Isaac *goes to him. They embrace.*

Lily Careful.

Gideon She thinks I'll break in half. Perhaps I will. An hour ago I thought this Gideon Sachs must be an unusually talented leader if it's so hard to replace him. But if after more than a year and a half in prison –

Isaac Four hundred and seventy days.

Gideon Exactly – no one has emerged, clearly emerged . . . there must be something wrong . . . about how . . . in the past . . . (*To* **Lily**.) Water, please.

Lily *goes out.*

Gideon Lily's love for me makes her overlook what is obvious. Tell me the obvious.

Silence.

Lily insists she will stay. But like me she's at risk. (*To* **Isaac**.) Surely you are prepared to stay? Yes or no? Only yes or no. Ah. Good. Yes, yes, yes, yes, yes. So?

Isaac No – please, go. I can keep out of the army. I have a job in the Ministry of – something and – for the love of God. I – . Clerk grade seven but the prospects with my abilities . . . give me a number, any number. Go on. Give me one.

Gideon Enough. You know quite well I won't agree to that. To help me? No. It makes everything pointless.

Lily *comes in with a glass of water.*

Gideon   Promise me that none of us who have lived and studied so closely together, almost as one man with one mind, none will ever be the servant of any state – capitalist, fascist, social democratic, any state at all – until . . . until . . .

Isaac   Until what?

Gideon   Until. Promise.

Lily   Do it.

Isaac   I promise.

Lily *gives* **Gideon** *the water. He drinks it off at one go.*

Gideon   Moreover there is another way. (*To* **Lily**.) Please – my case.

Lily *goes off.*

Gideon   It is an error to believe that all parts of a floor are equally hard. I have learnt this. There is always one corner that is softer, warmer, where a man can sleep easier. Always. Otherwise life would truly be . . . (*He is looking at* **Hannah**.) You never joined us. Why?

Hannah   Someone must earn a living. He can't.

Gideon   Oh?

Hannah   His head's in the stars. After a week or two, they throw him out.

Gideon   But anyone can sweep the streets. Or make boxes. Even a man with a brain. Am I wrong?

Lily *comes in and gives* **Gideon** *a small case.* **Gideon** *opens it and takes out some papers. He holds them out to* **Isaac**.

Gideon   A comrade from Riga died in my cell. I managed to snatch his papers before they hauled out the body.

He holds them out to **Isaac** *who takes them.*

He's registered dead. They can't conscript him. Burn your own. Then who are you?

Isaac *opens the papers.*

Isaac   Isaac Jahuda Levine.

Gideon   So – you can stay. Get a job. It doesn't matter what. Keep it. That is an instruction. Save. Join us. It is not given to everybody to make a large contribution. It is given to no one to know how large his contribution has been. But to recognise when it can be made and to make it – that is everything.

Lily   Lennie will collect his pass in the morning. He rides as far as the second stop. Gideon will be carried there by Jacob in his cart. Lennie –

Isaac   Isaac.

Lily   Isaac gets out. They exchange.

Gideon *takes the ticket from his pocket and holds it out to* **Isaac**.
Hannah *grabs it and picks up the two from the ground.*

Hannah   I knitted and knitted. I sewed and sewed. Look at my hands. This finger will never move again. Look. Bent like a duck's beak. To buy these. But I'll tear them up. If he stays I'll never see him again.

Lily (*screaming*)   Give them to me!

Gideon (*to* **Lily**)   No, no. Please ... The subjective in history. How it seems. How it feels. It feels good, it feels bad. Blow up the bank, cut his throat, that man is indispensible, this one can be allowed to die. In some respects, you know, watching someone make a choice, throw every single card into the ring, it makes me grateful still to be alive. If I ramble ... still weak ... forgive me ...

Hannah   Come into the bedroom. Lie down.

Gideon   I've recovered. Still ... still ... still. Husbands and wives. You know, surely we were capable of giving that up long ago. But I have none. It is not for me to say. It is not for me to say. Sisters, husbands, wives. It can be a source of great strength. That at least has been shown. And you will need your strength. Besides which, it solves another problem. If I am not going anywhere we can cut short this struggle to elect a successor. (*To* **Lily**.) Go and tell them. Tell them!

Lily, *furious, goes out.* **Hannah** *packs* **Isaac**'s *clothes into the suitcase and closes it. Meanwhile,* **Isaac** *offers the papers back to* **Gideon**.

Gideon   Keep them. The army might stop you at the border. Why take risks? So. I hope you will all be happy in the United States. Promise me one thing. You will remember that we are workers. Not bosses, employers. Whatever temptations. And Jews. All national oppression must be resisted with all your hearts. Then I am with you. And who knows, perhaps I *have* broken in half. Perhaps they know it. Perhaps they will leave me in peace.

Lily *comes in. She walks up to* **Hannah** *and glares at her in fury.*

Gideon   So. Do you agree with what I have said? Come, comrades. Criticise.

Scene Five

1976. The front stoep and lawn of **Mike** *and* **Rose**'s *house in a suburb of Salisbury. On the stoep is a swing-couch, a table and chairs. It is mid-afternoon.*

Albert, *wearing a smart suit, is dozing in a chair. His attaché case is lying on the grass. On the table is a tray with a cup of tea from which he has been drinking.* **Paul** *runs on dressed in track suit and training shoes. He runs on, stops, does ten press-ups, stands and runs off in the direction from which he came on.* **Rose** *comes on.* **Albert** *starts awake.*

Rose   Mr Mike's late again. Every Saturday the same. What can I do?

Albert   Never mind, Mrs Rosie. I don't mind to wait. It's a lovely day.

Rose   Is it? Did you see Master Paul?

Albert I didn't.

Rose I'll make some fresh tea.

Lily *comes on.*

Rose Lily!

Lily Paulie's home? Where is he?

Rose Who told you he's coming?

Lily He's my nephew. I heard.

Rose He came. But he isn't here. Did you hear me? You've no reason to stay. (*She picks up the tea tray and starts to go out.*) No, look, I have to ask you.

Lily Ask.

Rose They came to your house for cash for our boys on the border. You told them to leave.

Lily I surprised you?

Rose You know what *I* do? I organise raffles, bridge tournaments, I bake sausage rolls, knit jersies – . There's Jewish boys in the army too. But none is your son. So. What did you come here for?

Lily Today's yontif. I thought to go with my family to shul. Why you're hiding him from me?

Rose Don't go in the house! He's out running. Up and down all the streets. A soldier needs to keep fit. When he comes – well, he makes up his own mind. He's a man.

Rose *goes out.* **Lily** *watches* **Albert** *for a moment.*

Lily You do this every week? Sit in the shade, listen to the water running, running through the pool ... To sleep away the whole afternoon, you don't mind it?

Albert Mr Mike likes me to be here when he gets home.

Lily This garden's your heaven. Don't deny. You sit, you dream: one day this all will be mine. Am I right?

Albert   We don't see you at this house much, Miss Lily.

Lily   Why should I come? You dream much more sweet without me. Oh, Albert.

Lily *is suddenly exhausted. She sits.*

Albert   Hot?

Lily   Cool as a willow tree. It's nothing.

Mike *comes in carrying an attaché case like* **Albert**'s. *He sees* **Lily**. *He stops, takes this in.*

Mike (*to* **Albert**)   I'm sorry, my friend. What must I do? Throw my customers out on the street? (*Calls.*) Rosie! Bring food! (*To* **Lily**.) What did I always tell you? Between owner and employee, even a manager like Albert, it's a whole world. I don't blame him. He's first class and knows it. But on his door it says, Saturday one o'clock close. So one o'clock – closed. He done what the book says. But on my side of town? The till's ringing, two o'clock, they're pouring in, three, half-past three . . . (*Calls.*) And something for Albert! (*To* **Lily**.) Keeping well?

Lily   One hundred per cent.

Mike   All over the country, business? Dead. Do they moan and complain? But us? We go in, gloves off, fight it out. And a number one, first-class bonanza, third week in a row. (*To* **Albert**.) And by you? Show the worst.

Albert *holds out his file to* **Mike**. **Mike** *kicks off his shoes, takes off his jacket and cravat, sits, takes the file, puts on his glasses, examines it.*

Mike   So, so, so, so . . .

Albert   Alarm clocks is up ten per cent.

Mike   I told you: push digitals. You pushed them?

Albert   I pushed.

Mike   I drove past the shop. No posters, no banners. You know what I must do to get digitals into this country?

Rose *comes in with a tray of tea.*

Mike (*to* **Rose**) That's all? The whole day I'm out hunting. I bring home the wild beast from the bush.

He winks at **Albert**. *He thumps his stomach.*

The big chiefs are starving for meat. Meat! Meat!

Rose There's cold meat and salad in an hour.

Mike Why wait? Bring it now. (*To* **Albert**.) Get stuck in.

Albert My wife's also waiting.

Rose (*to* **Lily**) You're also eating?

Lily I got to go.

Rose You told me you're coming with us to shul.

Lily If I said so I'm coming!

Rose Why is it? Nothing ever goes how I plan.

Mike (*calling after* **Rose**) Where's Pumpkin? Tell him come.

Rose *goes off.*

Mike (*to* **Lily**) You're coming to shul with us? Can't answer. So where you going to now? A meeting? Listen – I want no trouble. Lily? I'm asking you.

Lily *hurries out.* **Mike** *picks up* **Albert**'s *file.*

Albert Mr Mike, I can tell you – this week, not first class but in the circumstances –

Mike I can pay my debts with circumstances? I sign in blue that means it's good, in black that means merely correct.

Mike *selects a pen and signs the file.*

This week black. Next week? Blue. We're agreed?

He hands the files back and eats. **Hannah** *and* **Isaac** *come on.* **Hannah** *supports* **Isaac** *who walks haltingly with a stick.*

Isaac   You talking business?

Mike *goes to them.* **Albert** *stands.*

Mike (*kissing them*)   Ma. Dad. Come. Sit.

Hannah (*of Isaac*)   How he looks? Better? Worse?

Mike   He looks fine.

Hannah   Pale, no?

Isaac   I don't want to interrupt business.

Mike (*to* **Isaac**)   How you feeling?

Hannah   He feels like a king.

Isaac   Where's Paul?

Mike *goes back to his chair.*

Hannah   And Rosie? Inside? She's cooking? She wants I should give her a hand?

Hannah *goes into the house. There is silence for a moment as* **Mike** *eats.*

Mike   Lily's here.

Isaac   And why not? Albert, you know what Jewish festival is today?

Mike   He knows.

Albert   Yom Kippur.

Mike   What I told you?

Isaac *chuckles.*

Isaac   Albert, you know what's Yom Kippur?

Mike   Come on, he's a bigger Jew than you are. You should see him on Saturday morning. Is he in my shop selling watches? Nah, he won't work on the shabbes. He's preaching out in the streets. Half the blacks in the township got already bar mitzvah. He knows what's Yom Kippur.

Isaac   Yom Kippur is the Day of Atonement. It's the day Jews don't eat.

Mike (*to* **Albert**)   Starts after sunset, don't worry, you're in the clear, eat.

Isaac   It's the annual stock-taking of our tribe.

Mike (*joining in*)   – of our tribe. For two days shut up shop, search our souls for our errors. Track them down, put it right. God signs, stamps, files you away till next year. (*To* **Isaac**.) I got it correct? Sh, sh! Rest.

Isaac *chuckles.* **Paul** *runs on. He's been running hard.*

Paul   Breathless!

Mike   To see him, it's like the sun came out.

Paul *collapses on the ground and lies panting.*

Isaac   Paulie!

Paul *sits up, sees* **Isaac**.
Isaac *opens his arms to him.* **Mike** *goes to* **Paul**.

Mike   Look at him! What you say? Isn't he marvellous? Look at this boychick. This comes from me? When were we specimens. Make a fist. Go on. Show your old man what they done to you. Paulie!

Paul *makes a fist.*

Mike   We done something good here. Hey? We made a lion, isn't so? (*He embraces* **Paul**.)

Rose *and* **Hannah** *come out with trays laden with food and tea.*

Hannah   Mikey – look! Lovely food Rosie made.

Mike *releases* **Paul** *who lies back on the ground.*

Rose (*to* **Paul**)   Don't catch cold.

Hannah   Isaac! It's Paul. (*To* **Paul**.) Give grampa a kiss.

Rose (*to* **Mike**)   Don't forget – swim before shul.

Mike   . . . nag, nag . . . I swim, she nags. We both get our exercise.

Rose   But you *need* . . .

Mike   I need, yes. I will, yes. But first build up my strength. Like our soldier boy.

Mike *sits at the table and eats.* **Rose** *and* **Hannah** *distribute cups of tea, plates of food.*

Hannah   The mayonnaise – a little bit sour. (*To* **Mike**.) You like it like that? Since when? But the salad dressing? Mine is also something. But this one! For my taste too much mustard. She likes it! Does it hurt anyone?

Rose (*to* **Paul**)   Come sit here.

Hannah (*to* **Paul**)   Sit by your grampa.

Mike (*to* **Paul**)   Mr Muscles – come, eat!

Paul   Ah! Ah!

Rose   What is it?

Mike   Is it cramp?

Rose   Where?

Isaac   Something wrong with him?

Mike   Cramp. Nothing.

Isaac   Look his face. That's nothing?

Rose *has run to* **Paul**, *pulled off his shoe, started massaging his foot.*

Paul   Rub it, man.

Rose   Better?

Paul   Easy! Easy! That's it.

Albert *is still standing.*

Hannah (*to* **Albert**)   You're eating or not eating?

Mike   His wife's waiting. He was always a good boy.

Hannah   Your wife cooks like so? Sit, my friend.

Albert *sits.*

Rose   Come on now. Lean on me.

Paul   ... not hungry.

Rose   Even a little. You coming?

Rose *goes back to the table.*

Isaac (*to* **Rose**)   He's all right?

Mike (*to* **Rose**)   He asks: he's all right.

Rose   He's fine.

Mike (*to* **Isaac**)   He's all right.

Hannah (*to* **Mike**)   You know what? Rosie keeps a lovely house. Clean, tidy. Beautiful. Who wants a sandwich? (*To* **Isaac**.) But why not? (*To* **Rose**.) It's no good. He won't eat what you cook. (*To* **Isaac**.) Why upset her? (*To everyone*.) Ask me why?

Rose (*quietly*)   What did he tell you?

Mike   Who?

Rose   Paul.

Mike   What should he tell me? (*To* **Paul**.) You waiting a gold invitation?

Paul   Ah! Ah!

Rose *goes back to* **Paul**.

Rose   Same place again?

She starts massaging.

Paul (*to* **Rose**)   Ma, you want to hear about me and Shortie Pretorius? That's a one for all time. So Shortie ... this was the first time – no, wait ... yes ... ur ... that's it. We were up a tree. So we looked down and there he was. The ... So I said to ... no, Trevie ... no – hang on ... um ...

Rose (*to* **Paul**)   You're needing a shower.

Mike (*to* **Paul**)   Come tell your old man what's new in the world.

Paul *sniffs himself and grins.*

Paul (*to* **Rose**)   You're damn right. Phew! Is this me?

Paul *stands and starts to go out.*

Mike   You didn't hear me?

Rose   He's tired.

Paul   Me? Fresh as a fart. You want to hear about Shortie or not?

Rose *and* **Mike** *exchange glances.*

Paul   Got the message. (*He goes out.*)

Mike   Must the boy polish the stoep in the afternoon? . . . smell makes my stomach go hard. I can't eat. (*He pushes his food away.*)

Albert (*to* **Isaac**)   Mr Levine, you'll agree with me. You can't ignore history. Isn't that so?

Mike   Leave an old man in peace.

Albert (*to* **Isaac**)   I push digitals, I push bicycle lights, I push alarm clocks. But at this moment in my people's history –

Mike   History's got nothing to *do* with it. Next week I'll spend with you in the township. Next Saturday's receipts will be up – what? Not too ambitious. Fifty per cent? The lesson of history is: put your head down and slog. Slog! It's like I tell you, Albert. All right, fail – at least try. Us, we can only do so much. We've done a lot for you people. Education . . . If you don't *want* to improve yourselves . . . ? Meantime, your children will eat – what? It's always the children who suffer . . .

Mike *stands.* **Hannah** *starts gathering plates.*

Mike   Time for my swim. (*To* **Albert**.) Monday, your office, at eight. And don't monkey around. Get some rest. We're going to work hard, make some money together. Don't look so blue. We'll have fun. (*To* **Isaac**.) You want to count how many lengths I do? It won't strain you, I promise. I'd give the boy a tip to do twenty lengths for me. But it's my lungs need exercise. Come.

Mike *helps* **Isaac** *off.*

Rose (*to* **Hannah**)   Leave it for the boy.

Hannah   I like to. Unless you don't like ... ?

Rose   If you like.

Hannah   I like to help people. That's what I'm like.

Hannah *takes some plates out.*

Albert   Mrs Rosie, I'm nothing special. I'm a simple man. But in my life I see the same thing happen time and again. Politics gets unstable – people with money buy gold. Bracelets, watches, necklaces. Mr Mike's shops do well. But by us? It's hard to squeeze, squeeze.

Rose   You want a parcel of food to take home?

Albert   No, I'm quite fine. I had lunch, tea. I'm full up to here. Happy Yom Kippur.

Albert *takes his file and goes.* **Rose**, *alone, sits for a moment staring into space. Then she finds she is crying, dabs at her eyes with a serviette, blows her nose.*

Paul *comes in draped in white towels.* **Rose** *looks up, hides the serviette, brightens.*

Rose   So? Feeling fine now?

Paul   'mall right.

Rose   How's your foot?

Paul   't's OK.

Rose   Do your back?

Paul *shakes his head.*

Rose Your hair?

Paul . . . 'mall right! . . . 'f you like.

Rose *takes a towel off his shoulders and rubs his hair with it.*

Rose Too hard?

Paul 't's good.

Rose You're wet all *over*.

Paul 't'll dry.

Rose I'll do you properly.

He yields. She rubs his back with the towel.

Rose Isn't that terrific? What girl would give you that? Free? Hm? What other girl? What happened there?

Paul *takes the towel back from her and moves away.*

Paul Fell off a ladder.

Rose You never tell the truth! What's happened? Tell me. The minute I saw you my heart stopped, I swear.

Paul *grins.*

Rose I'm dead now. If you don't wake me. How *can* it be nothing?

Paul It's nothing.

She slaps him lightly.

Rose Your bloody lies.

He is still grinning.

Rose I'll go mad. Quick, man. We won't get a moment alone. You're the only one I care about, ever cared about. Is it another of your jokes? No. You're scared. You? Scared? Tell me why?

Paul . . . don't take commands from women.

She raises her hand to slap him. He grabs it and twists it behind her back and up. She half stifles her cry. He lets her go.

Rose   . . . don't hurt me.

Paul   . . . warned you.

Rose   . . . hurt *me*? I beg you. Tell me! Yes, you're strong, you're beautiful. So what's wrong?

Paul *doesn't answer.* **Rose** *turns and goes quickly.* **Paul** *stays looking out.* **Lily** *comes on. She watches* **Paul** *for a moment before she speaks.*

Lily   My angel of peace.

Paul *looks around for some excuse to get away. He finds nothing. He looks at* **Lily**.

Lily   I've been searching up and down the streets for you. Where's daddy? You told him what you wrote me? No wonder he's jumping.

Paul   Please – don't tell him.

Lily   You wrote only to me?

Paul   I didn't write to you!

Lily   That you, *you* should feel so. By us we had a tradition. Teachers, scholars. But you? From where you got it? To see so clearly, write so simple, so true.

Paul   Where's it? You got it on you?

Paul *grabs her handbag, opens it.*

Lily   No, sweetheart.

She takes a piece of paper from her pocket. **Paul** *throws the handbag down.*

Lily   You're ashamed of your feelings. Why?

Paul   Tear it up . . . Warning you.

Lily   You think you're alone? We're many! I keep it by my heart.

Lily *slips the paper down the front of her dress.* **Paul** *stands undecided, then lunges at her, pulls out the paper, looks at it, crumples it.*

Lily   This is Lily! I'm the one *with* you!

Mike *comes on, dressed in a bathing costume and a towelling gown.* **Paul** *puts his towel over his head to dry his hair.*

Mike (*to* **Paul**)   Look at me!

Paul *doesn't move.* **Mike** *whips the towel out of* **Paul**'*s hand.* **Paul** *turns to look at* **Mike**.

Mike   Something's wrong?

Paul   No . . .

Mike   No who?

Paul   . . . Dad.

Mike   You're sure? I want the truth.

Paul   Yes . . . Dad.

Mike   So why behave like this?

Lily   What by you he done wrong?

Paul   Dad, did I tell you about me and Shortie Pretorius –

Mike   You want to hurt me?

Paul *grimaces.*

Mike   You do? Hurt your mother. I feel it, I promise you.

Paul   . . . won't.

Mike   His mother's *arm*! My God, I'll break yours!

Lily   He didn't mean to hurt. That's how they train him. He's still confused.

Paul   Don't fuckin' dare . . . Fuckin' dare . . . There's nothing wrong with me. Just don't talk, talk, talk about me all the time.

Paul *starts to go in.*

Lily   He told you what's paining him?

Mike (*concerned*)   Paining? (*To* **Paul**.) You hurt yourself running?

Lily *takes the letter from her handbag.*

Lily   In the past, he's unhappy, he came to me.

Mike   You? What for? (*To* **Paul**.) Is it true? (*To* **Lily**.) How many times?

Lily   Always. Now he's unhappy, he can't come, he wrote.

Mike   He wrote to us also. So?

Lily (*to* **Paul**)   You want to hurt him? Hide from him your heart. Be false to your own soul. That's how. (*She holds out the letter to* **Mike**.) Take. Read.

Mike *pours himself a drink.*

Lily   One thing is sure. He won't go back to camp.

Mike *drinks, takes the letter, reads.*

Mike   Unhappy, we knew that. Can't spell. We knew that as well. (*He turns to the second page and reads.*) 'Won't go.' 'Right, wrong?' What the army is? A philosophical walking tour? He wrote the same to us. I told him: this is life, sweet as it gets. You can't run away. (*He pockets the letter.*) First sign of stress – snap. A twig in the breeze. (*To* **Paul**.) You know what I done? You know what I done it for? Every last breath I take for? (*To* **Lily**.) A weakling.

Paul   Just let me tell you what I did with Shortie.

Mike   Shortie. We know Shortie. Like we know Pinny and Ninny and Pinky and Porky and all the rest you made up. He's making it up. Shortie! This I know! And the truth? He won't fight. That's all it is. He's afraid to fight. I must fight. I must build. But will he spend a couple of years protecting me, you, what we got?

Paul   So Shortie and me . . .

Rose *comes in.* **Paul** *sees her and stops talking.*

Lily   So. You won't help him?

Mike   My own son? I won't help him?

Lily   You'll send him back?

Rose   Of course he'll go back. Of course he will. Oh, I can't bear it. (**Rose** *is crying.*)

Mike (*to* **Lily**)   She's crying. Tears. (*He pours a drink for* **Rose**.) Drink. (*To* **Lily**.) You see what you're doing here?

Rose *drinks.*

Mike   I don't want a big discussion. What I want is he knows his dad is a rock he can lean on, help him climb over the hard times, the first few months –

Lily   He's been more than a year.

Rose   . . . the worst thing . . . my whole life . . . All of you despised me . . .

Lily   Me? Never.

Rose   I'm dirt! A farm girl. No feelings. I'm compost. Chuck me on your seeds, make them grow. I can't . . . go on. Even my son!

Mike *pours another drink for* **Rose**.

Mike (*to* **Rose**)   What can I say? After all, it is a war.

Rose   Why must you always *explain* to me?

Mike *pours drinks for himself and* **Lily**.

Mike   I don't say a big war. Not what a Jew calls a war. But a war. Is it easy? Be patient. He'll make up his own mind. He'll go. (*To* **Lily**.) Am I right?

Rose   No.

Mike   Rosie.

Rose You're not right. He's changed.

Lily What I told you?

Mike How changed? Muscle? Bone? Sure. Hardened,
developed . . .

Rose Changed! Changed to me. (**Rose**'s *arm hurts her. She
rubs it.*) Ow . . .

Mike *throws up his arms and sits.*

Mike How could a fella predict it? His captain –
Rawlings, Rawlinson, Raw-raw-raw – he phoned. They
don't know what's wrong with the boy. Won't even pick up
a gun. So? What? Court martial? They'll shoot him? Nah,
psychological causes. What it means? He's a little
meshuggah. Tell me, who isn't? But they're fanatics, they're
sending him home. Perhaps his own doctor . . . I pleaded.
For some cock-eyed theory – in front of his pals? Wait.
Yom Kippur is coming . . . (*To* **Paul**.) Want a drink?

He opens a can of beer, pours some into a glass and gives it to
Paul.

Paul So Shortie and me –

Mike Drink!

Paul *empties the glass.*

Mike That's the stuff. (*He gives him the beer can.*) What are
you? Nervous? Don't be nervous. You're a young ox.
Daddy loves you. But daddy's tochus is frozen, he's got to
get dressed. (*He starts to go.*)

Paul (*in anguish*) Daddy.

Mike Pumpkin?

Paul Don't worry.

Mike . . . not worried.

Paul I'll go.

Mike (*to* **Rose** *and* **Lily**) You see? I know him. He'll go.

He fondles **Paul**. **Paul** *accepts it.*

Mike   Fetch his clothes . . . mine . . .

Rose (*to* **Paul**)   Why do you torture me?

Mike (*to* **Rose**)   We're standing here naked.

Rose *goes.*

Mike   Pumpkin? Another beer?

Mike *opens a can and pours it for* **Paul**. **Isaac** *comes on. He looks very tired.*

Isaac   Talking business?

Mike (*to* **Isaac**)   Nah. Making a celebration. Nice walk? Lovely. Something to drink? Why not? Get it all down before sunset.

Mike *pours a drink for* **Isaac** *and himself.*

Mike (*toasting*)   To Pumpkin! To Paul!

Mike *drinks.*

Lily (*to* **Paul**)   When you don't show up, they'll send military police.

Mike   He said he'll go back. You didn't hear?

Lily   He'll hand you over, if you want or not.

Mike (*to* **Paul**)   Relax. Three days leave? Forget it. I'll ring up Raw-raw-raw, sell him my best watch cost price, he'll give you the week.

Lily   You need to hide? Come. I'll hide you.

Mike   Hide? From who?

Lily   You got to flee from the country? I'll find cash, what you need. (*To* **Mike**.) You can't say no. We were his age when we left our home. (*To* **Isaac**.) Tell him! (*To* **Mike**.) Your daddy was just like him. Not scared to say: 'This, I won't do it. A soldier? Not me.' We were proud of him. (*To* **Paul**.) Now we're proud of you.

Mike (*to* **Lily**) 'Hide him. Flee from the country.' You come to my house with these ideas in your head?

Lily It's his choice. He begged me: help him.

Mike Show! Where he wrote that?

Lily Not wrote. He feels it. (*To* **Paul**.) Speak! Like your heart speaks to me. (*She goes towards* **Paul**.)

Mike Keep your hands off my son! You had your chance to be one of us. You turned me down. So keep away. While he's weak, while he's leaning on me. Understand?

Paul (*to himself*) So this gook we'd sighted comes flit, flit, flit, bush to bush, tree to . . .

Rose *comes out bringing clothes for* **Mike**, *and* **Paul**'s *uniform, washed and pressed.* **Mike** *takes trousers and T-shirt from* **Rose**.

Mike (*to* **Rose**) She wants to take him away.

Rose Take him where?

Paul *takes his uniform and starts putting it on.* **Mike** *pulls his T-shirt over his head.*

Paul (*to himself*) HQ Charlie Tango and out . . . throat's like a fuckin' goat's arsehole. (*He drinks.*)

Mike (*to* **Lily**) Get in the car. I'm taking you home.

Mike *pulls on his trousers.*

Rose She's got no child. She wants mine. Paulie, my Paulie.

Rose *embraces* **Paul**.

Lily Rosie, Rosie, there's more to life than bodies, than sex sex sex. (*To* **Mike**.) I want him because I can care for what's good in him.

Mike (*to* **Lily**) You want him? Fine. I'm a fair man. (*To* **Rose**.) Leave him. (*He elbows* **Rose** *aside. To* **Paul**.) You want to go with her, go with her. How does she seem to you?

Paul *can't speak.*

Mike (*to* **Lily**)   Got your answer? (*He starts to go in.*) I'm dressing for shul. (*To* **Lily**.) You coming with your family to shul or we should drop you off with your friends in the bush? What you want? I got a big heart.

Lily   I want my life! (*To* **Paul**.) I made a mistake with my life. I don't want you should do it too. I had a friend, a fine man. A leader. He led us. He wanted to come to this country. He didn't. Why? It was a choice – politics or family. The family – your granny, your grampa – they won. So I left him. Is he living? Dead? No one wrote me. I did his work. I wanted a school for young blacks in his name. But your daddy wanted a shop. So? First I lost my friend, then I lost my family as well. Politics, family. Why must the one fight the other? Keep still, darling. Listen to me. I don't say I done nothing. I done plenty. I don't say I got no one. I got some. But – with him . . . ? Could be Gideon came here, you wouldn't be dressing in those clothes. Could be no wars, no blood, no fighting. Could be politics together with family. Who wants to tell me it can't be? But we lost it. I lost it. Then one day – your letter. I been so long on my own, sweetheart. Come.

Paul *doesn't move.*

Lily   Don't come. But don't let them push you the way they pushed me. In your whole life you got only one duty. Not daddy, not mummy, not aunty. Discover your choices. Choose, darling. You're free.

Paul *is now fully dressed in his uniform except for his boots.*

Mike (*to* **Paul**)   Ask what she wants of you. Who she is. Ask her.

Paul   So, OK . . . ur . . . (*He opens a can of beer and drinks as he speaks.*) Where do you actually come from then?

Isaac   He doesn't know? Paulie, where you come from?

Paul   Salisbury, Rhodesia –

Isaac   Oy, oy. I told him our stories, our history –

Paul   – Africa, the planet, the universe, the mind of God . . .

Isaac   Kovna, Lithuania.

Paul   Where's that?

Isaac   You remember nothing?

Lily   Today it's in Russia.

Paul   Why don't you say Russian then?

Lily (*to* **Isaac**)   He thinks we got something to hide.

Paul   You must have. Everyone does.

Mike (*to* **Paul**)   Sit down. Take it easy. You're doing well.

Paul *sits.*

Paul   So why did you come here?

Isaac   Why? We had nothing. You come from a very poor family.

Paul   I don't. You do. Hey, Dad?

Lily   Listen, we came to this country –

Paul   Big mistake.

Isaac   I think so too.

Paul   Leaving where they know you . . . like you . . . what makes you tick . . . a man without his pals . . . I couldn't . . .

Paul *is so exhausted he can't speak.*

Lily   Paul!

Isaac   He's asleep.

Lily   Wake up!

Lily *goes towards him.* **Rose** *blocks her way.* **Paul** *partly wakes.*

Paul That was your number one tactical error . . .
vacating base camp . . . your supply lines ran down . . .
you've been taken out . . . finished . . .

Still half asleep, **Paul** *gets up, kisses* **Rose** *and* **Mike**. *Then he
turns to* **Lily**.

I made my choice.

Lily *stands, looks at nobody, goes.*

Rose There. I can breathe again.

Paul *sits at the table, takes a handful of nuts from the drinks tray.*

Mike (*to* **Paul**) The sun's gone down, Pumpkin.

Paul . . . starving.

Mike Don't eat!

Paul *puts the nuts in his mouth.*

Mike Eat.

Rose Never mind shul tonight. Look, he's exhausted. (*To*
Paul.) Wait, I'll go turn down your bed.

Rose *goes out.* **Isaac** *stands.*

Isaac So. It's late. I'm tired. We're going home.

Paul You know what I was thinking? I remembered my
bris. Is it possible? I looked up. A face – like a sweaty old
cheese. And a knife. Shining. I thought: I'm going to be
peeled like a grape.

Isaac (*to* **Paul**) So. When I'll see you?

Paul *doesn't answer.*

Mike Tomorrow at shul.

Isaac Him.

Mike He'll be there.

Isaac And after? When you get leave again?

Paul   . . . dunno.

Isaac   A man could drop dead before that. Say goodbye.

Paul   . . . bye.

Isaac   Could be forever. A kiss?

Paul *looks at* **Mike**. **Mike** *motions with his head.* **Paul** *goes to* **Isaac** *and pecks his cheek.* **Isaac** *embraces him tightly.*

Isaac   Pauly, Pauly . . . I want to tell you once more so you'll never forget it. You know how we came to this country?

Paul *starts to shake.*

Isaac   What is it?

Paul   I can't . . . I can't . . .

Isaac (*to* **Mike**)   You see that? He can't. (*To* **Paul**.) Can't what?

Paul   So Shortie –

Isaac   Can't what, sweetheart?

Paul (*wailing*)   I'm trying to tell you.

Mike *goes to* **Paul**.

Mike   He's worn out. Come inside.

Isaac   He can't rest out here?

Mike   Then let him sit.

Isaac   It's so wrong if he stands?

Paul *breaks away from the two men.*

Paul   Four of us in the jeep, Shortie, Bennie, Trevie, me, all Jewboys . . . nothing you can't fix if you know how. Other jeeps far behind, in front, to hell and gone, who knows where. Us four, grey trees, mile after mile, deeper and deeper up this track. Bush, grass, more trees. Then – one mud hut. Push the door in. No one there. Move on. Just the four of us, knocking over doors, no one there,

moving on. Then – one more door. Packed full of bodies.
Whimpering! The stink, man. They pour out, stand in
front of us 'cause they know if they don't we knock the hut
flat, them inside. I ask Trevie: what now? We've found
them. God knows whose side they're on but we've found
them. So? Now? Trevie's staring, can't think. Shortie's
started to shake. Benny says: I know what I need . . . opens
his pants, has a damn good piss, there, in front of them,
pointing at them. We're on this raised part. The water runs
down in a little stream over the dry sand. We watch it go.
We look at their faces. Now they're really scared. One
turned . . . ran . . . no, man, no. Mistake! The firing
started. No, it wasn't us . . . swear . . . other guys . . . they
fell . . . crawled . . . fell . . . up and fell . . . I couldn't shoot.
Why? (*To* **Mike**.) Tell me. They did. I couldn't shoot.

Isaac Anyone can pull a trigger.

Paul I can't.

Isaac Explain to me why.

Mike Paul –

Isaac You don't want to listen his story?

Paul I can't.

Isaac Can't shoot? Can't explain?

Paul Standing amongst them . . . outside the hut . . . I
saw Lily.

He wipes his nose with the back of his hand.

We're back in our jeep . . . speeding . . . Shortie rips off
his shirt, out the window. Why? . . . Beating his hand on
his chest, crying out. Benny driving . . . foot slips, the jeep
bucks. I fell out . . . sick, all over a little dry bush with red
berries. Shortie stripping off clothes . . . Trevie trying to
stop him, hitting him . . . Benny just ran off in the bush.
We sat there, waiting. Bennie comes back: 'That's one
bunch of commies we done for.' Laughs. Commies. I look
up. Aunty Lily. I'm crazy? In her hand a glass of water.

'Boys, you want a drink?' ... walking towards us ... 'Boys, want a drink from Aunty Lily?'

Isaac   You see? By you he's just muscle. Nah. He's a thinker. And why shouldn't he? 'To fight, to build.' All over the world people do it – I don't want to hurt you – any peasant can do it. To think! That's our tradition.

Mike (*to* **Isaac**)   You're a thinker?

Isaac   My first words: 'What is the meaning of "mamma"?' I'm not lying to you.

Mike   A philosopher. All your life. Tell me, what did you think about?

Isaac *thinks.*

Paul   I got back to camp. Bone in my left foot is snapped. Hospital bed. The bone's healed. Get up! Can't. Screaming at me. Get out! Kill the damn commie gooks, man. Trevie's out and gone. Bennie. Shortie. Out and gone. Get out of bed!

Isaac   All right. I won't argue. But this one – you're right. He's not an Isaac. He's better. He's a Gideon. He wants to – he can't. He doesn't think only, he acts. He takes a moral position.

Mike   First give a full stomach. Then talk about morals.

Isaac   You got a full stomach.

Mike   They're trying to take it away! Can't you hear what he's saying? What's he got? Today? Me. I got cash in the bank. God forbid I should die, but I will. God forbid they should burn down the banks, but they do? What's he got then?

Isaac   With such a brain, what he needs?

Mike   I can't talk to you! All your life – you'll take money, you'll spend it, but talk, think about where it comes from – make even a little yourself – you won't. It's polluted, unkosher, unclean. I make it, it's fine, you can touch it. And the dirt? It all stays with me. You think, I work. You're clean, I'm dirty. And you want to talk morals? I'll show you morals. Paulie. Come here.

Paul *hesitates then goes to him.*

Mike   Do you love me?

Paul *says nothing.*

Mike   Then there's nothing in the world left to say. (*He sits.*)

Paul   Can't go back. So where? Jail? Bin? No. Got to get out. Where? Across the border. Got to. (*To* **Mike**.) Why can't I do it? You looked after us. I want to. Can't. (*To himself.*) Won't. Got to go. Got to fly. Got to take a drink from Aunty Lily.

Mike   How many times, I was your age, I'd have loved just to take off. Like a bird. When things got tough. Fly to the mountains. Lie in the sun. If I'd done what I wanted where would we be? Ma, my ma, my dad, Lily – you? Where? You want to run from your camp. OK, run. But the camp's got a barbed-wire fence. You know when you're out. Life goes on . . . and on . . .

Paul *runs off. Only* **Isaac** *sees him go.*

Isaac   Tell me, what you wanted in your life that you didn't do?

Mike   Me? I wanted the sun. The shade of a tree. A wooden table. A chair. A jug of fresh milk. All my life. To read. Take a few notes. To think. Let the whole world go by. But I had to look after my family. You didn't know? (*He turns, stands.*) Pumpkin? Paulie! Where he went?

Isaac *doesn't move.*

Mike   Paulie!

Mike *runs off.* **Isaac** *watches. He takes a handful of nuts and eats them.* **Mike** *runs on.*

Mike   He went into the house?

Isaac *shrugs.*

Mike   You saw him!

Isaac   You heard what those boys did – Shortie, what-ya-call, the other one? You heard? Jews?

He spits three times.

Mike   They're my sons! They did it for me! This is mine. I've dug earth, I've drawn water, I've struggled, I've won. That's our tradition as well!

Hannah *comes on.* **Rose** *follows.*

Hannah (*to* **Isaac**)   I'm waiting. Rosie's yawning. (*To* **Mike**.) Why out in the cold? Where's my little soldier boy? Kiss him for granny. (*To* **Isaac**.) Come.

Hannah *kisses* **Mike**. *She goes to* **Isaac** *and kisses him.*

My two strong boys. Thank God – my family gave me a good life. I wish the same to everyone. (*To* **Isaac**.) Come.

Isaac *and* **Hannah** *go.*

Rose   Where's Paul?

Mike   He went – to a friend. He's not inside?

Rose   I didn't hear him. (*She sits.*)

Mike   Look what we got here.

Rose   It's late.

Mike   Lovely house ... gardens ... pool ... everything ... Adam in Paradise. How could anyone run away?

Rose   I'd like to sleep for a hundred years.

Rose *stands, walks towards the house, turns to* **Mike**.

Mike   I'm going to stay.

Scene Six

1980. The dining room of the Levines' house. The seder table is partly laid for Passover dinner.

Rose*, wearing an apron over her clothes, is laying places at the table. She holds a published guide to the seder which she consults.*
Mike*, in suit trousers and a white shirt, is sitting at the table doing calculations, surrounded by books and maps.*

Rose   Salt water? I got it.

Mike   Salisbury to Beitbridge – 421 miles.

Rose   Roasted egg? I got it.

Mike   Beitbridge to Jo'burg – 342 miles.

Rose   . . . don't move, I can't finish.

Mike   Wait.

Rose   Mikey.

Mike   I'm mapping our route. Jo'burg to Cape Town – 1,156 miles. Total – *(He adds the figures.)* – 1,919 miles. Done.

Mike *closes his books and gets up.*

Rose   Roasted shank bone? I got it. Horse radish. Not possible. I went through all the shops . . .

Mike   Oh. *(He takes a small packet from the pocket of his jacket hanging over a chair and holds it out.)* Happy pesach from Albert.

Rose *takes the packet, opens it and reveals a large horse radish.*

Rose   . . . glad somebody's happy.

Mike *puts on his jacket and tie.*

Mike   He is. His brother's been elected to Parliament. Turns out he's quite a bright chap. Albert put him through school.

Mike Look at these forks. (*Calls.*) Gertie! You'll have to clean these again. Now *she's* gone independent. (*Calls.*) And turn the oven down to three! You hear what I'm telling you?

Isaac *comes in.*

Rose (*to* **Isaac**) Where are the prayer books? Do you know where to start, where to finish? . . . getting dressed. (*She goes out.*)

Isaac I'm resting in your boy's bedroom. What is it? A shrine? Nothing happened in there for five years. Clothes laid out on the bed . . . He's gone? Let him go. Your mama, may she rest in God's peace, she was here, not any more. Do I put out her nightie by the bed every night? I didn't even do it when she was alive. Anyway. Pesach. We see who isn't here.

Mike Look, it's not that I want to go. But are they going to take over my business or aren't they? Some say yes, some say no. Business is confidence.

Isaac And you got neither? Don't tell me.

Mike I can't take out my money. They watch all the banks. So what must I do? Take risks? Nah. I found this Indian in Cape Town. He wants to come here. A rich man. Good luck to him. We swap. He takes this house, I take his. He gets my bank account – So it goes . . .

The doorbell rings. **Mike** *pours drinks and hands one to* **Isaac**.

Isaac Where you learnt it, this swapping?

Mike The details I improvise. The spirit from you.

Lily *comes in carrying packages and parcels.* **Rose** *follows her in.*

Lily Sorry, sorry so late. I'm training up a little choir for independence. We don't yet know will they be part of the main celebration, so I want them tip-top. Perfect. They are. Sweetheart. (*She gives* **Rose** *a cake tin.*) Kirschkuchen. Baked special for you. To find kirsch these days isn't easy. But you know someone who knows someone. These days I do.

(*To* **Mike**.) You moved Albert into head office? This has a meaning? Don't tell me. Where? When? Don't tell me that either. (*To* **Isaac**.) And you?

Isaac   You want I should tell you?

Lily *puts her arms around* **Isaac** *and kisses him.*

Lily   Such an old bird. Not afraid to take flight?

Mike   And you?

Lily   Me? Ah, no. This time I stay.

Rose (*wailing*)   I want to go. I want to stay. I want to go. I want to stay.

Lily   Come, sweetheart.

She leads **Rose** *to the table.*

Isaac (*at the table*)   Only four chairs?

Lily   It's all we got left.

Isaac (*to* **Mike**)   Put one more.

Mike *moves a fifth chair to the table.* **Mike** *and* **Isaac** *put on skull caps and prayer shawls. They all sit.*

Isaac   So. Now we're ready?

He opens his prayer book. **Isaac** *starts intoning the Passover service in Hebrew. He rocks backwards and forwards as he reads.*

All who are hungry, let them come to this table, let them celebrate Passover with us.

He intones in Hebrew.

Now we are in a foreign land. Next year may we be in Israel. In this passage Israel doesn't mean in fact Israel. By this family, Cape Town is Israel. By me, a Jew is a Jew. What difference where?

He intones in Hebrew.

Now we are slaves. In the year to come may we be free.

Desire

for Judith Cornell

Characters

Kindo Goredema
Rosemary, *his older daughter.*
Shupi, *his younger daughter.*
Ambuya, *his mother.*
Gaudencia Kambada, *chairman of the village committee.*
Danger, *her son.*
Wireless Chikambo
Lena, *his wife.*
Freedom, *his daughter.*
Jericho Zindoga, *a government employee.*

The play is set in a village in the Zambezi Valley in the far north of Zimbabwe in 1980.

Desire was first performed at the Almeida Theatre, London, on 10 May 1990, with the following cast:

Rosemary	Vicky Licorish
Freedom	Marcia Myrie
Shupi	Pamela Nomvete
Ambuya	Corinne Skinner-Carter
Lena	Cassie McFarlane
Kindo	Louis Mahoney
Gaudencia	Cleo Sylvestre
Jericho	Cyril Nri
Wireless	Bazil Otoin
Danger	Michael Buffong

Directed by Andrei Serban
Designed by Richard Hudson
Lighting Design by Gerry Jenkinson
Choreography by Stella Chiweshe
Music by Torera Mpedzisi and Earl Waungana

One

Before dawn.
A bridge over a stream.
Rosemary *waits in the darkness.*
Freedom *rides in on a bicycle, dismounts. She wears military camouflage.*

Freedom (*calling softly*)   Rosemary!

Rosemary   I'm here.

Freedom   You've come! (*She holds out the bicycle to* **Rosemary**.) Get on.

Rosemary   I've come to tell you: I can't go with you.

Freedom   Why? All your friends are with me in the bush. They're full of fight.

Rosemary   Don't try to pressure me!

Freedom   You want to be with us.

Rosemary   Do I?

Freedom   I know your heart. Let's move. This place is dangerous.

Rosemary   Who can see us?

Freedom   There are always spies.

Rosemary   I'm going home.

Freedom   But why?

Rosemary   I've got a pain.

Silence.

Freedom   What kind of pain?

Rosemary *takes* **Freedom**'s *hand, shows her.*

Freedom   That's nothing.

Rosemary   Feel!

Freedom   It's fear. We're all afraid.

Rosemary   Of?

Freedom   Dying. Time passes, it's gone.

Dawn appears over the mountain.

The sun is rising. People will start moving in the village. (*She holds out the bicycle.*) Take it.

Rosemary   If I'm with you, who'll look after my father, wash his clothes, cook his food?

Freedom   Who cares? This is a war!

Rosemary   My mother's dead. He needs me.

Freedom   We all need you. To be strong! To fight!

Shupi (*off*)   Rosemary!

Rosemary   Too late.

Shupi (*off*)   Rosemary!

Freedom *mounts the bicycle.*

Freedom   I've loved you since you were so high. When it's dark, look for me. I'll come for you again. (*She rides off.*)

Shupi *runs on. She is crippled in her right leg.*

Shupi   Rosemary!

Ambuya *and* **Lena** *run on.*

Ambuya   Did you look by the river?

Shupi   She's not there.

Ambuya   In the fields?

Shupi   I ran down to the gully.

Ambuya   Try the other way.

Shupi *runs off.*

Lena   Maybe she took a walk?

Ambuya So early? What for?

Lena The war's over. The curfew's lifted. If people want to put one foot down then another and go on and on, no matter what the time, they can just go.

Shupi (*off*) Rosemary!

Lena You think she's run away?

Shupi *runs on.*

Shupi She's nowhere.

Ambuya Where could she run?

Lena Back to that man's bed.

Shupi She wouldn't do it.

Lena It's what she did before.

Ambuya Poor girl. Always the same. She hasn't got a mother she can turn to. Something's wrong, she puts on her shoes, runs.

Shupi She could have run back to him any time. Today she'll hear the judgement of the court: is she allowed to go to him or not. What good's running away?

Lena My daughter didn't run. They shot her. She was on her bicycle. She fell. Died. On this bridge.

The sun rises.
Rosemary *is sprawled on the bridge. They see her. They stand astonished. After a moment,* **Rosemary** *wakes, leaps up. Silence.*

Lena Why are you lying here?

Shupi Your hair's a tangle. Look. Her dress. It's torn.

Lena Why there? Why on the spot I found my daughter's body? A! (*She picks up a clod of earth.*) Her blood! The rain can't wash it. It's thick in the earth where you were lying. What's going on? What are you trying to do?

Kindo *rides in on a bicycle exactly like* **Freedom**'s. *He has a hoe over his shoulder. He stops.*

Lena (*to* **Kindo**)   Your daughter was sleeping on the spot I found my daughter. I want to know the reason.

Kindo   Rosemary?

Rosemary   I couldn't sleep. I came out for fresh air. Maybe I lay down.

Kindo   Her neck is bleeding.

Lena   Bleeding?

Ambuya (*going to* **Rosemary**)   Where?

Kindo (*to* **Ambuya**)   Mother, I told you: look after her!

Rosemary *is about to faint.*

Shupi (*going to her*)   Rosemary!

Kindo *throws down his bicycle, takes* **Rosemary** *from* **Ambuya**, *steadies her.*

Kindo   OK. OK. (*He takes off his shirt, uses it to staunch the wound on her neck.*) Keep still.

Ambuya   It's just a scratch. Maybe she scraped it on a tree.

Lena *throws down the clod of earth.*

Lena (*to* **Shupi**)   But this is where we found the body. Isn't it? Right here. Right on this bridge.

Rosemary   I'm sorry, father, if I've worried you.

Kindo   Me? Worried? About what?

Rosemary   Did you think I'd run away?

Kindo   I plant maize, weeds grow, *that* makes me worried. I know you won't leave me. (*He throws his shirt to* **Ambuya**.) Wash it. When it's dry bring it to me. (*He mounts his bicycle, starts to ride off.*)

Shupi   Father.

Kindo *stops.*

Shupi Don't forget. The court will judge Rosemary's case at ten.

Kindo But it's the people's court. Not so? Then it must wait for the people. (*To* **Ambuya**.) Take her to rest. I'm going to cut my weeds. (*He rides off.*)

Two

Mid-morning. A clearing under a tree in the centre of the village.
Gaudencia, *chairman of the village committee, sits on a wooden chair, sewing.* **Shupi** *sits near her. She takes the minutes of the court proceedings.*
Rosemary *and* **Ambuya** *sit together as do* **Lena** *and her husband* **Wireless**.
Rosemary's *husband* **Jericho** *sits to one side.* **Kindo** *sits on the other.*
Apart from **Jericho** *and* **Rosemary**, *everyone's clothes are in tatters.* **Rosemary**'s *dress is old but whole.* **Jericho** *wears a smart khaki uniform and holds a metal spray gun.*
Gaudencia *raises her right fist.*

Gaudencia Forward with the new committee!

Everyone raises their right fists.

All Forward!

Gaudencia Forward with the year of reconciliation!

All Forward!

Gaudencia Down with treachery and lies!

All Down with them!

Gaudencia Forward with democracy!

All Forward!

Gaudencia Good. Before we begin. I know you all feel deeply about what we're going to hear. But everyone in this valley is hungry. Since sunrise we've been in our fields. We need to rest before the sun gets cool and we can work

again. So, comrades, do your level best to keep your
speeches brief. Good. Number two. People keep asking me:
during the war no one could farm, our government
promised till the harvest comes they'd send us rations,
where are they? I'm chairman of this village. Yesterday I
caught the bus. I went up the mountain to the District
Office. I asked those young men: 'Where are our rations?'
They said: 'You're not forgotten. Sign this docket. Trust us.
Your food will come.'

Jericho *takes off his jacket.*
Gaudencia *finishes what she is sewing.*

Lena (*to* **Wireless**)   How does she look to you?

Wireless   Worn out. Like you, like me.

Lena   If you'd seen her on the bridge.

Wireless   I'll watch her, hear what she says, then I'll try
to work out what it means.

Shupi *takes off her blouse – she wears a vest beneath – and holds
it out to* **Gaudencia**, *who holds out a length of thread.*

Gaudencia   That's all that's left.

Shupi   Try at least.

Gaudencia   My dear, I can't work miracles.

Shupi   Uh uh. I know you.

Gaudencia *takes the blouse, starts sewing.*

Gaudencia   Comrade Jericho, you brought this case. I
hand over to you.

Jericho   Forward with democracy!

All   Forward!

Jericho   OK. I don't know where to start.

Gaudencia   At the beginning.

Jericho   OK. I was born with a smile on my face. All my
life I've been quite free and easy. But this business with

Rosemary . . . OK, I'll keep it brief. Rosemary is my wife. She's lived with me a mile along the road, there at the flygate where I work, one year. One day she said she wants to see her grandmother, her sister and so on. She came here. Now she wants to come home. There's an obstacle. Her father. He says no.

Gaudencia   Comrade Kindo, I hand over to you.

Kindo   A! A! A! Look! I thought the ground was dry. It's wet. My pants are wet. Shupi, go home. Bring me another pair.

Shupi   You haven't got another pair.

Kindo   I mean my trousers. You can't mean I haven't got even one other pair? Well, go home anyway. I'm hungry. Cook me some eggs and meat.

Shupi   We've got no food.

Kindo   A! A! A! No food. He's got a uniform, a government job, they give him food, a house, a salary. What have I got? The fact is, it's her choice. She wants to be with me.

Jericho   You force her!

Kindo   How? Are there chains on her feet?

Jericho   This is a court of law. Am I right?

Gaudencia   You're right.

Jericho   Let's look at law. I paid brideprice for her.

Gaudencia   You did?

Jericho   One hundred and twenty-seven dollars.

Gaudencia (*to* **Shupi**)   Write it down.

Jericho   One hundred and twenty-seven dollars. That's what he was paid. But what matters is I love her, she loves me.

Kindo (*to* **Rosemary**)   Tell them why you came here.

Silence.

Jericho   The point is she's got some kind of pain.

Gaudencia   Then why not go to the clinic?

Wireless   Excuse me, chairman. What I want to know is, what kind of pain is this? Maybe it's the kind they can cure at the clinic, maybe not.

Jericho   We went to the clinic.

Gaudencia   What did they say? Rosemary? Ignore these people. Think of me as though I were your mother. Talk only to me.

Rosemary   They gave me pills. I went back. Three injections. I was still suffering. My grandmother knows about roots and leaves.

Ambuya (*laughs*)   That's true. I do.

Rosemary   So I came home.

Wireless   Did she help you?

Rosemary   She did.

Ambuya (*laughs*)   That's true.

Wireless   Thank you. That's what I want to know.

Jericho   She got well. A month went by. Another. 'My one and only joy, come home, I'm missing you.' I went to find her father there, there, there, far, far hoeing his field. 'You want her? Finish paying.' 'Are you mad? I've paid!' 'There's sixty more to come.' Another sixty dollars!

Gaudencia (*to* **Shupi**)   Write the numbers down. (*To* **Jericho**.) So did you pay?

Jericho   Love makes a man a fool.

Gaudencia   And did she go?

Jericho   You can see she's here! See what I mean?

Rosemary *grimaces with pain.*

Jericho   And then, you see what happens? She got sick again.

Kindo (*to* **Rosemary**)   Look at me.

She looks at him. He pulls a comical face. She smiles.

She's feeling better. My face is all the medicine she needs.

Jericho   I'm a stranger in this place. My home is on the mountain. But I want to trust this court. The policy of our government is: any man wherever he may go must get fair play. Is it fair I should pay and she stays in his house and weeds his field?

Shupi   Do you want someone to weed or do you want Rosemary?

Jericho   I want justice. (*To* **Gaudencia**.) They voted for you. It's your job to give justice to me.

Rosemary, *in pain, tries to speak.*
Wireless *goes to her.*

Jericho   I want her home!

Wireless   Stop the court! She's in pain.

Jericho   No! It's a trick. You're all plotting against me.

Kindo   OK, he paid. Yes, OK, he did. But that was not for marriage. It's a fine.

Jericho   For what?

Kindo   Seduction of a virgin.

Jericho   My god!

Gaudencia (*to* **Shupi**)   Write!

Jericho   Blue lies!

Kindo   It's true! One night war came to this village. I was headman. Eight guerrillas came to talk to me. Other headmen ran straight to the whites and made reports. I supported independence. I pledged my life to help the struggle. And my daughters helped me. Shupi went with

the guerrillas to the bush. She learnt to fight. Rosemary
stayed here to organize supplies. (*Indicates* **Jericho**.)
Everyone knows he was a sell-out. He lived there at the
flygate with the white police.

Jericho   Tell me, did I invent the tsetse fly? Was it my
idea that if a tsetse bites a cow that cow will bite the dust?
It's my job to spray every car (*He sprays*.), bus (*Sprays*.),
truck (*Sprays*.) that goes up and down the mountain to kill
tsetses, to stop the spread of their sleeping disease.

Kindo   We ate bark. We slept on stones. He ate meat
and rice and cuddled in clean sheets.

Jericho   Because there was a war, should I run from my
job? No. I took chemicals from whoever had them, black
or white. I did my job. That is what my conscience asked
of me.

Kindo   I was on a mission. He came armed to my house,
forced her to go with him.

Jericho   The truth is I found her lying on the mountain,
frightened, starving, her clothes soaking wet. She'd run
away from here. I didn't ask why. I gave her food, warm
blankets, a place to sleep. Who could dream we'd fall in
love? We did.

Gaudencia (*to* **Rosemary**)   Did he force you or did you
run to him?

Wireless   No one will blame you if you tell the truth.

Rosemary   Father, you're very kind. But so is he. You
love me, I know you do. But so does he. You miss me
when I'm not with you but there's your other daughter.
He's only got one wife. The war was bad. I was afraid. I
ran. He found me.

Gaudencia   So do you want to stay or go?

Rosemary *looks at* **Kindo**, *then goes to stand with* **Jericho**.

Jericho   Forward with the year of reconciliation! Forward
with democracy!

Gaudencia (*to* **Shupi**)   Write. They love each other. He paid for her. (*To* **Jericho**.) Take her. (*To* **Rosemary**.) Go with him.

Jericho   Forward with the new committee! Thank you.

He puts on his jacket. **Rosemary** *goes. He follows.*
Gaudencia *gives* **Shupi** *her blouse.*

Gaudencia   That's the best I can do.

Three

Evening, a week later.
Jericho's *yard.*
Rosemary *is cooking over a fire.*
Jericho, *wearing his uniform, sits playing with his spray gun, watching* **Rosemary** *in silence.*
Rosemary *sweeps the yard, then goes back to cooking again.*

Jericho   Three months ago, each day twenty, thirty, jeeps and trucks went up and down this road. These days? A wheelbarrow (*He sprays.*), a donkey (*He sprays.*), a cart (*He sprays.*) What goes by? My life. I long to take you home. I must stay here beneath their stars, their skies. They mean nothing to me. I love to watch you working. You sweeping my yard, you cooking my food. (*Silence.*) Talk to me. (*Silence. He throws the spray gun down.*) Don't do that!

Rosemary   I'm cooking.

Jericho   You make believe you're somewhere else. It drives me crazy. Where do you think you are? On your moon?

Rosemary   I'm here.

Jericho   No. I can't live this way. I've got a good heart. What I love is talking, drinking, having a good time.

He looks at her, then goes to her, puts a hand on her. She pulls away.

Rosemary There's people on the road.

Jericho No one can see us.

Rosemary There are always spies.

Jericho Let's go inside.

Rosemary So you don't want food?

Jericho I want it. And I want you. And I want peace.
And I want you to be peaceful. And I want you to be
peaceful peacefully.

She goes on cooking. He moves away from her.

So one more night I'm going to sleep alone. Oh god, give
me a transfer out of here. I'm young. This valley is a pit of
witches, liars, thieves. (*He sits, plays with his spray can.*) A
bread van (*He sprays.*), a bicycle. (*He sprays.*)

Rosemary *brings him a plate of food.*

Jericho Do you want to get rid of me? This doesn't just
kill flies. It wipes out dogs, cats, drivers, passers by. (*He
sprays, coughs.*) Where's my strong soap?

*She brings him a bowl of water and soap. He washes his hands, then
smells them.*

I stink of death. Feed me.

She feeds him with a spoon.

You're losing weight.

Rosemary No.

Jericho I can feel. You were like a sow. Now you're a
young pig. (*He takes the spoon, tries to feed her.*) Put this in you.

*She pulls away. He grabs her, holds her tight. She struggles to get
away.*

Open up.

Rosemary I ate while I was cooking.

Jericho Liar! Don't fight with me. Why must you always fight? I want you to be strong and happy. Open your mouth, my apple.

She breaks away from him, looks out.

Rosemary Shupi! Shupi!

Shupi *runs in.*

Rosemary I've told you, it's not good for you to run.

Shupi I'm in a hurry.

Rosemary Your leg needs rest.

Shupi You're wrong. It's only when I'm still this one shoots this way, this one that. If I run I'm on wheels.

Rosemary It doesn't hurt?

Shupi Only here, where the bullet went in. The bone is strong. And if it does? I've got a job to do, I'm late. So it hurts me, so?

Rosemary Where are you going?

Shupi A meeting of the youth. We've had a message from headquarters. We must elect a leader.

Jericho What for?

Shupi There's work for us. (*To* **Rosemary**.) Why don't you come?

Rosemary Me? Do you want me to?

Jericho Her? Youth? (*He laughs.*) She's a married woman. What work is this?

Shupi To organize the people.

Jericho Organize? No. These people? They go their own way. Organize but if they change their minds, want something else, that's it, end of story, bash your head on a wall.

Shupi But you've organized what you want.

Jericho In a way.

Shupi   Me too. (*She runs off.*)

Jericho *has been feeding himself.* **Rosemary** *takes his empty plate from him.*

Jericho   I wish you were a water melon. I would eat you skin and flesh and seeds.

Rosemary *puts his plate by the fire, starts to go out.*

Jericho   Where are you going?

Rosemary   If I don't fetch firewood, you'll beat me.

Jericho   Beat you? Me? When did I even raise my hand? Beat you? Fetch firewood, fetch anything, just go. Just go! No! Come here. If you hate me – I was a fool, I begged you, come back home – but if you hate me, why did you agree?

Rosemary   To be with my husband.

Jericho   I see. Is that someone I know?

Rosemary   The court didn't force me. I chose to be with you.

Jericho   The court can't order you to love. Love is fire. Yours has burnt away. I'm hot. Let me cover you just once, you'll burst into flame. Tell me you want to.

Rosemary   I want to.

Jericho   Every night I'm up there on my bed, you're on the floor. Tell me you'll get in my bed.

Rosemary   I'll get in your bed.

Jericho   But do you want to? Honestly? Tell me you do.

Rosemary   I do.

Jericho   Through the whole war I wished harm to no one. I wouldn't hurt a fly if my conscience didn't tell me: do your job. But you!

Gaudencia (*off*)   E – oi!

Rosemary   E – oi!

Gaudencia *comes on carrying a basket and her shoes.*

Gaudencia   How did you spend the day?

Rosemary   Good, if you did.

Gaudencia   I did.

Rosemary   Very good. You look worn out. Come, sit.

Gaudencia *sits, rubs her feet.*

Rosemary   Are you hungry? We've got plenty to eat.

She gives her the bowl of water, fetches her food. **Gaudencia**
washes her hands.

Gaudencia   My dear, you make me feel I've got a home.
Is no one else going to eat? (*She soaks her feet in the bowl.*)
That's better. (*She eats.*)

Rosemary   Where've you come from?

Gaudencia   My old home near the border. I've come
footing, footing the whole way.

Jericho   You didn't catch a bus?

Gaudencia   I did. But half-way the driver was so drunk
that fat conductor – you know him? –

Jericho   I know him.

Gaudencia   He grabbed the driver's key. He said: 'Not
one yard more.' They had to wait for him to sober up. But
me, my blood was running. I must move. This heel broke.
(*Indicates one of her shoes.*) Maybe you've got some string?

Rosemary *looks in a box.*

Gaudencia   You see, I heard the boys who went to fight
are now on their way home. My son is one.

Rosemary   No string. Glue.

She gives a tube of glue to **Gaudencia** *who mends the heel of her
shoe.*

Gaudencia He knows we who lived there near the border were moved out by the soldiers. He doesn't know where to. I went to leave a message in case he goes there. But there's no village.

Jericho Nothing at all?

Gaudencia They burnt it. Then grass and rain did their work. No, nothing, just the round earth floors.

Rosemary How will he find you? What's his name?

Gaudencia Herbert. He'll find me. Then I'll be the lucky one. It won't just be you.

Rosemary Am I so lucky?

Gaudencia Of course you are. You've got water in your taps, electricity. And food.

Rosemary Did you eat enough? This pumpkin will go off. And these potatoes. (*She puts them in* **Gaudencia***'s basket.*) Tell me about him.

Gaudencia Herbert?

Rosemary Do you miss him?

Gaudencia How can I answer you? Painfully. On the other hand he was fighting for my rights. Because of that he's always been with me.

Rosemary Did he write letters?

Gaudencia His enemies gave him no time.

Jericho I make a point of writing to my mother once every two years. If I'm busy or not, once every two years I drop everything.

Rosemary How long has he been gone?

Gaudencia He left when he was sixteen. Thirteen years.

Jericho You think you'll recognize him? I don't think so.

Gaudencia He can come back with a thousand other boys, blind my eyes, I'll walk straight to him. (*She puts on her shoes.*) There, my friends, like new.

Rosemary Don't go.

Gaudencia When I think about my son my blood runs. I must move. Thanks for the food. Stay strong. (*She goes.*)

After a moment **Rosemary** *starts to wash the pots and dishes in silence.*

Jericho It seems you've got something to give to everyone but me.

Silence. Then she goes to him.

Rosemary I'm here.

Jericho Are you? (*He embraces her.*) Oh, I want to sing. Nothing must ever come between us. Nothing. Come, lie with me. (*He lays her on a mat, puts a hand under her clothes.*) Oh, skin and flesh and seeds. (*After a moment.*) What? What is it?

Rosemary Nothing.

Jericho You're crying. Why?

Rosemary The pain.

Jericho Where?

She takes his hand, shows him. He pulls her clothes open.

Who did this?

Rosemary No one.

Jericho Tell me! Who fought with you?

Rosemary With me?

Jericho Bruises. Scratches. I want the truth. More! Red as blood. You're bleeding.

Rosemary *breaks away from him.*

Rosemary Don't touch me! Don't touch me!

Four

Night.
Ambuya's *yard.*
Ambuya *is sitting with* **Lena** *and* **Wireless**.

Ambuya   Death is always bitter. I'm old. I've suffered. Why should I want to live? But when they cover me with earth, even my heart will cry. The earth is full of murdered children. At night I hear them. Even by day, if I'm in the field, I open my mouth, I can't sing.

Lena   Our daughter was so young. She hadn't had even one child.

Wireless   Not even one.

Lena   That's why she wants to come home.

Ambuya   Yes. But to who?

Silence.

Wireless   Everyone is hungry. Many girls are sick.

Lena   You didn't see her. She was lying on the spot! There was blood on the earth. What else can it mean?

Wireless   Unless you know which way to look at it, it can mean anything.

Lena   So you don't want to talk to Tandiwe?

Ambuya   Was that her name?

Wireless   That was what we called her. It was only when she went to fight she took another name. Others were called Scorpion, Bazooka, Terror. They called her Freedom. (*To* **Lena**.) Talk to her? I want to.

Ambuya   To kill a girl before she's given birth. They're cruel, they're very cruel. (*She gets up, looks up at the sky.*) Rain?

Lena *and* **Wireless** *look at the sky.*

Wireless   I don't think so.

Ambuya   You'll need money to pay drummers, to buy beer. My hut was burnt and all my things. You'll need to buy new cloths, black and white.

Lena   Her husband has money. If it's her, he'll pay.

Ambuya *sees something moving.*

Ambuya   Go in.

Wireless *and* **Lena** *go into the hut.*
Rosemary *runs on, throws herself at* **Ambuya***'s feet, pulls open her clothes.*

Rosemary   Look at me!

Ambuya   Who did this? You don't know?

Rosemary   Do you?

Ambuya   Come to the light.

She takes **Rosemary** *into the light, examines her, then takes tubs of ointments from a basket. As she oils* **Rosemary***'s body, she sings to her. Then:*

Now?

Rosemary   I feel cool.

Ambuya   And the pain? (*She goes on oiling her.*)

Rosemary   Sometimes it's here, or here. Sometimes I'm well, I'm even smiling, it's still somewhere.

Ambuya   And your husband? Does he want to sleep with you?

Rosemary   I want to sleep with him. I used to lie on his white sheets, all those pillows, read his magazines. It was the best time of my life.

Ambuya   That time is gone. The dead are very jealous. After all, you can't have more than one person in you. (*She laughs.*)

Rosemary *leaps up.*

Rosemary   You think it is?

Ambuya   Could be. Come here. Poor girl. You always want to run.

Rosemary   Don't tell anybody. Please!

Ambuya   Why? If there's one in you, you'll be so peaceful. He'll have no wars to fight, no plates to wash, no yard to sweep. I know. (*She laughs.*) I've got one in me.

Lena *and* **Wireless** *emerge.*

Rosemary   Have you told them?

Ambuya   What can they learn from me? They know you and their daughter were so close. Bread and butter, tea and sugar. She had many friends. It's you she wants.

Rosemary   Who wants me?

Lena   Freedom.

Rosemary   Freedom's dead!

Wireless   Yes. But she doesn't want to be.

Lena   She also wants to wear new clothes, eat food, lie with her husband.

Ambuya (*to* **Lena**)   Sh! (*To* **Rosemary**.) Remember? You were small. The bush. The well. You and her used to climb trees. She's there. Now. Longing for you. Suffering.

Lena *goes to* **Rosemary**, *pulls her clothes open, looks at her.*

Lena   Don't fight her! She can kill you! Let her come!

Rosemary   I can't!

Wireless   Only you can.

Rosemary   She doesn't want me. My pain has gone. That's what I came to say. It's gone! There's nothing wrong with me. (*She runs out.*)

Silence.

Ambuya *looks at the sky.*

Ambuya   Rain?

Lena *looks at the sky.*
Rain falls heavily.

Five

Afternoon, a week later.
Wireless'*s yard.*
Lena *is cooking.*
Kindo *wheels on his bicycle. Strapped to the back is a box of*
bottled beer. He and **Wireless** *are drinking.* **Kindo** *hands*
Wireless *the box and lays the bicycle down.*

Kindo   Who's going to be the chairman?

Wireless   I propose you.

Kindo   Seconded.

Wireless   You propose me.

Kindo   As what?

Wireless   Secretary.

Kindo   You can't write.

Wireless   It's a drinking committee. There's no need to
talk. So I've no need to write down anything.

Kindo   Good! Forward with inebriation!

Wireless   Forward!

Kindo   Forward with intoxication!

Wireless   Forward!

They drink.

(*To* **Lena**.)   What's to eat?

Lena   Wild mushrooms, wild okra.

Kindo *gives her a bottle.*

Wireless   Very good with beer.

Lena   You don't want food?

Wireless   We're drinking. Why eat?

Lena   Bottled beer? What good is it? You can drink and die.

Kindo   Rosemary is better. No more aches and pains. Her husband's happy. He sent money to me. What must I do? Just sit and feel grateful? To him? I won't. I'll drink it away. (*He drinks. Indicates* **Wireless**.) I asked him what he wanted. (*He takes lengths of black and white cloth from the box.*) And needle. And thread. (*He gives these things to* **Wireless**.) Someone's going to dance. He won't say who.

Lena *takes the cloth, needle and thread, sits and starts to sew the two pieces together lengthwise.*

Wireless *sits and drinks.*

Kindo   You see? I'm like the sun. I'm somewhere else, you think you don't need me. In your darkest hour I pop up again.

Shupi *runs on.*

Kindo   Yes? You're always hanging round. What now?

Shupi   I'm coming from a meeting, father. I'm just passing through.

Kindo   Why don't you greet your sister?

Shupi   Where is she?

Kindo (*holding up a bottle*)   Here! (*He drinks, then speaks in falsetto.*) Hullo everyone. My name is Rosemary. (*He laughs, drinks. Own voice.*) Oh what daughters I've got. One sick, one a cripple, leg like a chicken bone. (*Falsetto.*) Hullo everyone. My name is Rosemary.

Shupi *starts to go.*

Kindo   Hey! If you're going why not take my bike?

Shupi Father, please. (*She moves on.*)

Kindo You didn't hear me? I said take my bike. Can't you see I'm drunk? Don't quarrel with me.

Shupi *picks up the bike.*

Kindo Jump on it and go!

Shupi *tries to mount the bike, falls.*
Lena *leaps up.*
Kindo *laughs.*

Shupi I don't know why you're so harsh with me. (*She runs out.*)

Lena It was on that bike my daughter died. When she fell, my heart stood still.

Kindo *picks up the bike, dusts it down.*

Kindo I bought it the day my father died and I became the headman of this village. My people saw her gliding down the hill: 'A! It's the headman. If we've done something wrong we'll get hot hell.' Four, five times the handle-bars broke. I fixed them. The chain snapped. I learnt how to rivet. Wheels buckled. I got a crowbar, bent them straight. Over the years I screwed on five new seats. So the guerrillas asked me: 'Can I borrow your bike?' 'Of course, if you need it. I support the struggle. I'll give you everything.' Look how I got her back. Rusted. Brakes gone. Bumpers missing. Twisted. Bent. So, now we've got committees. I'm not the headman any longer. Who needs it. Throw away the beast. (*He lets the bicycle fall and drinks.*)

Danger (*off*) E – oi!

Wireless E – oi!

Danger *comes on. He wears military camouflage, carries a shoulder bag.*

Danger Friends, you don't know me. I'm passing through this valley. In a week I'm back again. I saw you from the road and came to ask: can I borrow your bike?

Silence.

OK, I'll hire it. How much do you want for, let's say, seven days?

Kindo *picks up a bit of earth, holds some out to* **Danger**.

Kindo Eat.

Danger What's that?

Kindo A bomb damaged your ears? I told you: eat!

Danger Is this a joke?

Kindo Not if you want my bike.

Danger *takes a bit of earth, licks it.*

Kindo How does it taste?

Danger Like shit.

Kindo *eats the rest of it.*

Kindo It's honey to me. That proves you're not from here.

Danger You could have asked. I would have said. What kind of man are you?

Kindo That's what *I* want to know.

Danger In the war I was called Danger. I'm from this valley but not from here.

Kindo From where? This side or that?

Danger From over there.

Kindo Then you can't take my bike. (*He laughs.*) I never liked those people who live there.

Danger My! Ten years of struggle and we're still divided? This side of the valley, that side. Has nothing changed?

Kindo You comrades buggered up my bike. I won't lend it again.

Danger (*to* **Lena**)   I've walked far. It seems I've got to walk again. Can you spare something to eat?

Kindo   There's no food.

Danger   None at all?

Kindo   Scratch in the bush. Pick your own roots and weeds.

Wireless   It's true. We've got nothing. We're still waiting for our rations to come.

Danger   Oh ho! Now I know where I am. (*He laughs.*) Goodness. My my my.

Kindo   What are you laughing for?

Danger   Oh, bad news, bad news. Do you want to hear? Before I walked down the mountain, I took a breather at the District Office. They were almost dead from laughing. Shall I tell you why? Village chairmen from all over go there, make demands for food, get it next day. Your chairman is so shy! She sits on the grass in the back yard, gets out some knitting, never says a word. One day a comrade went to ask, what does she want? She hardly looked at him. 'Nothing. Please don't let me waste your time.' An hour passes. She folds up her knitting, walks down to the bus, goes home again. Oh my, they're laughing there. But then they stop laughing and wonder: what kind of men are you? We gave our blood so you could vote. You vote for her, you throw our blood away.

Kindo *picks up his bicycle, tries to mount it, can't manage it, holds it out to* **Danger**.

Kindo   Take it. Ride to the District Office. Tell them, me, Kindo, I was headman. I'm coming now to get food for my people.

Danger   Me ride up there? For you? But I'm from that side of the valley. (*He picks up his bag.*) I left my people thirteen years ago. I'm going to find them. Comrades, stay strong. (*He goes.*)

Kindo Forward with democracy! The chairman lied! Throw her chair over! Someone else goes in! I'll do it! Forward with the new committee! (*He tries to mount the bicycle, fails, throws it down.*) I'm too old for this game. (*He sits.*) Tell me why I'm thinking of my wife. She could take a bag of maize seeds, sow an acre in an afternoon. She knew every kind of fertilizer, how to mix them, how much to use. She could cook a goat (*Snaps his fingers.*), and it was done. Maybe I'm just hungry. Maybe.

Lena *is still sewing,* **Wireless** *drinks.*

Gaudencia (*off*) E – oi!

Lena E – oi!

Gaudencia *enters.* **Rosemary** *follows carrying a sack of vegetables.* **Gaudencia** *is knitting as she walks.*

Gaudencia You're here?

Lena I'm here.

Gaudencia Look what I've got. Onions, potatoes, turnips. I'm just one. Let me share them with you. (*She takes the bag, opens it.*)

Lena A! A! You've saved our lives. (*She claps and ululates to* **Gaudencia**.*)

Gaudencia (*of* **Rosemary**) Thank her. She gave them to me.

Lena *looks at* **Rosemary**.

Gaudencia She's got so strong. She carried the whole bag from the flygate.

Lena *takes onions and potatoes from the sack.*

Gaudencia And she gave me this wool.

Kindo Still knitting.

Gaudencia It's a scarf. Do you like the shade?

Kindo For who?

Gaudencia My son.

Kindo Your son? Rosemary, I'm glad to see you. Come sit here, talk to me.

Rosemary *goes to* **Kindo**.

Kindo You've got nothing to say? You want to drink?

He opens a bottle for her. She shakes her head.

You'll take nothing from me?

Rosemary It makes me ill.

Kindo Your husband said you were better.

Rosemary I am.

Kindo So, chairman, your son. He's coming home, is he?

Gaudencia All the boys who went to fight are on their way.

Kindo They've come already. Months ago.

Gaudencia Not all. Herbert will be here soon. (*Of her knitting.*) I want this done by then.

Kindo I see. And our rations?

Gaudencia Any day.

Kindo Your Herbert, which side did he fight on?

Rosemary Father, let's go look at your field. I want to see how high the maize is. Come, I'll help you weed.

Kindo (*to* **Gaudencia**) Did you see his uniform? Did you? Many boys come home. 'Where have you been?' 'We ran to join the comrades.' Rubbish. They just ran.

Gaudencia My son told me: 'Mother.' 'Yes?' 'I have to go and fight.' To take a knife and cut would hurt him less than to ask for who. Where's Shupi? I've got piles of paper work. She can give me a hand.

Kindo If a boy is not back yet, he won't come.

Rosemary   Father!

Gaudencia   No, no.

Kindo   Like our rations, that boy's gone for good.

Gaudencia   I know he will.

Kindo   How do you know?

Gaudencia   I heard him in the wind.

Kindo   The wind? (*He laughs.*)

Gaudencia   'Mother,' he said, 'Don't give up. Wait for me.'

Kindo   So that's how they did it.

Gaudencia   Did what?

Rosemary   Chairman, I'll help you with your papers. Let's go.

Kindo   They took him in a helicopter, tied a rope around his neck, kicked him out into thin air, let him swing. That was the cry you heard.

Gaudencia   Herbert will come!

Without anyone noticing, **Rosemary** *goes.*

Kindo   Where are our rations?

Gaudencia   I went to see them on the mountain. I signed the docket. They promised me.

Silence as everyone looks at her.

Kindo   Nothing will come. Nothing. (*He takes onions and potatoes from the sack and throws them into the air.*) Bombs were falling! Hand grenades! Watch them go! I lost my wife, my job as headman, my bike, Rosemary. Who says the war is over? It's burning inside me.

Lena *has finished sewing the black and white cloth.*

Lena   It's done. (*She puts it over her head.*)

Shupi (*off*)   Rosemary!

Wireless   Freedom.

Shupi (*off*)   Rosemary!

Wireless   She's calling Rosemary.

Shupi runs on.

Shupi   What's going on? I saw Rosemary running away.

They look round. She's gone.
Kindo *gets on his bicycle.*

Kindo   Where did she go?

Shupi   Into the bush.

Kindo *rides off.*

Wireless   Help me find her.

He runs off. The others follow.

All   Rosemary! Rosemary! Rosemary!

Six

A clearing by a well.
Freedom *wears military camouflage. Her bicycle lies on the ground.*

Rosemary   I went to look at you. You were lying on the bridge. Your blood ran into the river. Your arms and legs were broken, twisted round the bike. I couldn't look. I ran. I didn't stop till I was on the mountain.

Freedom   What can I tell you? I have to stay in shadow. Heat's a problem, more so than in life. I want to dive into the river, drink, get cool. I can't. If it rains the grass makes my feet itch, I don't know why. I only have one feeling.

Rosemary   Tell me.

Freedom   Desire.

Rosemary   For what?

Freedom   The life I could have led. And for revenge.

Rosemary   On who?

Silence.

Freedom   Your father's coming.

Rosemary   Here? You better go.

Freedom   He can't see me. I'll sit here by the well.

Rosemary   Just let me talk to him, explain why I'm going, then I'll come.

Freedom   That's what you said last time! 'Just let me tell my father.' We waited. Did you come?

Rosemary   They keep on asking, 'Do you want to live like this or that? With this one or with that one?' No! The answer's no! I'm here now in the bush. I won't go home. I only feel at peace when I'm with you.

Kindo *rides on, dismounts.*

Rosemary   How did you find me?

Kindo (*he laughs*)   The others ran, one there, one here. In my mind I saw two little girls. The tree, the well. Where else could you be? (*He sits.*) Ah, this grass is soft. The sun is warm.

Rosemary   You're not angry?

Kindo   I peddled for a while watching the sky. Wide. Empty. I turned on to a path. Trees, shrubs, animals. In the whole world there's no one left who wants to use me or to kill me. It's so still. I can hear thorns growing. Leaves. So here we are. Tell me. Why did you run away?

Silence.

I'm thirsty.

Rosemary *goes to the well, brings him water in her hands. He drinks.*

Kindo It's sweet. Water from you is always sweet. My father's father came out of this earth. This water is my blood, these rocks my bones. But that's over and done. I try to hold on, hold on to what's dead and gone. Maybe that's what's wrong. (*He lies on the ground.*) Rosemary, don't leave me.

Freedom *mounts her bicycle, rides round and round, then stops.*

Kindo You love him so much?

Rosemary Who?

Silence.

Freedom Come.

Rosemary I can't choose between you.

Freedom Come!

Rosemary I don't want to die.

Freedom I don't want you for death. This is for struggle. I have to struggle to come here. I need your strength (*She picks up* **Kindo**'s *bicycle and holds it out to* **Rosemary**.) All your friends are with me. They're full of fight. Let's move. This place is dangerous.

Rosemary Who can see us?

Freedom There are always spies.

Rosemary *takes the bicycle, mounts it.*

Freedom That's it! You want to. Oh, you want to.

Rosemary *is riding* **Kindo**'s *bicycle.* **Freedom** *mounts her own. They start to ride round and round each other.*

Voices (*off*) Rosemary! Rosemary!

Freedom *rides off.*
Rosemary *goes on riding round.*
Wireless, **Shupi**, **Lena** *and* **Gaudencia** *run on.*
Kindo *leaps up, watches.*

Rosemary Forward with the struggle of the people! Down with racism and exploitation!

Wireless   It's her! She's come!

Rosemary   Forward with the struggle of the people!
Down with racism and exploitation!

Wireless   We'll brew beer! We'll play the drums! You've
come! Freedom, you've come!

Seven

Night, two weeks later. **Wireless***'s yard.*
To one side stands a large metal drum full of beer.
From nearby comes the sound of drumming.
Gaudencia *is sitting on a chair, her head bowed.*
Rosemary *runs in, crouches on the floor. Draped over her head
and shoulders is the black and white cloth* **Lena** *made. Her body
heaves as she struggles for breath.*
Wireless *comes in.*

Wireless (*to* **Rosemary**)   But why did you stop dancing?
(*He draws beer from the drum, offers it to* **Rosemary**.) You can
drink all night. This beer won't harm you.

Rosemary   I'm hungry.

Wireless   Good. Hunger is good.

Rosemary *runs to one side, retches, vomits.*
Gaudencia *goes to her.*
Ambuya *dances in. She is dressed in a long black and white dress
trimmed with ribbons.*
Wireless *crouches and claps in greeting to* **Ambuya**.

Wireless   Grandfather, you have come. Grandfather, you
are welcome.

Ambuya *draws beer from the drum, drinks, then goes on dancing
quietly to one side.*

Wireless (*to* **Rosemary**)   That's good. Make your body
empty. Then fill it with beer.

Rosemary *pulls off the black and white cloth.*

Rosemary I can't do it. Please!

Gaudencia She's exhausted.

Lena *runs in, crouches, wails in a deep voice.*

Wireless (*to* **Rosemary**) Watch her! She's fighting.
Don't fight! That's why she's in pain. (*He crouches and claps
to* **Lena**.) Old woman, why do you hurt my wife? (*To*
Rosemary.) It's her mother's grandmother. (*To* **Lena**.) Be
gentle with her. Everyone has come to greet you, from the
east, from the west, from the village, from the bush. We're
asking all the old ones: solve the problems of this house.
Do you think we don't welcome you? We do!

Lena *cries out in her own voice.*

Wireless Lena? Or who?

Lena Me.

Wireless Dance. She'll come again.

Lena I'm going home. I want to sleep.

Wireless *draws beer, holds it to her mouth, forces her to drink.*

Wireless Dance! You want to. She'll come!

Lena *starts to dance again. She and* **Ambuya** *dance quietly
together.*

Wireless Forward with the old ones! I'm chairman of
this business. I've got work to do. (*He goes out.*)

After a moment, **Jericho** *comes in carrying a small box. He draws
beer from the drum, drinks, spits it out.*

Jericho Sour! Didn't I tell them: 'Wait until your maize
is ripe?' No, I must hire a truck, push it up the mountain
and half-way to town. The only grain I found was three
years old. Stale grain won't make sweet beer. (*He drinks,
grimaces, drinks again.*)

The drumming stops.
Lena *and* **Ambuya** *rest.*

Jericho I turn my back, they knock off. Damn those boys! I pay for them to play. (*To* **Rosemary**.) Listen, this game of yours is costing me. Don't hide here. Dance! Let's go! Get out there! (*He tries to pull* **Rosemary** *to her feet.*)

Gaudencia Leave her.

Jericho In five hours she's hardly moved a foot. I must do something. There's not long to go.

Gaudencia Your suffering's as great as hers. Don't punish her for that. If she won't dance maybe it should be you.

Silence.

Jericho I'll just run to the gate and check if anything's come up. When I'm back, if nothing's happened, I'll write the whole thing off as a bad job. (*To* **Rosemary**.) Don't be cross. I want you well, that's all. (*To* **Gaudencia**.) Look after her for me. (*He goes.*)

The drumming starts.
Ambuya *dances over to* **Rosemary**, *gently raises her to her feet, dances round with her, pulls the cloth back over her head, then dances out.* **Rosemary** *dances out after her.*
Lena *is dancing quietly by herself.*
The drumming gets louder.
Gaudencia *draws beer, drinks, spits into her hand.*

Gaudencia It burns and comes up yellow. What does that mean?

Shupi *comes in.*

Gaudencia Poor girl. You're worn out. Sit with me.

Shupi I can't. She'll speak. I'll miss her. (*She starts to go out.*)

Gaudencia Are you ashamed of me? You think I betrayed you. I did. What was I afraid of? Young men in suits? I was elected chairman of this village, me a stranger, why? Because of my courage in the war. I look at my clothes, I look at theirs. I'm sorry, I can't speak.

The drumming stops.
Kindo *runs in.*

Kindo (*to* **Shupi**)   Where is she?

Shupi   Dancing.

Kindo   No. She's run off. Find her!

Shupi *runs out.*

Kindo   Her clothes are wet. Her forehead's white with salt. She's shaking, crying. How can this be good? (*He drinks.*)

Wireless *comes in carrying a bowl.*

Kindo (*to* **Wireless**)   Your daughter's dead. You want to kill mine!

Wireless *ladles beer into the bowl.*

Wireless   No, comrade. No, no, no. The old ones, what are they actually? They're a committee. They're very wise because they're very dead. They want us to be strong. And why? They want beer. They can smell it on our breath. They want drums. They hear them in our ears. (*He gives the bowl to* **Kindo**.) Drink.

Kindo *drinks.*

Wireless   Drink!

Kindo *drinks again.*

Wireless   Take it to the drummers. Go.

Kindo *goes, taking the bowl.*

Wireless   I'm fighting hard. I'm shouting to my daughter: 'Don't torture Rosemary for nothing! Make her feet jump! Get in!'

Ambuya *comes in, dances quietly.*

Wireless   And you?

Gaudencia   How can I dance here? This is not my home.

Wireless These days the whole country's your home. Dance if you want.

Gaudencia I want. But it's up to him. If he wants he comes. What can I do?

Wireless *takes a bundle of clothes from under* **Gaudencia***'s chair and unties it. It is a black and white dress. He lays it over her. The drumming starts.*
Lena *has been resting. Suddenly she leaps to her feet.*

Lena Oh, my brothers! Oh, my brothers! I am suffering! Aah! Aah!

Ambuya (*to* **Lena**) Grandmother, you've come?

Lena I'm here! I've come!

Ambuya Stamp your feet. Hard! Harder! Feel the pain.

Lena I feel it.

Ambuya Pain is life.

Lena Yes.

Ambuya Life is death.

Lena Yes.

Ambuya Death is joy.

Lena Yes.

Ambuya Joy is pain.

Lena *stands panting and moaning.*
Ambuya *claps her hand over* **Gaudencia***'s mouth, holds it there. When she releases it* **Gaudencia** *gasps for breath.*

Ambuya Breathe the air. Deep! Deeper! Is it sweet?

Gaudencia It stinks! It's rotting!

Ambuya Good! Dance! She'll come.

Ambuya *and* **Lena** *moan, wail, dance round.*

Lena *dances out.*
Gaudencia *is wailing with pain.*

Gaudencia   Ah! Ah! Ah! Ah!

Wireless   Come, grandmother. Come, put on your dress.

Wireless *pulls the black and white dress over* **Gaudencia**'s *head.*

Your arm. Push through the hole. That's it. Now this one. Please, grandmother.

Gaudencia   Oh, my brothers!

Wireless   Wait! The buttons!

Gaudencia *gets up.*

Gaudencia   Oh, my brothers!

Wireless *picks up a ritual axe.*
Gaudencia *dances out.*

Wireless   Wait! Your stick! (*He runs out after her.*)

The drumming gets louder.
Rosemary *dances in.* **Shupi** *follows.*

Shupi   If you don't want to, don't. No one can force you. Come, I'll take you home.

Ambuya   Don't touch her! (*To* **Rosemary**.) Come, my darling. Come, my sweet one. Come, my strong, brave fighter. Come.

Ambuya *lifts* **Rosemary**, *dances round with her. They both dance out.*
Alone, **Shupi** *tries to dance.*

Shupi   Freedom, she doesn't want you. She never did. I'm the one who helped you, fought beside you. I want you. Come to me. (*She is still.*) I can't do it. Is that why you don't want me?

Danger *comes in. He is wearing camouflage and carrying his bag. He watches.*

Shupi   Make me dance. Come, Freedom. Come. Take me.

She sees **Danger**.

Who are you?

Danger   Comrade Danger. I've walked all day. I'll die if I don't drink.

Shupi *gives him beer. He drinks.*

Danger   Sorry about your leg. Was it the war?

Silence.

I'm asking how you were wounded.

Shupi   I was shot. The day Freedom was killed.

Danger   Comrade Freedom? Is that so? You knew her?

Shupi   This was her home.

Danger   Is that so? We were together maybe three, four years.

Shupi   It's her they're trying to bring back.

Danger   Is that so?

Shupi   You think it's wrong?

Danger   Some people say: 'What did we fight for?' To wake the masses, to cleanse their minds of superstition. If that was it we failed. Utterly. Everywhere I've been all over the valley they're drumming, drinking, bringing back the dead. On the other hand, we also fought to give them back a sense of who they are, their culture, history. For myself – I trained in Finland, Cuba – it makes me uneasy. (*He drinks.*)

Shupi   If you didn't come to dance, what are you doing here?

Danger   I'm searching for my mother. So far I've drawn a blank. I'm glad to meet a friend of Freedom's. I better go.

The drumming gets louder.

Rosemary *runs in wearing a black and white dress, waving a ritual axe.*

Gaudencia, **Lena** *and* **Ambuya**, *all possessed, all wearing black and white, all waving ritual axes and sticks, dance in. The dancing is now violent and warlike. The mediums dance and whoop.*

Wireless *and* **Kindo** *run in and watch.*

The drumming stops.

The mediums are still.

Wireless *claps to the mediums.*

Wireless   Welcome, grandmothers, grandfathers. We've got a problem. Your grandchild is ill. Who sent this illness? That's what we want to know.

Silence.

Danger   Oh god.

Shupi *(to* **Danger***)*   What?

Danger   Mother!

Shupi   Sh!

Wireless   Who's that? *(To* **Danger***.)* What's wrong, comrade?

Danger   My mother. She's in pain.

Wireless   They're all our mothers and fathers. I'm the chairman of this business. If you're quiet, you can stay here. If not, time to go.

The mediums seem exhausted. They shake themselves gently as though to free themselves from sleep.

Ambuya *groans.*

Wireless   Speak. We want to hear.

Silence.

All the Ancestors   Aah! Aah! Aah! Ooh! Ooh! Ooh!

Shupi *(to* **Danger***)*   Keep still.

Danger   I've got to help her. Mother!

Shupi   Sh!

Danger   Then let me go.

Wireless (*to* **Danger**)   Sit down!

Danger *does.*

Wireless   Don't be angry, grandfathers. We're children. We know nothing. We can't live without you. Speak.

Silence.
When the mediums speak they use voices deeper than their normal ones.

Ambuya   Are you – ?

The ancestors laugh and make hooting noises.

Wireless   Grandfather?

Silence.

Ambuya   Are you well?

Wireless   We are. Only our legs – haai! – from the dancing. And our heads – hoo! – from the drinking. That's how we are. And you?

Ambuya (*wailing*)   Oh, my brothers! It's dark. It's so dark!

Kindo   Must I light a lamp?

Wireless   They don't want lamps. It's your father's grandfather. Talk to him.

Silence.

Kindo   Grandfather, of all my father's sons only I am living. I am dying now because of what is happening to this one, this daughter. I'll do anything to help her. Tell me.

Ambuya   Water.

Kindo   He wants water.

Wireless *pours water into a cup and gives it to* **Ambuya**.
Ambuya *takes water into her mouth, passes the cup to another
medium, then sprays the water out of her mouth. In turn the other
mediums do the same.*

Ambuya (*wailing*) You treat me so badly. Why? Oh oh
oh oh. Why? You cry, cry, cry, complain, complain. How
have I hurt you? How, my children? How?

Danger Mother, stop this. Mother, talk to me.

Gaudencia (*indicating* **Danger**) That's the one! That's the
one who's trying to kill us!

Danger What do you mean?

Gaudencia They want to finish us!

Wireless Who, Grandmother?

Gaudencia The young ones like him.

Wireless Who are they?

Gaudencia They live – there! – on the mountain. They
speak half-half. Half you can hear, half no one can
understand. And they are proud. You must do what they
say. But they do nothing. They want to finish us! They do!

She throws herself at **Danger**, *hitting him.*

Wireless *and* **Kindo** *pull her off him, settle her down.*

Danger (*to* **Gaudencia**) Mother, don't you know me?

Silence.
Jericho *runs in.*

Jericho What the hell is going on? (*To* **Kindo**.) Why
didn't you call me?

Kindo Throw him out! Don't let him in.

The ancestors groan and wail.

They want him out!

Wireless If they want it, let them say so.

Jericho   Who's in charge here?

Wireless (*of* **Ambuya**)   Him.

Jericho (*to* **Ambuya**)   Grandfather, I'm her husband. Don't hear what they tell you. I love her, believe me. Help my wife.

Ambuya   This one is not my blood.

Jericho   What did he say?

Ambuya   This one did not come out of my earth.

Jericho   No, I was born on the mountain. But I paid for her. And I went to the shop and bought you beer.

The ancestors laugh.

Ambuya   The beer is sour.

The ancestors laugh.

Lena   It's sour!

Gaudencia   It's sour!

Ambuya   It's full of lumps. It's sour!

The ancestors laugh.

Lena   Is it brewed from maize we grew for you?

Jericho   No. It's too early.

The ancestors laugh.

Gaudencia   You can't wait?

Lena   He can't wait!

The ancestors laugh.

Jericho   We can't. She's ill. (*He takes a black chicken from the box he has been carrying.*) I brought you this black chicken. I know you'd rather have a goat. All the goats round here were slaughtered by the soldiers. Please, take this instead.

Ambuya *takes the chicken.*

Ambuya   You think I've come to slaughter you?

Danger (*to* **Wireless**)   What do I say?

Wireless   No.

Jericho   No.

Ambuya   Or to slaughter your wife?

Wireless   No.

Jericho   No. But she hasn't eaten for a week. Who can live without food?

Ambuya   Me!

The ancestors laugh.

Ambuya
Gaudencia   } Me! Me!
Lena

The ancestors laugh.

Ambuya   She didn't eat. But did she die? No. Because I care for her. So why do you cry, cry, cry, cry, cry, cry, cry, cry cry? She can speak if she wants. We're going. We've had enough of you.

The men clap as they speak.

Kindo   Don't go! We need you!

Wireless   Grandfather, don't leave us.

Jericho   Stay with us, Grandfather! Help us!

Danger   I've had enough. I've got to go.

Suddenly **Rosemary** *begins to shake. She rolls on to the ground, cries out, rolls over and over hitting the ground violently with her arms.*
The mediums surround her, shaking themselves and hooting softly.
When they move aside, **Rosemary** *is sitting on the ground with the black and white cloth over her head.*
Silence.

When **Rosemary** *speaks, it is as if each word must be dragged up from the depths, as if each word causes pain.*
She wails.
Wireless *claps.*
Silence.
Rosemary *wails.*

Wireless   What's your name?

Rosemary   Nedondo.

Wireless   Who?

He claps. **Kindo** *and* **Jericho** *clap.*

Thank you, thank you for coming.

Rosemary   Oh, I am the country. Oh, I am the nation.

Wireless   Who are you?

Rosemary   Nedondo.

Wireless *claps.*

Wireless   Welcome, Mother, welcome.

Rosemary   I live deep in this earth. Men walk over me, walk their boots over me. My face. My breasts. My thighs. Stick their steel spades into me. Dig me, drill me. Rip, tear my guts. Oh, my children. They hurt me. Me, Nedondo, mother of the country. Zimbabwe. Oh! Oh! Oh!

Silence. She laughs.

Let them dig deep. They can't reach me.

Silence.

Wireless   No. That's not the one. That one's trying to block the one who wants to speak.

He claps. **Jericho** *and* **Kindo** *clap.*
Rosemary *makes guttural meaningless noises, falls silent.*
She tries again to speak, fails, falls silent.
She gets up, wanders round as though looking for something.
She finds **Danger**. *At his feet is his bag. She opens it, takes out a camouflage jacket and cap, puts them on.*

Silence.

Danger *and* **Rosemary** *look at each other.*

Danger   Who are you?

Silence.

Tell me.

Silence.

Comrade.

Rosemary   Ah! You know!

She laughs. The ancestors laugh.

Danger   State your name distinctly. Do it.

Silence.

Rosemary   My name is Freedom. Comrade Freedom.

Danger   Oh god. Bring me something to drink.

Wireless *brings him beer. He drinks.*

Danger   Where are you?

Silence.

Precise co-ordinates of your position. Give them to me.

Rosemary   In the bush.

Danger   I said precise.

Rosemary   Outside the village.

Danger   Which one?

Rosemary   My father's.

Danger (*to* **Wireless**)   I can't go on.

Wireless   Go on!

Danger (*to* **Rosemary**)   You recognize these people?

Rosemary   I do.

Danger   And you can trust them?

Rosemary   I can.

Danger   You've got information for them?

Rosemary   I have.

Danger   Good. Make your report.

Rosemary *makes incoherent sounds.*
Silence.
Rosemary *makes incoherent sounds.*

Danger   Comrade! Put your back straight. That's it! Be proud of who you are. This is a debriefing. Tell us what you've got to say. That's an instruction!

Silence.

Choppers overhead! Dive for cover!

Rosemary *throws herself on to the ground.*

Danger   All clear. No, there's another. Dive!

Rosemary *does.*

Danger   Good. Comrade, can you hear me?

Rosemary   Yes.

Danger   Tell me what you want.

Rosemary   I want this country free.

Danger   It is free!

Rosemary   I never saw it! I want to see it! This woman, this girl, this Rosemary. I made her ill.

Danger   Why?

Rosemary   Someone did something wrong.

Danger   To who? To her?

Rosemary   To me.

Danger   What did he do?

Rosemary Betrayed me. This woman, this girl, this Rosemary can't be well until he has admitted what he did.

Danger Who is it?

Rosemary The one who betrayed me.

Danger Who was it?

Rosemary Someone.

Danger This is an order. Tell me.

Rosemary I've got other orders. I must go.

Danger Who did it? Freedom! Who betrayed you?

Silence.

Wireless Please don't go, my daughter. Freedom! Stay with me.

Ambuya Fool! How can she?

It is dawn. The sky goes white. A deep red glow lights the faces of the mediums.

Gaudencia The sun!

Lena The sun!

Ambuya The sun!

The sun rises.
One by one the mediums go. As they leave and the shadowy world of the mediums dissolves into the day-to-day world of the village, the tatters and tears in their black and white clothes can be seen.
Shupi *is fast asleep.*
Kindo's *bicycle is lying on the ground.*
Mugs, cups, bowls, dishes are scattered round.
Danger *and* **Jericho** *sit on the chairs.*
Wireless *and* **Kindo** *stretch, drink another mouthful of beer, wash their faces, rinse out their mouths with water, sit out in the sun.*
Lena *comes on in her everyday clothes.*

Wireless (*to* **Lena**) You need some beer?

He gives her beer. She sits and drinks.

OK?

Lena   OK.

Wireless (*to* **Jericho**)   Don't forget to pay the drummers.

Jericho *goes out.*
Kindo *stretches, yawns, takes off his shoes, rubs his feet.*

Wireless (*to* **Danger**, *of the beer*)   There's plenty. You
want some? (*He gives beer to* **Danger**.)

Kindo (*to* **Danger**)   So you came back?

Danger   I did.

Ambuya *comes on in her everyday clothes.*

Wireless   Ah! There you are, Grandmother.

Ambuya *starts to tidy up the mugs and cups.*
gives beer to **Kindo**.

Wireless   The first time, they never tell you everything.
Let her rest. In a month or two we'll try again.

Gaudencia *comes on in her everyday clothes. She sits next to*
Lena. *They whisper to each other.*
Ambuya *goes over to* **Lena** *and* **Gaudencia**. *The three women
laugh and whisper together.*
Jericho *comes on.*

Jericho   Who promised them so much. It wasn't me.

Kindo (*to* **Danger**)   So who are you?

Danger *goes to* **Shupi**, *wakes her.*

Shupi   Did she come?

Danger   She did.

Shupi   Why did no one wake me? Did she speak?

Danger   She did.

Shupi   What did she say?

Danger   Someone betrayed her.

Kindo (*to* **Wireless**)   Let's go to the river. I want to wash my feet.

Shupi   Who?

Rosemary *comes on in her everyday clothes. She sits.*
Lena, **Ambuya** *and* **Gaudencia** *fall silent.*
Silence.
The three women start whispering again.

Shupi   Who betrayed Freedom? Does anybody know? If you want Rosemary to get well, you have to say.

Silence.

Wireless   She was in the bush, I don't know where. She came into my house. She had a gun, this big. She asked me will I take it to someone on the mountain. I said: 'No. If they catch me, they'll kill me. Why not you?' She said: 'It's urgent. I can't go by bus, the soldiers know me.' She's my daughter. What could I do? At night I crept into his house, took his bike, gave it to her. He says he gave it to guerrillas. He'd rather give his teeth. She's gone. Next thing, soldiers! 'Comrades were here!' 'No, baas.' 'Don't lie to me!' Whaa! Whaa! I'm bleeding, my nose broken. 'Yes, baas, yes, there was. They went into the bush.' Whaa! Whaa! I'm on the floor. 'Don't lie! Who was here?' 'My daughter, baas.' Don't blame me. I had to save my life. 'Where did she go?' 'There. Up the mountain.' 'With others?' 'No, alone.' 'On foot? By bus?' (*Silence.*) 'On a bike.' (*He is crying.*) Who betrayed her? Me.

Silence.

Jericho   Any car, bus, bicycle that passes through the gate must first be sprayed by me. All I said to her was: 'Why not take your parcel off the carrier? I don't want to wet it with my spray.' She shot off down the road, round the gate, up the mountain. I can't make exceptions. Every cow in the land will die of sleeping disease. Then I saw there were jeeps after her. I shouted: 'Someone's taking tsetse up the mountain.' The jeeps were off. We saw her in the headlights. She knew she couldn't get away. She

turned, sped back so fast they kept on missing her. I could
have closed the gate when she'd gone through. A jeep can
knock it flat. Could I have saved her? I didn't even try. It's
no surprise she's so angry with me.

Silence.

Kindo They said no one may touch her. There she lies,
bullets in her brain, there she must rot. I thought: if they're
so cruel they can kill a young girl, how can we ever win? I
thought, the government will still be here when the war is
over. They're going to need a headman. I know the
people. It might as well be me. I went at night. I prised
open her legs, her elbows. The bones in her hands cracked.
I pulled my bike out, wheeled it home. The one she hates,
the reason that she wants to kill my daughter – me.

Silence.

Rosemary You pulled the bike from her. That's what I
saw.

Kindo You saw?

Rosemary I did.

Kindo That's why you ran away?

Gaudencia *has been watching* **Danger**.

Danger The person waiting for the gun Freedom was
bringing up the mountain – it was me. I waited for it. It
never came. So I was caught and beaten up and tried and
put in jail. After the war I lay in hospital. Mother, that is
where I've been.

Gaudencia I thought the sun was up.

Danger It is.

Gaudencia What world is this where the dead walk after
dawn? Or is the dead one me? (*She feels him gently.*) You're
Herbert?

Danger In the war I was Danger. If I'm Herbert it must
be peace.

Gaudencia *starts to dance.*
Rosemary *has been watching* **Gaudencia** *and* **Danger**. *Now she starts to cry. She cries and cries.*
Shupi *goes to comfort her.*
Ambuya *is comforting* **Kindo**. **Wireless** *and* **Lena** *are sitting together.*
Gaudencia *stops dancing, sits with* **Danger**.

Jericho So what happens now? Is Freedom at rest?

Rosemary *stops crying, recovers.*

Rosemary I feel better.

Jericho Good. Are you coming with me?

Rosemary *shakes her head.*

Jericho I said it was a waste of cash. She's no better than she was. See what I mean?

Rosemary (*to* **Wireless** *and* **Lena**) You got her back, then I took her away. At least you've got each other. (*To* **Kindo**.) What can I do for you? (*She wanders over to* **Kindo**'s *bicycle, runs her fingers over it.*) The truth is – what I feel is – I'm so damn hungry.

Lena Me as well.

Gaudencia Me too.

Danger Of course. Your rations didn't come. Blame your foolish chairman. Where is she?

Silence.

Gaudencia I'm here.

Danger I mean the chairman of this village. Mother, is it you?

Everyone laughs, except **Rosemary**. *They laugh and laugh.*
Rosemary *has lifted up the bicycle. Now she gets on it and rides round.*
Everyone watches her in silence.
Rosemary *stops.*

Rosemary When I ran away, I went up the mountain. It's time I went again. I'll go to the District Office. I'll get our food. I won't be afraid of anyone. (*To* **Kindo**.) Don't worry about your bike. I'll bring it back.

Kindo My daughter, I give it to you.

Rosemary *rides round.*

Gaudencia Forward with the year of reconciliation!

All Forward

Gaudencia Forward with the struggle of the people!

All Forward!

Rosemary *rides out.*
They watch her go.

Shupi Freedom, keep going! Keep going, Rosemary!

The Ends of the Earth

in memory of Arthur Day

Characters

Daniel, *thirty, a geologist.*
Takic, *twenty-five, a musician.*
Nico, *forty, an hotelier.*
Pintilje, *forty, a dentist.*
Yosip, *fifty.*
Cathy, *thirty, a teacher.*
Rosa, *a cook.*
Dusja, *eight.*
Valley People
Mountain People
Soldiers
A Guard
Musicians

Time: the recent past
Place: London and the Balkans

The Ends of the Earth was first performed at the Royal
National Theatre in the Cottesloe auditorium on 23
February 1996, with the following cast:

Daniel	Michael Sheen
Cathy	Samantha Bond
Nico	Kevork Malikyan
Takic	Declan Conlan
Rosa	Etela Pardo
Pintilje	Tom Mannion
Yosip	Karl Johnson
Dusja	Dunja Fehimovic/
	Elena Stevanoski
A Guard	Ivan Vanja Albahari
Valley people,	Boris Boskovic, Ivan Marewich,
Mountain people,	Lawrence Werbner,
Soldiers	Igor Zvonic
	Michael Esswood, Goran
	Kostic, Andrew Russel
Musicians	Joe Townsend, Ben Grove,
	Pete Watson

Directed by Andrei Serban
Designed by Richard Hudson
Lighting by Simon Corder
Music by Adrian Johnston
Choreography by Kate Flatt
Sound by Christopher Shutt

Part One

Scene One

A village square. Dusk.
The restaurant of a small hotel. Lights in the trees.
Daniel *and* **Cathy** *eat and drink.*
Musicians play.

Daniel Oh God.

Cathy Good?

Daniel Heaven. (*He puts food on her plate.*)

Cathy No, I've got plenty.

Daniel Have more.

Cathy We've ordered too much.

Daniel We'll order more.

As they eat she watches him. He sees her watching. He caresses her face.

Daniel Have your eyes changed colour?

Cathy (*laughing*) Yes.

Daniel They were brown, no? Now they're blue as the sea. Oh, the sea, the sea.

The sound of the sea.

Cathy (*taking his hand, kissing it*) How do you feel?

Daniel Oh, I feel so . . . (*He drinks all the wine in her glass.*) Like that. Waiter! Garçon! Ragazzo! Prundig! What country are we in?

Cathy What do you want?

Daniel Vino. Vino, vino, vino. Where's the brute?

Cathy Oh, do you think? I thought all the men seemed rather . . .

Daniel   Niet. Nada. Noodoo. Wait till you see the men of the mountains.

Cathy   Well, why didn't you take me to the mountains? Dodo.

Daniel   I will. Tomorrow. Dodo. (*He leans across, kisses her.*) I wanted a day a deux with you.

Nico, *the hotel keeper, comes on. He is in his forties, swarthy, heavily built, his manner by turns ingratiating and ironic. He puts a dish on the table.*

Cathy   No, that we didn't order. (*To* **Daniel**.) Did we order that?

Nico   No, this you don't order. This the cook makes for you as a gift.

Daniel   Oh, how kind of him.

Nico   He is my wife, this cook. Taste first. Maybe it won't suit you. Then I divorce her.

Daniel *tastes it.*

Nico   Am I still a married man?

Daniel   Oh. (*He puts some on* **Cathy**'*s plate.*)

Nico   Thank you. I'll tell her.

Daniel   *I'd* like to tell her. Where is she?

Nico   She stays always at her place in the kitchen.

Cathy   But why's no one here? Your hotel looks comfortable and the food's delicious.

The music stops.
Nico *exchanges a look with* **Daniel**.

Nico   It's the wind.

Daniel   'The wind.'

Nico   All day it blows hot, it blows dry. People stay home.

Daniel Can't you make it stop?

Nico Stop the wind? (*He laughs.*) You know a way?

Daniel Perform sacrifices.

Cathy Sacrifices? (*She laughs.*)

Daniel Burn things. Throw them into the sea.

Nico We're poor people. We've got nothing to throw. If we had we would. For you. (*He starts to go.*)

Cathy Waiter.

Nico I am Nico.

Cathy Nico. More wine, please.

She hands him the empty wine jug. He goes.

Cathy Wait a minute! Nico! Did you tell him we want to phone home?

Daniel Tomorrow.

Cathy No, now.

Daniel We'll do it in the mountains. We can bounce it off a satellite, it's easy. Here to do anything is agony.

The music starts.

Daniel Do you want to know why no tourists come here? Because ... (*He rocks his hand.*)

Cathy What? Do they have earthquakes?

Daniel No! 'Earthquakes'. (*He laughs.*)

Cathy Don't laugh at me.

Daniel (*laughing*) Sorry but, you know ...

Cathy Don't.

Daniel That's you. Everything's taken so literally.

Cathy Well, take this literally. I want to phone now.

Daniel   Oh, you do?

Cathy   I want to know how Sally is.

Daniel   How she is. Is she missing her mummy?

Cathy   Don't you care at all?

Daniel (*getting up*)   Nico! Telefono, per favoro por madamo. Nico! (*He hears the music, starts to dance.*) Come!

Cathy   No. I'm exhausted.

Daniel   Oh come!

She doesn't. He turns to **Takic**, *one of the musicians – sultry and watchful. He dances in front of him.* **Takic** *dances with him.* **Cathy** *goes to* **Daniel**, *dances with him. Then she dances with* **Takic**. *After a moment she breaks away. The music ends.*

Cathy   If you're so cheerful, why did I fly all this way?

Daniel   You flew for the moon! For the men of the mountains! (*Silence.*) In the morning –

Cathy   Yes. Tom'll come with the jeep, we'll drive to the mountains. You told me. Yes. (*Silence.*) Where's the guidebook? (*She opens it.*) What's there to see here?

Daniel   Nothing a quarter as gorgeous as you.

Cathy   What?

Daniel   My underpants have got up the crack of my bum.

Cathy   At least you're wearing them. (*She laughs.*) Did you put them on in my honour?

Daniel   And what are you wearing? That's for you to know and me to find out.

He kicks off a shoe and, under the table, puts his foot between her legs.
Takic *is hovering.*

Cathy   Danny! Um ... The square in Novi Mesto sounds interesting. 'Encircled by high trees ... Statue of the local hero riding a horse. Each night musicians play.'

Takic This Novi Mesto.

Cathy (*giggling*) What did he say?

Takic Novi Mesto, this. Statue there. See? Anton Lubovic.

Cathy I see. Oh, here he is. 'Anton Lubovic. Poet. Confectioner. Founder of the nation.'

Takic Big man in valley. Big for fighting, big for chocolates. You want buy chocolate? I get good price.

Nico *comes on with a jug of wine. He speaks sharply to* **Takic** *who returns to the musicians.* **Nico** *fills their glasses.*

Nico If you are interested in sacrifice, next time you must come in Easter. What happens then is remarkable. The men of this village make a cross of wood. One climbs on.

Cathy Who climbs on?

Nico God must choose. It can be anyone. He can be old, he can be young. What they do is this. They nail his hands like so.

Cathy They nail him?

Nico Bang, bang. They tie his ankles. His skin goes pale as milk. They carry him through the fields, through the vineyards. All the men follow singing, through the streets, round the hill, back up here to the church. There on his cross he hangs until dawn. Would you like to see this? You must make reservations. I have only six rooms. (*He clears their plates to another table.*)

Daniel Don't speak. I've come all over my trousers.

Cathy Danny!

Daniel I couldn't help it. Two such powerful emotional experiences.

Cathy You liar. You haven't. Let me feel.

Daniel *smashes a plate.*

Daniel   I never want this moment to return. I never want to be so happy again.

Cathy (*to* **Nico**)   I'm so sorry. That lovely plate.

Nico   You're happy? (*He smashes a plate.*) Then I too am happy.

Daniel (*embracing* **Nico**)   You are so beautiful.

Cathy   Of course he is. Come, let's go in.

Nico   Ah. My wife also adores me.

Cathy   Is our room ready?

Nico   Naturally.

Daniel   Thank you. (*He kisses* **Nico**. *To the musicians.*) Thank you. I want to die. Thank you.

Cathy *leads him out, he limping.*
Nico *folds tablecloths. The musicians leave.*
Daniel *limps back on, takes his shoe, blows a kiss, starts to limp out.*
Takic *plays and sings a few lines of 'The Crow Song'.*

Nico   You know what it is?

Daniel   What? No.

Nico   It's a song of the mountains. The mountain people sing it when they're frightened.

Daniel   Is he from the mountains?

Nico   He is.

Daniel   What's he frightened of?

Nico   Of nothing. (*He laughs.*) He's practising.

As **Takic** *sings the song* **Nico** *translates.*

Nico
  'Outside the window
  The crow waits in a tree
  If the window won't open
  It will smash its way in
  By singing we oil the window
  The warm night air
  Tastes of red chillis
  The crow flies in.'

Takic *speaks.* **Nico** *argues with him.*

Nico   I say you are happy. He says in your heart is great sorrow.

Daniel (*to* **Takic**)   Is that in the song? Or is he talking to me?

Nico *translates.*

Nico   To you. He has something to tell you.

Daniel (*to* **Takic**)   Tell me.

Takic   Come see old man.

Daniel   Which old man?

Nico   He speaks of a man who lives high in the mountains.

Daniel   Why should I want to see him?

Takic *speaks.*

Nico   Because of the pain in your heart.

Takic   You want see him. I know you.

Cathy *comes in.* **Takic** *speaks.* **Nico** *takes* **Daniel** *aside.*

Nico   He says in the morning wait for him outside the butcher. You know where that is?

Cathy   What's going on?

Takic *speaks.*

Nico (*aside to* **Daniel**)   He's hard to reach, this old man. But if you fail to go, your sorrow will never leave you.

Cathy   What's he talking about? Danny?

Daniel   Sh! Go away!

Nico   Trust him. He is your guide. He will lead you to him.

Scene Two

A hotel bedroom. One hour later.
Daniel *sits at a table.* **Cathy** *lies on the bed — both in their underwear.*
Daniel *is smoking. He stubs out his cigarette, looks for another, finds his packet is empty.*
The sound of the sea.

Cathy (*bitterly*)   'The sea, the sea.'

A heavy lorry rumbles past.

Cathy   I want to say one thing. If you go to see that man, whoever he is, I go with you.

Daniel   He told you. Women aren't allowed there.

Cathy   Says who?

Daniel   It's a rule.

Cathy   Who makes these rules?

Daniel   Not just you. All women. Local women.

Cathy   How will they stop me? Is there a wall? Is there broken glass on the ground? No, because women here don't argue, they do what they're told, is that it? Shit! (*She slaps a mosquito on her arm, sprays herself.*)

A knock at the door. **Cathy** *draws a sheet over herself.* **Daniel** *pulls on his trousers, opens the door.* **Nico** *comes in.* **Rosa** *follows with a jug of wine.*

Nico (*beaming*)   To make our apologies for the delay my wife offers you her special wine.

Rosa   Special wine.

Rosa *puts the jug on the table and deftly tidies the room, putting clothes on chairs etc.*

Daniel   What I asked is that you get your telephone working.

Nico   For local calls I would be happy for you to use this. (*He shows a mobile telephone.*) But long distance have to go through the town hall. What can we do? (*He lifts the telephone receiver, jiggles the button.*) Hullo? Hullo? (*He speaks.*) Ah, now it is working.

Daniel   You said that an hour ago.

Nico   I assure you the old lady is trying and trying your number. Perhaps there is no one at your home? (*Silence.*) Meantime, our bar is open twenty-four hours. Whatever you need Rosa will bring. I want you to be happy again. Break the jug if you want to.

Cathy   You've been very helpful. Thank you.

Nico *and* **Rosa** *go.* **Daniel** *pours the wine, drinks.*

Cathy   Can't we, Danny, can't we forget the whole thing? Let's sleep, let's get up early, let's take a bus at dawn. We'll go to Fezia.

Daniel   Fezia.

Cathy   It says in Fezia – Fezia, Fezia – they cook a special squid. And the beach –

Daniel   Beach? Fezia's in the mountains.

She looks up an entry in the guidebook, reads. He drinks.

Cathy   OK, enough bullshit. Who is he? You must know who he is. Then why do you want to go with him? He's a trickster, a charlatan, obviously.

Daniel   Who is?

Cathy The one who sings. All of them. I've got one full day here. One. You go up the mountain while I sit in this dump and wait for you and ... You can't stand me to be with you. Admit it.

He picks up the telephone receiver, listens. There's no reply.

Cathy (*harshly*) What do you want? Sorry. I mean, do you want something from the bar?

He gestures: a cigarette. She takes cigarettes from her bag, throws them to him. He lights one, smokes, coughs.

Daniel Didn't you hear what he said? He wants to see me.

Cathy He didn't say that.

Daniel It's what he said.

Cathy It's not!

Daniel Shit. Shit. I'll fucking kill you, do you hear me?

Silence. She dresses, is about to go out.

Daniel Cathy ...

Cathy Shut up. How dangerous is it?

Daniel Is what?

Cathy It. Out there. At night. Tell the truth.

He makes the gesture of rocking his hand.

Cathy Has there been any fighting?

Daniel Do you mean with guns?

She laughs.

Only at night.

She laughs.

Not every night.

Cathy And you want to go into the mountains? Alone?

Daniel I live in the bloody mountains. Not the old man's mountain. There's a thousand bloody mountains.

Cathy But you're safe, is that it, because you have some special insight? You see into their souls, isn't that what you do? You don't speak a word of their language but you have a special rapport with these people, with the mountain people, with everyone in the world except me. With me it's too much to even return my phone calls.

Daniel Where we are it's wooden huts, that's all it is, you'll see. We're out at the site all day. Who can take phone messages?

Cathy And your famous satellites? Don't they have an answering machine? Paul hears from Tom.

Daniel Oh, does he?

Cathy (*she laughs*) And Tom had no trouble phoning me. What's happened to you? I didn't hear for weeks. Are you in the land of the living? Then he phoned. And told me the state you're in. You won't get up in the morning. That's not like you. The first thing that goes wrong – and he says most things have gone wrong, is that true? – you give up and sit staring into the mountains.

Daniel I like the mountains.

Cathy So what I did ... I bought a ticket for you on the same flight back as me. The day after tomorrow. At three.

Daniel Don't ask me rubbish.

Cathy It's not rubbish.

Daniel How can I leave? I have a job to do. These people need water.

Cathy Yes, they do. But why, Danny, why, why, why do you use them, your work, anything, everything to cut yourself off from me?

Daniel Do I do that?

Silence.

It's not something I choose. I don't seem able to choose anything. It's like everything I could do or ever did is lined up. It's in a line, my whole life. I've done it all up to this point, do the next thing.

Cathy   But why's the next thing always, always, always, always, being angry with me?

Daniel   My child is dying.

Cathy   She's not dying! She's ill. She's not dying. And did you hear what you said? Did you hear what you said? She's ill, Sally's ill so you blame me. You're angry with me.

Daniel   She's not ill. She isn't ill.

Cathy   I'm sick of it. I'm just –

Daniel   There's something wrong with her.

Cathy   I've had enough.

Daniel   It's genetic. It's not an illness. Don't you understand anything?

Cathy   I'm sick of it! Sick of you! You!

Daniel   Do I blame you for that?

Cathy   Are you asking me?

Daniel   If I did, if I do, it's unfair of me.

Cathy   'Unfair' of you?

Daniel   Yes. Yes, it would be.

Cathy (*silence*)   What?

Daniel   You always ask 'what?'

Cathy   Well, tell me.

Daniel   It came into my mind. I imagined Sally playing in the sea.

Cathy   We'll bring her here. She'll play in the sea.

Daniel   It *is* unfair. I do blame you. It could be me. It could be both of us. I think it's me. So I have to do something. I have legs. There's a mountain. I can climb it.

I have ears. I can hear what this man tells me. If he tells me anything. What if he can help her?

Cathy (*gently*) Who? Who can help her?

Daniel You want me to go. You want me to hear what he has to say. You won't admit it but you want me to go, don't you?

Cathy You know what? You're the bloody dictator, worse than any of the politicians here. You. You've got to decide. You've got to control. God, God, God, God, God, God, I hate you. (*A long silence. She takes off her dress.*) Come and lie with me.

He takes off his trousers, gets under the sheet. She strokes his hair.

Cathy Goodness you get into a state. Poor you. You've got so thin.

Daniel Have I?

Cathy Skin and bone.

Daniel Good.

Cathy Feel. No, don't play with yourself.

Daniel Why not?

Cathy Because . . . Why? Because it's insulting to me. Because I'd rather, if you want sex, that you'd have it with me.

Daniel (*he lifts the telephone receiver*) Oh. Hullo. Yes. I wanted . . . What did I want?

Cathy Cigarettes.

Daniel Cigarettes. Not local ones. American. And my call. Please put it through. (*He puts the receiver down.*)

Cathy I do try with you. I try. I try. What can I do? It's as if you don't like me, or want me, want to be with me. It's as if you don't like women.

Daniel I don't like you so I don't like women?

Cathy   So you don't like me.

Daniel   No, I do quite like you. But I don't like women, no.

Cathy   So what does that mean? Would you rather be with men? Are you gay? You spend all your time with men. Do you go to bed with men?

Daniel   No.

Cathy   Do you want to?

Daniel   How many ... No. No. OK? But how many heterosexual men, do you think, really like women? Really, really.

Cathy   What don't you like about us?

Daniel   You make me uneasy.

Cathy   Me? Or us?

Daniel   I can't somehow relax with you.

Cathy   Don't be silly.

Daniel   It's true.

Cathy   With me? Or with my whole sex?

Daniel   You're wet. No, listen to me. You asked, I'm telling you.

Cathy   Wet?

Daniel   You're a marsh. You. You. You're full of juice. I like things to be hard. And brittle. And dry. I do. The fact is I don't like men much either.

Cathy   So what do you like?

Daniel   I like my daughter. I like Sally. (*The phone rings. He answers it.*) Yes? Yes, well put it through then. Mum? Yes, clearly. Very hot. How's Sally? What? What? I don't ... You what?

Cathy   What's happened?

Daniel How could you do that? (*Covering the phone.*) You fucker! You, you – Shit her! Shit her!

Cathy (*taking the phone*) Doreen? Oh. Oh. Did it bleed? Is there a bruise? Oh. I see. Yes, she likes it if you do that. Kiss it for me too. And? Is that all? Good. Danny, he's ... He's ... Yes, but what's new?

Daniel Give it to me!

Cathy (*she gives him the receiver*) Danny, you're having some sort of a breakdown. Do you understand what I'm saying to you? You're cracking up. Do you realise that? So is this the best time for you to shout at her? Would it help her? Would it help you? (*He gives it back.*) Doreen? Good. Good. We'll call again tomorrow. Yes, we'll call you. And, Doreen, thank you. (*She puts the receiver down.*) She was playing with her. She bumped her head. It's a tiny bruise. She called the doctor. She'll pull through.

Daniel How could you leave her?

Cathy (*silence*) You know I didn't want to.

Daniel But you did! Fucking women! What are you good for? Nothing!

Cathy No. No. No. No, no. I left her – why? I wouldn't leave her for anything, not for the world. I left her because I was so worried about you! (*She's crying.*) I love you. I do! That's what breaks my heart. Oh God. It's so sad. I love you and you despise me. You do!

Daniel Cathy, how long can it take? Up the mountain, down the mountain. An hour?

Cathy Liar! You're such a liar! You'd say anything to get your way, anything!

Daniel Two hours. That's all. Then we'll go to Tringano. Look it up. It's a lovely place. There's a beautiful bay. We'll relax. We'll swim. The water's blue. (*Howling.*) What's wrong with me? I have done nothing! I can do nothing! I will leave nothing!

Heavy trucks go past. She strokes his hair. He pulls away from her. He throws up. She goes to him.

Daniel Leave me.

Cathy All that lovely food.

He washes out his mouth with wine from his glass. He lights a cigarette, smokes.

Cathy What do you think? He knows medicines? He can cure her? Is that what you think? (*She laughs. She sighs.*) If you go up there tomorrow, will you come home with me after?

Daniel Yes.

Cathy Then go.

Daniel (*silence*) Funny, now I don't want to.

Cathy (*silence*) The wind's dropped. (*She laughs. She kisses him.*) OK, then forget about him. In the morning we'll wait for Tom. He'll drive us up your mountain. We'll see your camp, your dam. In the morning he'll drive us down again. We'll go home.

Daniel All right. All right. That's what we'll do. All right. All right, you win.

Scene Three

Next morning. **Daniel** *and* **Takic** *high in the mountains.*

Takic These mountains, good, huh?

Daniel Oh, yes. I love these mountains. I could live here. Me, live here, I could.

Takic Live? No. Live? Too hot, too dry. Rabbit live here. You rabbit, huh, you? (*He jumps, sniffs, laughs.*) Rabbit, you, huh?

Daniel I want to keep going. Is this the way? Or is it a dead end? No! Yes! I can see the way through. Let's go.

Takic (*pointing down*) Hotel. Look. You. Look there. Wife, you wife. Bye bye, wifie. You big, wifie so so so so, only so small. Too small. There, butcher. Me, I work there. Cut meat, cut meat.

Daniel But now? You work with him?

Takic Huh?

Daniel You work with old man?

Takic Huh? (*Silence.*) We ... We, we ... Look, look, yes? We, us, mountain people. Valley people like to kill us. (*He laughs.*) Kill us, kill us. Why?

Daniel I don't know. But I'd like to know why.

Takic Valley people make for us everything very bad. So we live here. To live there, down there, for us is ... Heaven? Hell? Which?

Daniel (*pointing*) Heaven, hell.

Takic Hell. Bloody fucking hell.

Daniel So why do you go there?

Takic Here, up here, no shop, no what what, no beer, no nothing. Me ... (*He imitates the sound of his instrument.*) For who I play? For God. But God ... You know God? Does God pay good money? (*He laughs helplessly.*) But God loves me. And you love me, huh? No?

Daniel Um ... Yes, I do.

Takic You no love me?

Daniel No, no, I do love you. I love the mountains.

Takic (*pointing far down*) You see rock there?

Daniel Which one?

Takic There! We call that 'cat'. You see 'cat'? There, that rock we call 'donkey'. Between 'cat' and 'donkey' water will come.

Daniel What do you mean?

Takic You know. You don't know? You know. (*He imitates digging the earth.*)

Daniel (*laughing*) You know about that?

Takic Yes. You, I see you!

Daniel Does everyone know? What do they think? If that is where the reservoir is put ... If water, the lake did come there, will it be good or bad?

Takic Good! For us very good. (*Pointing down.*) For them, bad. Bloody fucking bad. (*He laughs.*)

Daniel Why? Do you ... ? Do they ... ?

Takic (*pointing up*) Village.

Daniel Oh?

Takic My village.

Daniel Oh. It's far.

Takic This country, this bloody fucking country, God made everything far. (*He whistles.*)

Dusja, *eight years old, appears.*

Daniel You said women aren't allowed on this mountain.

Takic This, woman? No. This daughter. Dusja. Little Dusja. Pretty little Dusja. So friend, what you brought for old man?

Daniel Brought? No, I ... Brought for him?

Takic You give little Dusja, she give him.

Daniel Sorry? No. I'm not sure I ... (*He takes out money, holds it out.* **Dusja** *takes it.*)

Takic Good.

Daniel Can we go now?

Takic   Yes. No.

Daniel   Um ... Take me to him. If you do, I'll pay you. OK?

Takic   Pay me! You. Pay me now! Now pay me!

Silence. **Daniel** *holds out money.* **Dusja** *takes it.*

Daniel   So can we go?

Takic   Old man, he like watch. Watch-watch. Watchie-watchie.

Daniel (*laughing*)   You're kidding, I'm not giving him my ...

Takic   Watchie-watchie. (*He laughs.*) Old man like watchie-watchie.

Daniel *laughs.* **Takic** *laughs.* **Takic** *stops laughing.* **Daniel** *takes off his watch, gives it to* **Dusja**.

Takic   Old man, he like shirt. Beautiful shirt.

Silence. **Takic** *speaks to* **Dusja**. *She takes a knife from under her dress, hands it to* **Takic**.

Takic   Old man, he like beautiful, beautiful shirt.

Daniel   I want to see him! Put that away! Where is he?

Silence. **Daniel** *runs off. He runs back.*

Daniel   Which way? I don't know the fucking way!

Takic   Old man, you want him? This is old man. (*The knife.*) He like money. He like things. You give nice things for old man?

Silence. **Daniel** *takes off his shirt.* **Dusja** *snatches it, puts it on.* **Takic** *picks her up, dances with her, kisses her, caresses her.*

Takic   Ah! Pretty Dusja. Look, look. Pretty, pretty Dusja. (*He laughs, flourishes his knife.*) So. You love old man. Here he is. I know you. You want give him trouser, shoe, money, money. You want give him everything.

Scene Four

The village square. Midday.
Village men sit at tables drinking. One plays a guitar.
Nico *serves beer.* **Rosa** *peels fruit.*
An **Old Man** *with a white beard and a* **Young One** *sit apart,*
their heads back, dental apparatus in their mouths, white cloths draped
round their necks.
Pintilje, *a dentist, sits at a table eating a meal. A large, powerful*
man, he eats as he does his dentistry with delicate and sensual
discrimination.
Yosip *is older, clean shaven, slighter, ascetic but not severe. He sits*
to one side reading as he eats his meal.
Daniel, *distraught, still without his shirt, comes in. The guitar*
playing stops.

Nico   Mister, where have you been?

Daniel   Where's my wife? Cathy! (*He starts to go in.*)

Nico   She's not here. Mister! Your wife is with your
friend. The one from the mountain.

Daniel   What friend?

Nico   With glasses. With the long hair.

Daniel   Tom!

Nico   Yes, Tom. Mr Tom. They didn't find you?

Daniel   She's with Tom! Where are they? Are they here?

Nico   They waited for you all morning yesterday. They
had a swim, then lunch: sardines, white wine, bread. At
four they drove off in the jeep to see if you were coming.

Daniel   Did you tell them where I'd gone?

Nico   Everyone was asking: where are you, where is he?

Daniel   Did you tell them?

Nico   Mister?

Daniel   You knew!

Nico   I knew what? I knew nothing.

Daniel   I went with that musician! Why didn't you tell my wife which way we'd go? You said, go with him into the mountain. He's a thief!

Nico   No.

Daniel   A thief.

Nico   No, mister.

Daniel   Yes, yes! He robbed me!

Nico   Who robbed you?

Daniel   He took my money, my shirt. And left me. I was lost high up in the mountain for a day and a half! There were no people, there were no villages. Who is he?

Nico   Mister, this is the square of musicians. Some I know, some are good men. Others . . .

Daniel   Look at me! No wallet, nothing!

Nico *speaks to* **Rosa**. *She goes in.*

Nico   Last night, she phoned.

Daniel   Who phoned? Cathy? So you know where she is?

Nico   She was asking where are you, are you here? Two hours ago she phoned again.

Daniel   From where?

Nico   The army base. She said 'I'm going somewhere'. The line was too bad to hear.

Daniel   Call the base. Will you do that?

Nico   For you I'll make one thousand phone calls.

Daniel   Ask them to find her. Ask them to tell her, don't come here. Go directly to the airport from wherever she is.

Nico   To the airport. So you are leaving? I'll tell Rosa pack your suitcases.

Daniel Tell her I'll meet her at the airport. And bring me a beer.

Nico Don't worry, mister. We'll find your wife. In this place, everything always works out fine. One cold beer!

He goes. **Rosa** *comes out, gives* **Daniel** *a shirt.*

Daniel This isn't mine.

Rosa You need? Take.

She watches as he puts it on then goes.

Daniel (*to* **Yosip**) Excuse me. The plane to the city, do you know when it leaves?

Pintilje My friend, in a country in crisis, it is inadvisable to have one of your own. (*He pours spirits into two glasses, offers one to* **Daniel**.) Drink. Go on. Hoy!

They drink.

How do you find it?

Daniel (*gagging*) Strong.

Pintilje (*refilling* **Daniel***'s glass*) You swallow, it seems to go. In fact it lingers. When you are back in your own country of green fields and sweet meadows, you'll feel again its fire and think of us devils in this land of stones. Igor Pintilje.

Daniel Daniel Croft.

Pintilje (*of* **Yosip**) Do you know him?

Daniel No.

Pintilje So why do you talk to him?

Daniel I thought he might help me.

Pintilje You ask just anybody? What does he know? He owns nothing, he earns nothing. Now, if I may assist you. The plane from our dusty little aerodrome to the great city, is that it? It leaves at three-fifteen.

Daniel Do you have the time?

Pintilje For some to be free others must wear chains. (*He consults his pocket watch.*) One twenty-three.

Daniel Shit! How can I get to the airport? Is there a bus?

Pintilje It travels once a day but has already left, naturally.

Daniel What can I do?

Pintilje Despair. Or ask. And receive. It's up to you. When my work is done my car is at your disposal. We'll leave, let's say, in five minutes?

Daniel It's very kind of you.

Pintilje No. To do this is nothing. I have two sons, Peter and Karoli, fifteen and twelve. Each Friday I fetch them from their school. It is less than a mile this side of the airport. They are good boys. I try not to be late for them. You must be starving.

Daniel No, really. I'm fine with this.

Pintilje Remember where you are and how things stand. When food is offered, eat.

Nico comes out with beer.

Pintilje Nico, our friend needs to regain his powers. In your kitchen is there no marmalade, no cheese?

Nico Jam! How is jam?

Pintilje Mr Croft?

Nico My wife is cooking some. As soon as it's ready she'll bring it right away. (*He goes in.*)

Daniel What I want is a cigarette.

Pintilje (*offering him one*) No, no, keep the packet, my good Mr Croft, please.

Daniel *lights up. He smokes and relaxes.*

The guitarist starts to play.
Rosa *brings out a suitcase and a rucksack.*
Pintilje *works on the* **Young Man**, *removing apparatus from his mouth. When the work is finished, the* **Young Man** *pays, then joins the other men, talks and drinks with them.*
Meanwhile:

Pintilje   You are working on the dam? I'm no mind reader. What else in this place could a person of culture do?

Daniel   I'm a geologist, yes.

Pintilje   So there you are. It's fate we should meet.

Daniel   In what way?

Pintilje   In the family of science, geology and dentistry are sisters. Both unearth secrets which lie deep. We put in our probes, we analyse data. The objects of your study are earth, water, fire. Mine, alas, are decay, disease. Amongst these people I uncover a good deal. (*He works on the* **Old Man**.) And how does your work proceed? Successfully?

Daniel   Not very.

Pintilje   Interesting. Is there some particular problem?

Daniel   Sabotage.

Pintilje   But who is doing this? You have suspicions.

Daniel   People can't seem to get it into their heads that when this dam is built it'll give water not to one group, mountain people or valley people, how could it?

Pintilje   Indeed?

Daniel   But to the whole region, the mountain *and* the valley.

Pintilje   Did you survey the Hajda Valley? From here you take that road to the black hills. You go down, you go down, you go down, you go down. At last you come to a plain where there is nothing but my ancestral vineyards, my fields. Under whose control will our water be? That is what we in the Hajda Valley are asking and asking.

The **Old Man** *cries out in pain.* **Pintilje** *shouts at him.*

Pintilje (*to* **Daniel**)   You saw me! I did to him exactly what I did to that one. Did he scream? This one screams like a pig. Why do you scream, old man? That's how I'm paid for being gentle with him. (*After a moment.*) May I ask something that has always troubled me? God made the mountains who knows how many years ago. He made the wind. It blows. Rain falls. Here comes lightning. Here comes ice and snow. Is this correct, what I am saying? Centuries pass like a bird flaps its wing. The mountains crack up into rocks. The rocks become stones. They roll down the hills. They reach the sea. In the waves they rub together until all that's left is sand. Here's what I want to know. I'm sure I'll put it crudely but it's important to me. If things have gone so far and all that was great is now small, are we near the end of the life of this earth? Or is it possible somehow that the mountains can be restored and the earth can go, I speak like a child, back to the beginning again?

The **Old Man** *removes the cloth round his throat revealing his long white beard. He gives* **Pintilje** *money and sits with the other men.* **Daniel**, *transfixed by the sight of the* **Old Man**, *follows him.* **Pintilje** *packs his equipment into bags.* **Nico** *runs out with a mobile telephone.*

Nico   Mister! I have her! She's here, mister, here she is, she's on the line!

Daniel (*to* **Nico** *of the* **Old Man**)   Who is he?

Nico   Who?

Daniel   Is that the old man?

Nico (*laughing*)   Are you still looking for him? No. He's no one. He's my Rosa's father. He's my father-in-law, the butcher. That's who he is.

Daniel (*laughing*)   The butcher. His father-in-law. (*He takes the phone.*) Cathy? My love. Yes. Yes. Yes. Me too, I can tell you. Fine. Really! (*Still laughing.*) No, it was all utter balls, it was nothing. There was no old man. I don't know what got into me. I keep seeing old men all over the place. There is no old man. I was a bit … crazy. Yes, maybe. I'm so, I'm so, I'm so, so sorry.

Pintilje   I'll have your luggage put in my car.

He calls **Rosa***, gives her keys. She carries the suitcases off.*

Daniel   But I'm better now. Yes, I swear. Good idea. No, don't, don't, don't. There's no time. Go straight there. We've got, what?, an hour. Someone will drive me. No, it's fine, it's arranged. Me too. Me too. I love you too.

He hands the telephone to **Nico** *who gives him the bill.*

Pintilje   Are we ready?

Daniel (*to* **Nico**)   How can I pay you? Do you want my shoes? (*He offers them.*)

Nico (*tearing up the bill*)   You pay me nothing. You are my friend. Come back in Easter and pay me nothing also. You are happy now? You are. I can see.

Pintilje   My Peter, my Karoli are waiting. Come my friend.

He carries his bags off.
Daniel *turns to go, turns back for a last look.*
Takic *comes in carrying a basket.* **Daniel** *watches as he shows his purchases to* **Yosip***.*

Daniel   Nico.

Nico   Mister?

Daniel   There he is!

Silence. **Nico** *calls to* **Takic** *who goes to him. They talk.*

Nico   Of course, this man I know him. He says he waited for you outside the butcher's shop. You didn't come.

Daniel   Waited for me? I waited for him for an hour. Then he came. He led me up the mountain. You know you did. You took my money. You took my watch.

Nico He speaks no English.

Daniel He speaks English! Speak!

Takic *speaks.*

Nico He says he has no watch. He's a poor man with no money.

Daniel Ask him if he has a daughter. That high. Ask him.

Nico *speaks.* **Takic** *answers.*

Nico He says yes. He has a daughter. But every one of these men have daughters.

Daniel *hurls himself at* **Takic***, knocking him down. They wrestle on the ground.*
The men shout out as they watch. **Rosa** *and* **Pintilje** *hurry back in.*
Yosip *separates* **Daniel** *and* **Takic***.*

Daniel Old man! Where's the old man? (*He takes a knife from a table.*) Here's the young one. Where's the old one?

Takic *speaks. Everyone bursts out laughing.*

Daniel What did he say?

Takic *speaks. Everyone laughs again.*

Daniel Tell me what he's saying! Tell me!

Yosip My friend, some things it is hard to translate. This is impossible.

Yosip *speaks. Everyone laughs.*

Yosip He took your watch, your money? Perhaps you were lucky. If you had made it up the mountain, that old man, what would he have taken from you? (*He pours a glass of water.*) Take this from me.

Daniel *doesn't move.*

Pintilje   You see? This is our tragedy. The government takes everything it can lay its hand on — our land, our streams. The people follow their example. We have become a nation of thieves. Your wife is waiting.

Daniel *throws down the knife and goes.* **Pintilje** *speaks. A burst of laughter and chatter among the men.* **Pintilje** *goes.*
Takic *plays the guitar.* **Rosa** *dances with the men.*
Daniel *comes on. Silence falls.*

Nico (*angry*)   Mister? You forgot something?

Daniel (*to* **Takic**)   I hit you. I'm sorry. I was angry with you. But I'm sorry I hit you.

Nico   Go. It's nothing. (*The car hoots.*) Go! Forget him.

Nico *and* **Rosa** *go.*
Daniel *drinks* **Yosip**'s *glass of water. He sees* **Yosip** *watching him.*
The car hoots. **Daniel** *starts to go, stops. The car hoots.* **Daniel** *wails as if his heart will break.*

Yosip   My friend, if you find it impossible to go, then stay. (*Silence.*) Come to me.

Daniel *turns to him.* **Pintilje** *comes on.*

Daniel   I'm not coming!

Pintilje   No, Mr Geologist. Really, you should get out of this country. You should leave. You know why? You see that statue? You know who he is? Anton Lubovic. You have heard of him? A poet.

He sings. The men join in. **Takic** *goes.*

And here come the horsemen
Brave, from the east
On great black horses
Ai!
And it's me, Anton, and my brothers
Racing across the plains
On great black horses
Ai!

And he was a marvelous confectioner. He made soldiers
out of chocolate, complete in every detail. What a man he
was! What a horse he rides! What a famous, extraordinary
battle he once fought! In my dreams, waking and sleeping,
I am up there with him. My sons sit astride. Peter in front,
Karoli behind. With good old Anton Lubovic we ride and
ride across the valleys. We look out over our country. How
beautiful it is! Oh God, with what lands you have seen fit
to entrust us. We will look after them, Mr Builder of
Dams. Mr Despoiler of Valleys. You wish to stay? Well,
you are in safe hands. I wish you well of them. (*He drinks.*)
Hoy!

He goes. All the men follow. A car starts up, drives off. **Rosa** *runs
on.*

Rosa   Suitcases! He got suitcases!

Daniel   It doesn't matter! Leave them! Forget about
them!

Yosip   No, that's foolish. You have possessions. Why lose
them?

*He goes off, shouts to the men. A heavy truck starts up, rumbles
away.* **Rosa** *goes off. Only* **Daniel** *remains.* **Yosip** *returns.*

Daniel   How much difference does it make where you
live? The weather, the climate. Say you had some task to
do, some destiny, something that would use all your
strength, all your cunning. If you lived in the wrong place,
too cold, too wet, then not only would you fail to do it but
you'd never even catch a glimpse of what it is. Might be.
Might have been.

Yosip   You are crying. Why? Everything has a reason,
not so?

Daniel   I'm sorry. (*He lights a cigarette, smokes, coughs.*)

Yosip   Have you done something wrong?

Silence. **Daniel** *stares at him.*

Yosip   Or are you sorry that you're going to miss your
plane?

Daniel Do many people come and see you?

Silence.

Yosip One day someone came. He was the first. Later there were others. Perhaps the last has been. Who knows? (*Silence.*) The thief, as you call him, was ill. I cared for him. Now he cares for me. That is how we live, is that not so? You give something, the one who receives feels – what? My English is not what it was. An urge to give something in return. Why? We don't know. But you feel the truth of what I'm saying, don't you?

Daniel Yes.

Yosip What is hard is to give and get back nothing.

Daniel To make a sacrifice?

Yosip (*he laughs*) No. One sacrifices. Why? You feel in your heart an emptiness. You give so it may be filled. Or there is a desire for something specific – health, knowledge, power. You give, you receive. No, to truly break the cycle one must give and desire in return absolutely nothing.

Daniel As if it had been stolen?

Yosip (*he laughs*) No. Towards the thief one feels self-righteousness. As you know. That is also something. As you know.

Daniel *laughs.*

Yosip (*harshly*) What do you want from me?

Daniel My daughter is ill.

Yosip Oh ... They told you I am a doctor? No. (*He starts to go.*)

Daniel I'm afraid she will die.

Yosip (*silence*) How old is she?

Daniel Five months.

Yosip A lovely girl.

Daniel She has bright red hair, brown eyes. Would it help to have a photograph?

Yosip In what way?

Daniel Damn! I had one in my wallet. She's been ill since she was born. It's genetic. Do you understand 'genetic'? The valves of her heart don't work. They're going to operate.

Yosip But that's good.

Daniel She's had many operations. Nothing makes her better. Nothing.

Yosip You have other children?

Daniel No.

Yosip Who is with her?

Daniel Her mother. Usually. Not now. She came to look after me.

Yosip She left her child? Brave woman. You and she love each other? (*Silence.*) Speak without thinking.

Daniel Yes.

Yosip (*silence, he laughs*) Well, you are young and much in your life is good.

Rosa *comes on with two bottles of jam.*

Yosip Have you met Rosa, the cook, the wife of Nico? She has life in her like a yard full of children. She is very dear to me. So is her jam.

Rosa Jam.

Yosip *takes the jam.* **Rosa** *goes.* **Yosip** *puts the bottles in* **Daniel**'s *hands.*

Yosip For your wife. And for you. Don't thank me. She collected all the ripe berries. What did I do? Take it.

Daniel (*in anguish*) Help me! I'm bad. I'm so bad. Help me!

Yosip The only sin is to believe happiness has gone forever. I'll put it more simply. After summer, autumn. But after winter, spring. That's not my wisdom. Who am I? What do I know? It's the wisdom of the mountains, the streams. (*Silence.*) When our friends with the truck return they'll take you wherever it is you need to go.

Daniel *walks away, is about to light a cigarette, finds he still has one lit, sits at his table, smokes.*

Yosip Do you go to church?

Daniel No.

Yosip But you pray?

Daniel (*silence*) Sometimes I do.

Yosip It doesn't matter whether you do or not.

Daniel When I'm desperate. It's a habit, that's all.

Yosip You speak as though habit were nothing.

Daniel I don't pray. Or if I do, I'm so full of doubt it's worth nothing.

Yosip Oh, doubt. Doubt will always be with us. I think but I'm not sure. (*He laughs.*)

Daniel *laughs, coughs.*

Yosip And who can say what is worth how much and to who? You smoke too much. Will you give it up?

Daniel *hesitates then throws down his cigarette, grinds it out. He empties the packet onto the ground.*

Yosip So. We'll see what we can do.

Part Two

Scene Five

A sitting room. Flowers in a vase. Evening.
Cathy *holds* **Sally**. **Daniel** *comes in.*

Daniel   How is she?

Cathy   Fine.

Daniel   How much did she drink?

Cathy   Everything.

She takes **Sally** *out.*
Daniel *sits at a table, starts marking exercise books.*
Cathy *comes in.*

Daniel   Asleep?

Cathy   Asleep. What are you doing? You can't do that.

Daniel   Why not?

Cathy   They'll know it's not my handwriting.

Daniel   Will they?

Cathy   Of course they will. That's the sort of thing you're extremely sensitive to when you're ten years old. Move over. (*She kisses him, takes his place, marks the books.*)

Daniel   How much do you have to get through tonight?

Cathy   Just let me do it, OK?

Silence. She smiles at him.

Daniel   Anything I can get you?

Cathy   Mm–mm.

Daniel   Drink?

Cathy   Mm.

He puts on his jacket.

Cathy   Where are you going?

Daniel   Round the corner to get . . .

Cathy   Is there nothing left?

Daniel   I wouldn't mind a walk. I haven't been outside all day. Which is fine. But . . .

Cathy   What about that whatever-it-is we brought back from . . . ? It's in the cupboard.

Daniel (*silence*)   Which cupboard?

He goes out.
She lights a cigarette, smokes.
He comes back with a bottle and two glasses. He tries to take the cigarette from her.

Cathy   Oh typical. You've given up so I have to.

She takes a puff, stubs out the cigarette. He pours drinks, hands her one.

Cathy   Cheers (*She drinks.*) Ooh.

Daniel   Strong.

Cathy   That it is. (*She works. He drinks.*) What?

Daniel   Thinking. Remembering.

Cathy   I knew you were up to no good. Why don't you . . . ?

Daniel   Do you think I'm drinking too much?

Cathy   What do you think? Oh yes. Did you notice, your journal's arrived? Why don't you read that?

Daniel   When's the last time you actually saw me have something to drink?

Cathy (*laughing*)   Why lay out money for an expensive magazine and not even take it out of its envelope?

He takes the journal from its envelope, glances at it.

Daniel   You think I do everything too much, don't you?

Cathy (*laughing*) No. Not at all. Depends what it is.

Daniel Cathy –

Cathy No, the reason you forgot about that bottle is it's my bottle. It's a tendency of yours to forget whatever doesn't owe its existence to you.

Daniel I forgot it because you hid it.

Silence. He reads.

Cathy I like the flowers, incidentally.

Daniel Shall I try to tell you how I feel?

Cathy And I don't see you drink because I'm never at home during the day, so what does that prove?

Daniel That's OK. I can take care of everything.

Silence. She watches him.

Cathy 'How you feel?' (*Silence.*) All right, tell me.

Daniel So happy.

Cathy Do you?

Daniel I do.

Cathy I'm glad.

Daniel *Are* you?

Cathy (*silence*) What do you think? That's wonderful. I'm delighted. Relieved.

Daniel But maybe not when I tell you the reason.

Cathy Then why not, for once don't tell me.

Daniel I think I'm happy for many reasons.

Cathy Because Sally's so much better.

Daniel Number one. Number one, number two and number three.

Cathy But number four . . .

Daniel   Reason number four for being happy is that at last I am clear.

Cathy   About?

Daniel   What I ought to do.

Cathy   Don't say it. It's not true so don't say it.

Daniel   The truth, Cathy, the truth. You see . . .

She drains her glass. He refills it and his own.

Daniel   . . . I never, never wanted to study geology.

Cathy   Here we go. So why did you?

Daniel   Because Tom was. And we'd been through so much together. And I love Tom. And I didn't know what else to do. If Tom had studied architecture I'd be an architect. I would.

Cathy   How can you say that? You love geology. You talk nothing but geology day after day.

Daniel   Is that so?

Cathy   Danny . . .

Daniel   No, do I? I can't remember everything. I'm asking you.

Cathy   You can't remember? What's this? (*She picks up a book.*)

Daniel   Why did you dig that out?

Cathy   Because . . . Because . . . (*She reads a bit.*) Listen to this.

Daniel   No. Please.

Cathy   How many other geologists have written a book that's had a really popular sale? That's been a hit?

Daniel   Oh come on.

Cathy   In the whole world, how many?

Daniel Many. Hundreds. Over the years. That's not the point.

Cathy I think it is.

Daniel No, the point is . . . Life. What is it? Life. Life is . . . It's things happening to us, isn't it? Most of the time. Meteors hurtling towards us from space. I don't want to stand there forever getting hit.

Cathy When did you ever?

Daniel Mm?

Cathy You're one of the most recklessly . . . No. Independent-minded . . . Pig-headed, actually. OK, resolute. No, I'd say pig-headed.

Daniel Is that so? No, I'm interested. Most of the time I feel like a sand castle watching the tide come in. No. That's what I used to feel.

Cathy What I think and feel is that you're spending too much time thinking and feeling. A bit of doing wouldn't come amiss. Like making supper.

Daniel Supper's made.

Cathy Oh.

Daniel Supper's ticking over gently in the oven.

Cathy Let's go and have it then.

Daniel But that's what I've been thinking. The food we eat, do we savour it? Do we feel the coolness or the warmth of the air we breathe? We feel nothing. We know nothing. 'Do things.' I don't want to do any more things, Cathy, without . . . Without what? Choosing them. We're slaves. No, at least slaves feel their chains. We, we seem unfettered. But – ! We think – we don't think! –

Cathy Sh!

Daniel – we're free. What?

Cathy No, go on.

Daniel   Did you hear her? (*He starts to go out.*)

Cathy   Don't run away. If there's more, let's have it.

Daniel   It's hard to say.

Cathy   Leave it then.

Daniel   Do you know how often I masturbate? Used to. How often a day?

Cathy   Do you want to tell me?

Daniel   Ah. Yes. Good question. (*He plays with the packet of cigarettes.*) Why do I want to tell you this now?

Cathy   With supper ticking over in the oven.

Daniel   Don't you want me to? No! What do *I* want? I want to tell you.

Cathy   And if I don't want to hear? What if it'll upset me?

Daniel (*silence*)   Well, any time you want to hear, I'm ready.

Cathy   To do what? Confess? Is that it? Do you still think it's a sin?

Daniel   If I feel that it is and still do it then, yes, it is a sin.

Cathy   Oh, my love. (*She laughs.*) Do you think I don't know you can't keep your hands off yourself?

Daniel   But now I can. I do.

Cathy   And how does that make you feel?

Daniel   So happy.

Cathy   Oh, oh, oh, oh, oh, oh. My darling, my sweet, the man I care about and love, really love, adore. I'm your friend. Apart from everything else, I am. If you're in pain, let me help you.

Daniel   How?

Cathy Talk to me.

Daniel Nothing to say. First I gave up smoking. Now this. Do you see?

Cathy You're giving up all your bad habits. Is that it?

Daniel Yes! No more habits, good or bad. Exactly. Live in the moment. Choose!

Cathy So is it a good moment to think about the future?

Daniel Yes, I want to.

Cathy Good. So the first question is: when are you going back to work? If not because *I* think you should, then because Tom needs you. He's written how many times? You ought at least to answer. And if he wants you back, to help out on the dam, if that means being away for a month or two, or more, you know – how can I put this and not seem unloving? – fine by me.

Daniel Oh, something really funny ... Did I tell you? When I was ... When you came to fetch me ... When I had what you call –

Cathy Your breakdown. Yes?

Daniel Those men! They got hold of your suitcase. They were bringing you to me. No, me to you. And I'd got the suitcase from ... wherever. The hotel. No, someone's car. Whose? We were putting it on this truck, a huge one, a beast. It fell open. I found a few bits and pieces, you know, specimens. I'd put them in with your things. They rolled out. Silence fell. Then the yelling! They shouted at me and shouted at me. They refused to take me any further. They thought I was stealing their stones! Bits of their land.

Cathy You were, in a way.

Daniel And in that moment, I wanted so much, so much, a cigarette. So I asked for one and lit it and when it was burning I pressed it hard, like this, against the palm of my hand.

Cathy Danny!

Daniel Until I could smell it sizzling.

Cathy You did what? No.

Daniel I chose to. So I did. And in that moment I was free.

Cathy That's not what you told me happened.

Daniel Have I smoked again? And the other thing is . . . About going back, no. I've been there. I've done that. I've learnt what they have to teach. I'm not going back. Is that clear? Ever. (*Silence.*) There's an old dichotomy. Perennial. You think it's been resolved, put to bed. Then you find it's got up again. It's this. Is God – whatever one means by . . . in or above, i.e. apart from, separate, outside the world? Or . . . It sounds like nothing. It drives people crazy. Take evolution. The old arguments. Did God make the world as something separate from himself, clay moulded in his hands, a sculpture of which he's the artist, into which his life was breathed? Or is life God? Life itself. How can I put this?

Cathy You put it very clearly. You suspect that you're God and you're checking it with me.

Daniel (*he laughs*) The same problem crops up in all religions: Islam, Judaism – the Kabbalah!

Cathy Now you're gabbling.

Daniel It's so important this. In Elizabethan England . . . When did the Renaissance truly begin? When the scientists, such as they were, struck the earth with a stick and said here, not in the heavens but here, down here, in the earth, (*Holding his body.*) here, here is where holiness is. Look, does God think it's wrong when I wank? Is he somewhere out there judging me? Or is the pleasure I feel . . . Or when I eat delicious food or breathe sweet air or make love to you, or simply am with you, talk with you. Like now. Is that pleasure, this huge pleasure – telling you after all this time, this long silence, this ice age, this death-like anger

between us, Cathy, how I feel, how I really, truly feel . . .
It's like, you know, I'm full of light. I'm going to burn with
it, burst with it. Cathy! Is this . . . Is this Him? (*Silence.*) Not
that I believe in Him.

Cathy Don't you?

Daniel That I think I can safely say.

Cathy I think you do.

Daniel Oh, fuck a duck, Cathy. What I'm trying to tell
you is that I feel I could do anything. The heavens are
open. And if I did it, it, whatever it is, and I did it well, as
well as I could, if I did it with love and for the love of
doing it and only for that reason . . .

Cathy Did what?

Daniel If I choose to do it . . . I drink too much? (*He
flings out the contents of his glass.*) 'Who shall ascend the
mountain of the Lord and who shall stand in his holy
place? He who has clean hands and a pure heart.' What is
it? What is it? Cathy? What is it?

Cathy Look, if you're feeling better, great. But, do
something for me, don't come off the pills straight away.
Because whenever you do . . .

Daniel (*silence*) Do you remember that old man?

Cathy (*she does*) No, what old man?

Daniel Who I went to meet on the mountain. Who I
met in the square.

Cathy Actually . . . It's been a long day . . . Sally, all my
kids . . . What I want more than anything – will you turn
the oven off? Good night – is bed.

Daniel It was him who told me to give up smoking.

Cathy (*surprised*) Was it? Him? The old man? So you did?

Daniel He didn't say: give up smoking and Sally will
live.

Cathy Danny . . .

Daniel Look at me! He didn't say that, but, but . . . I did. And she did. So now what I feel is . . .

Cathy Tell me. You have some sort of power?

Daniel No. No power. No. I don't know what I have. But I feel it's, yes, it's simpler than power. It's . . . What is it? I understand. You. How things are. I can see into things.

Cathy Come to me. I want to tell you something. I listened to you, now you listen. Put your arm round me. (*Of his palm.*) How is this? Not much better, is it? Do you scratch it? Put a plaster over it.

Daniel I did. It came off.

Cathy Oh, what a baby. (*She moves away.*)

Daniel (*wailing*) Why are you leaving me?

Cathy Because I'd rather sit over here, that's why. You believe you understood something there, do you? Do you remember that musician?

Daniel Which one?

Cathy I thought he was good looking. You called him a brute.

Daniel No, that was the waiter, the manager, Nico.

Cathy Was it? Anyway . . . I mean the one who took you up the mountain. What I wanted to tell you was . . . You insisted on going up the mountain. I'd left Sally. You left me. I was so alone. (*She is crying.*) I went to bed with him.

Daniel Did you?

Cathy You had to go! So go, damn you. Ten minutes went by, he sauntered in. Why did I do it? Did I want to? You say we should do what we want.

Daniel Did I?

Cathy What we feel. So I did. I thought, any second
you'd come in. Was I hoping you would? That would show
you. What? Many things. That it wasn't only you who can
choose what to do. So I did it. (*Silence.*) It wasn't very nice
actually. I wouldn't have said God was in him. You
reminded me of it when you talked about masturbating. It
felt as if that's all he was doing. Using me as a fist. You're
right. I didn't fancy him. Funny, you always remember
men more clearly than I do. But I was so angry. With you.
So what do you think? Was 'God' in there? Or was that
simply a bad thing to do? (*Silence.*) Because that's how I
am, you see. Bad. And you know what I feel? Shall I tell
you why I feel Sally was born ill? I know what I'm going
to say isn't true but it is true. There's something bad in
me. And it came out. And it got into her. I love her so
much but somehow it came out of me. And though we say
she's better and the doctors do, we know she's only better
than she was. She could get worse. Most likely she will.
Most likely she'll die. And that's because not all the
badness has come out of me. There's more. And all the
time it gets bigger and bigger, it grows and grows. What
does it feed on? Shall I tell you what I think? It feeds on
my loathing. Of you. Because I do loathe you. Your
weakness. So you see, you have to leave, you have to. I
want you to leave. Do you hear me? I want you to leave
us, Sally and me. I want you to go. Oh God, go. I do.
Please. I don't believe any of this, what I've said. I don't
believe it but I believe. So go. Now. Please. Please.

She goes out. She comes in. She is smoking.

Daniel How is she?

Cathy (*silence*) Asleep.

Scene Six

An office in a wooden hut. A desk, chai
walls. The room has been turned upsid

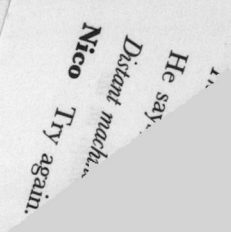

Men of the mountains stand about. Among them are **Daniel** *and* **Nico**. *All are warmly dressed, some with blankets round their shoulders. Some of the men smoke cigarettes.*
Nico *is writing.*
An armed **Guard** *stands over them.*
A strong wind blows.
In the distance: bursts of machine gun fire. A mortar explodes. Then, in silence, the song of a bird.

A Man (*to* **Daniel**)   *Itnis tara.*

Nico   Do you understand?

Daniel   Say it again.

The Man   *Itnis tara.*

Daniel   What's *itnis*?

Nico   I told you. Snow.

Daniel   *Itnis tara.* 'There will be snow.'

Nico   Snow is coming.

Daniel   When?

Nico *asks. The man answers.*

Nico   'With this wind, tomorrow.'

The man speaks.

'In the morning.'

Another man speaks.

He says, before midday.

Daniel (*laughing*)   How can they know so exactly?

Nico   They do. These men know everything.

The first man speaks.

listen.

gun fire.

Do you hear?

Daniel   Do you mean the bird? Is that it?

Nico *laughs, tells the men who laugh. One speaks.*

Nico   It's the snow bird. It lives in these mountains. When the wind is cold and it sings, snow is coming, they know.

Daniel   Snow is coming. *Itnis tara.*

Nico   Good.

Men laugh. The man speaks.

Nico   He says, 'That's why our friends fight so hard to set us free from here.'

Daniel   What does he mean?

Nico   When it snows they'll go.

Daniel   They'll go? They'll abandon us?

Nico   Against white snow they'll be such clear targets. How can they fight? What can they do? So they'll go.

Daniel   What will happen to us?

A man draws a finger across his throat. He sings. The men laugh.

Nico   He says,
  Spring flowers grow high where the snow was deep.

Daniel   Why did they laugh?

Nico   Who will lie under deep snow? We.

*An explosion nearby. Some of the men shout at the **Guard** who shouts back, pointing his rifle at them.*
Nico *has gone back to writing.* **Daniel** *glances at some of the pages he has covered.*

Daniel   What are they? Are they poems?

Nico   Poems? (*He laughs.*) No, not poems.

Daniel   What do they mean?

Nico   Those soldiers told you to write, didn't they?

Daniel   They did.

Nico   So fine, you explain why you're here, what we were doing in the mountains, you and me, they let you go. But me? They don't ask what I have to say. So I write not poems, look, menus! Starter, main course, dessert. Look! Brotik, it's cabbage soup. Sonno salavi, it's pork with potatoes fried with berries you find down there in the valley. Split banana, it's banana split.

Daniel *laughs.*

Nico   It's funny? Look! If they read these they'll remember how much they enjoy my food, they won't want to hurt me. Why should they? All these men, these mountain people worked for you. OK, if the dam is bad for the valley they must be punished. But me? Why should they take me prisoner? I'm not from the mountain, I'm not from the valley.

*Soldiers push in two **Prisoners** with sacks over their heads. Three men dash forward shouting, try to pull the **Prisoners** away from the **Guards** and to get their sacks off. The **Soldiers** push them back, drag the **Prisoners** out.*
*The **Guard** points his rifle at the men and shouts at them. In the next room, the **Prisoners** cry out as they're beaten. A man starts to sing 'The Crow Song'. Others, including **Nico**, join in, singing quietly. The **Guard** shouts at them. They go on singing. As the singing continues:*

Daniel (*to* **Nico**)   How do you know that song if you're not from the mountain?

Nico   My wife, my Rosa is from here. She taught me.

*The **Prisoners** in the next room cry out.*

Daniel   To marry a woman from the mountains, wasn't that dangerous?

Nico   All women are dangerous. (*He laughs.*) We can't live with them, we can't live without them.

Daniel *laughs.*

Nico   It's funny?

The **Prisoners** *cry out.*

Daniel   Do you have children?

Nico   With Rosa? No. We think Rosa is . . . That she is, that she cannot . . .

Daniel   So why do you keep her?

Nico   I need a good cook. (*He laughs. He is crying.*) And I have another reason. I love her. That's why I keep her. Now you know.

Nearby: machine gun fire.
Soldiers *run into the room. They shout. All the men stand.*
Pintilje *comes in. He wears camouflage and carries a rifle.*
He speaks to the **Soldiers***. They go out. He looks at each of the men in turn. He sees* **Daniel***.*

Pintilje   Ah.

He reaches into a pocket of his coat, takes out a portable telephone, looks at it, laughs, takes off the coat.

Pintilje (*of the coat*)   This isn't mine. Whose is this?

He speaks to the **Guard** *who takes the coat and goes out. The telephone rings. He answers it – furious. He barks orders, then puts down the phone.*

They told me there were no foreigners among the prisoners, that all you engineers had run away. You are from where? From America?

Daniel   From England.

Pintilje   From the pastures and meadows of England.

The **Guard** *brings in a second coat.* **Pintilje** *takes it, puts it on, reaches into a pocket, takes out a pistol. He laughs, then shouts at the* **Guard** *who runs out.*

Pintilje (*of the pistol*)   This is also from England. Very delicate, very light. So we pay big money. So we shoot, the trigger jams, we die. So I wish to ask you a question: in what do you people believe? Can you answer? (*He drinks from his hip flask.*) In what do you believe? We begged you: stop, stop, stop, stop, stop, stop, stop building this dam. What can we do? We climb the mountain, surround your camp. Your English, your Americans – a helicopter flies up, away they go. Who remains? These poor fools, these beasts of burden who dig your trenches and carry your stones. Do they care about land? No, they are herders of sheep. You flood a million of their acres, so what? But we, we who live below, we who will lose control of our water in our river, we cry to the government: you're our father, we are in pain, dry our tears. They are too far away to hear us. We don't wish to hurt anyone.

The **Guard** *has brought a third coat.* **Pintilje** *puts it on, reaches into a pocket, takes out papers.*

Pintilje   Ah! This is it. This is what I'm looking for. (*To* **Daniel**.) Is it you who wrote these?

Daniel   Yes.

Pintilje   You're surprised I have them? Well, they tell you write your life story, they expect a paragraph – name, religion, profession. You wrote a novel! Who has time to read? (*Silence.*) I have. All night long no sleep. So it comes down to a simple question: is what you write true? Answer me.

The phone rings. **Pintilje** *answers, speaks, puts it down. He reads* **Daniel**'s *papers at random. A long moment passes*

Pintilje   You were found wandering with a guide, our good friend Nico, in the mountains. Weren't you told that place was outside the war zone? (*Silence.*) This is no good! None of it is any good! You must do it again! (*He tears up some of the papers. He reads.*) You have written why you came to our country the first time. Why did you return? Is it here? Show me. Where can I read it?

Daniel   I didn't have time to write everything.

Pintilje You have it now. I am a generous man. I give it to you.

Daniel The reason I came back was to find . . .

Pintilje The old man.

Daniel He isn't that old. I don't think he's much older than I am. Maybe he is.

Pintilje You were following his orders?

Daniel He didn't give me orders.

Pintilje (*he reads from random scraps of paper*) 'He ordered me to give up smoking.'

Daniel I didn't write that.

Pintilje 'He ordered me to come back to this country.' Wait. Don't speak. 'He ordered me to build the dam.' My friend, there are a hundred thousand rivers, there are a hundred thousand valleys. Why choose ours? Answer please.

Daniel A survey carried out for your government suggested that was the best place for it.

Pintilje 'Suggested'? You were not sure?

Daniel We were quite sure.

Pintilje 'Quite'?

Daniel Absolutely.

Pintilje Ah! 'Absolutely.' That sounds like our government. You see, my friend, the Hajda Valley is the most beautiful place God left his fingerprints on. It is our duty to protect it. It was in the Hajda Valley Adam Lubovic fought his extraordinary battle.

Daniel You told me all about Adam Lubovic.

Pintilje I did? (*He stares at* **Daniel**, *then hands him his flask.*) Your face I know. Orientate me.

Daniel   The square at Novi Mesto. You told me about the statue under the tree. Your offered to take me to the airport. (*He sniffs the flask.*) We drank this.

Pintilje   And did you like it?

Daniel   Yes.

Pintilje   Then drink.

Daniel *drinks.*

Pintilje   What did I tell you?

Daniel   That Anton Lubovic wrote many fine songs. What a warrior he was. His sword. His horse. How you'd like to climb onto it, you and your sons.

Pintilje   My sons? You wrote about my sons? Show me. What did you write? (*He laughs.*) I told you nothing about them. How many do I have? Five? Or four?

Daniel (*showing him*)   Peter and Karoli.

Pintilje *reads. He speaks to the* **Guard** *who answers.*

Pintilje   He says you haven't eaten today. You've had at least a cup of coffee? (*He speaks to the* **Guard** *who answers.*) I'm sorry. These animals have drunk it all. Well, I did my best for you. (*Silence.*) I told you Adam Lubovic fought an extraordinary battle but what I didn't tell you is this: he was defeated. He lost everything. Even so he went on fighting. Why? Do you know? Because he was a man. What else can a man do? Moreover, and this is what is hard for you to understand, sometimes you have to lose to win. Listen to me. There is a battle over a piece of land, you fight, you win. The land is yours. Time passes. Someone offers a good price for it. You sell, why shouldn't you? Or, or there is a battle, you fight, you lose. You die. Your blood soaks into the earth. It's yours forever. No one can ever take it from you. In the Hajda Valley thousands of our brothers were slaughtered.

Nico   Eight hundred years ago! You see? They're crazy, these people. This was eight hundred years ago!

Pintilje   Eight hundred years. How time flies.

Nico   Igor, these people, they're nothing to me. This man wanted to find an old fellow. I showed him the way. I help anyone. I help you. With food. I serve you food. Look. Brotik, sonno salavi. I serve anyone! Everyone!

Pintilje   (*laughing*)   No, no, no, no, no. The Hajda Valley. Dig its soil, your spade sticks. Why? The mud is my tears mixed with my skin.

An explosion.

Soon, of your dam there will remain nothing.

Nico   Igor!

Pintilje   Sh! (*To* **Daniel**.) Now for you. Look at this. This is interesting. Yes. Here we are. Sally. Little Sally, your daughter. Yes, sh! Let me read. You gave up smoking? Interesting.

After a moment, he speaks to the **Guard** *who takes out a packet of cigarettes and a lighter and hands them to* **Pintilje**. **Pintilje** *lights a cigarette. All the men are smoking.*
In the distance: a burst of machine gun fire.

Pintilje   In this country you could make very good tests of the dangers of smoking. For us thirty, forty a day – nothing. (*He speaks to a man who answers.*) Eighty! And look how strong he is. That's how we are. We smoke, we drink, we die in the arms of our wives. Have one.

Daniel   *doesn't move.*

Pintilje   So now I understand everything. He didn't order you to build the dam, he didn't order you to return, he didn't order you to give up smoking.

Daniel   I'd struggled for years to give up. When he said what he said I was able to. That's all.

Pintilje   So you are free to do as you choose? Good. Then as an aquaintance, even a friend, I invite you. Join me.

Daniel *takes a cigarette, puts it back.*

Daniel   All right. He ordered me to give up smoking.

Pintilje   At last we know who we are. One of our enemies gives you an order, you obey. Now I'm ordering you. (*Silence.*) How is little Sally? You don't know. You've had no news for one, two weeks. Let me see your eyes. Show them to me!

After a moment, he speaks to the **Guard** *who offers* **Daniel** *a cigarette.* **Daniel** *doesn't move.*

Daniel   Why are you doing this?

Pintilje   You believe if you smoke your daughter dies? Is that what you believe?

Daniel *takes a cigarette, lights it, coughs, chokes, stubs it out. Silence.*

Pintilje   And we are the ignorant savages. We behave without logic, without reason. Take one! Smoke it! Do it!

Daniel *takes a cigarette.*

Pintilje   Put it in your mouth!

Daniel *puts it in his mouth.*

Pintilje   Must I tell you everything?

Daniel (*he takes the cigarette out of his mouth*)   I thought my daughter was dying. I could do nothing. The one time of my life I really needed to be strong –

Pintilje   You were weak. Be weak again. For me.

Daniel   I do not believe if I smoke she'll die.

Pintilje   It's what you wrote. Look! But if you don't believe it, do it! Why not?

Daniel   All he said to me . . . It was a metaphor. I was enslaved by a wrong way of looking at the world. By guilt. By habits of mind that were stale. I was blind. He showed me my life's in my own hands. All I had to do is take control of one, even one part, not do one thing I long to do, sacrifice even one thing . . . and I'll be free. He helped me. Why did I come back? To thank him. No. That's only part of it. I came because . . . (*Silence.*) What did I write there? (*Silence.*) Where's the fucking thing? (*He takes the cigarette from the* **Guard***, tries to light it.*) Cheap tobacco. (*He lights it.*) Oh God. I can do it. I'm free. (*He struggles to bring the cigarette to his lips, throws it down.*) It's no good. You'll have to shoot me.

Pintilje   You? Not you.

He speaks to the **Guard** *who goes out. He comes in pushing a* **Prisoner** *with a sack over his head.* **Pintilje** *shouts at the* **Prisoner***, shouts again. The* **Guard** *hits the* **Prisoner***, shouts at him.*
The **Prisoner** *exposes his upper body.* **Pintilje** *speaks. The* **Prisoner** *takes his shirt off.* **Pintilje** *speaks, then shouts. The* **Prisoner** *lets his trousers fall.*

Pintilje   God is great. Don't you think so? Look what he made. Strong. Beautiful. He is going to die for what he's done. Maybe you can save him. (*He points the pistol at the* **Prisoner***.*) One, two, three.

He speaks. The **Guard** *puts a cigarette in* **Daniel***'s mouth, ignites the lighter.*

Pintilje   One. Oh, my friend, it would be just one tiny sin. Don't you know, a man can commit a thousand and even so God says 'Come over here, beloved, sit on the side of the sheep'. Two. These men, one of these, maybe this one, went to my village, killed my sons, my Peter, my Karoli.

Daniel   Why?

Pintilje   Why?

Daniel   Why did they kill them?

Pintilje   I'm only their father. Why ask me? You build a dam. There's fighting. They must die. Now so must he. Do you want to see him?

He speaks to the **Guard** *who pulls the sack off the* **Prisoner**'s *head. It is* **Takic**. *He has been badly beaten.*
Gunfire nearby.

Daniel   Jesus.

Pintilje   You know him? Is he a good man? What did he do in his life? Did he curse his mother? Did he envy his neighbour? Did he steal? Did he commit adultery?

Takic (*to* **Daniel**)   Hey! You! Rabbit! Rabbit! You like live in mountain! (*He laughs. He rubs his crotch.*) Old man. Old man. This is old man. What you got for him?

Pintilje *speaks to the* **Guard** *who ignites the lighter.*

Pintilje   Myself I long to love everybody. In my heart is room for the world. Who do you love? Your daughter and that's it. One, two ... One, two ... Please. Do it. My sons are dead. Your daughter is alive. Why should your people live and we die? Let her die too. Let everyone die. Smoke. Do it!

A long silence. **Daniel** *takes cigarettes and lighter from the* **Guard**, *lights one, gives it to* **Pintilje**. *He lights another. He smokes. The gunfire stops. The wind continues to blow.*

Pintilje   So now she is dead. Now we're equal. Both childless, both alone. Good. So, tell me about science. You are a geologist, yes? The earth will last forever. Is that true? I think no. I think the earth is a piece of God's shit. Dry. Hard. Flying through space. Which is dark, which is empty. Except for the wind.

The phone rings. After a moment the **Guard** *answers it. He speaks to* **Pintilje**. *There is hubbub among the men.*

Takic *begins to sing a jubilant song. The men join in.* **Pintilje** *shoots* **Takic**.

Pintilje   What could I do? I always hated the way they sing.

Scene Seven

The square. Everything is covered in snow.
Daniel *sits at the only table peeling fruit.* **Rosa** *watches him.*
Cathy *runs on wrapped in warm clothes.*
Rosa *goes.*

Cathy You're not surprised to see me? (*Silence.*) The
ambassador's man is waiting by the church in his car. The
roads are terrible. He wants to drive back at once in case
there's more snow. (*Silence.*) You must be freezing.

She takes off her coat, puts it round his shoulders. He doesn't move.

They've been very good all the time you were here, kept
me in touch, phoned at least twice a day. You were in all
the papers. Do you want to see?

She opens her bag. He doesn't move. She closes it.
Rosa *comes on with a plate of food, puts it on the table.* **Daniel**
says a few words to her.

Daniel In fact they're closed.

Cathy Oh?

Daniel Nothing reopens until Easter.

Rosa (*to* **Cathy**) Eat. Eat.

Cathy (*she hesitates, then eats*) Oh . . . I remember this. Are
you the cook? It's delicious. As good as last time.

Nico *comes on carrying parcels.* **Rosa** *goes to him, takes the
parcels, embraces and kisses him.*

Nico You see how she loves me? As your wife loves you.
(*To* **Cathy**.) I told him you would come. How long will
you stay? It's nice and peaceful. Stay for ever, why not?
We have mountains, we have the sea. (*He laughs.*)

Cathy Thank you for looking after him.

Nico Or are you leaving at once? You are a kind
woman. You will be gentle with him. (*He speaks to* **Rosa**.
She laughs. He laughs.) Forgive us. We have only been back
together three days.

His arms round her, teasing her, they go in.

Daniel (*silence*)   When? When did she die?

Cathy   Who told you? Was it the embassy? I asked them not to!

Daniel   I didn't want to smoke. I wanted to. He made me. I had to. I didn't have to. What does it matter, want, not want? I did. (*Silence.*) It was night. A bird was singing. It was before the snow. I had a cigarette. It was four days ago. When did she die? Tell me.

Cathy   Two weeks ago. You'd hardly left. You left on a Thursday. She died the next day. In the morning.

Daniel   What must I do?

Cathy   Come with me.

Soldiers wander on with empty beer bottles. They shout for beer.

Daniel   Something odd. I've forgotten her name. Sara? Sophie? (*He laughs.*) I'll tell you something funny. We had this idea to build a dam. A dam! What can you hold back? Nothing!

Rosa *comes out and refuses to sell beer to the soldiers. They argue.*

Daniel   Sally! Sally!

He weeps. The soldiers jeer at him and throw stones.

Cathy (*to the soldiers*)   Stop it! Stop it! Leave him alone! I'll kill you!

The soldiers and **Rosa** *go.*

Cathy   We'll stay. Is that what you want? We can do anything we want to do. There's a plane back to London at midnight. We could get it. Shall we? Let's, Danny. What did you say? I didn't hear what you said. Speak more clearly.

The sound of the sea.

Scene Eight

On top of the mountain.
Daniel *sits smoking.* **Cathy***'s coat lies on the ground at his side.*
He watches **Dusja** *as she washes plates and cups in a tin bath full
of water. She wears black.*
Yosip *comes on with a pan of hot water. He pours it into the bath.*

Yosip   People sometimes ask me: how is it possible that at
the top of a mountain there can be a well.

Daniel   The pressure in these meso-toleaelic ranges
produces an exceptionally high water table. If fissures
occur, as they frequently do, water forces its way to the
surface.

Yosip   My answer is this. (*He makes a gesture.*) It can be
interpreted many ways. What it means is: 'How do I
know?'

He speaks to **Dusja**. *She replies and goes.*

Yosip   You say you lack wisdom.

Daniel   Yes.

Yosip   But wish to find it.

Daniel   I do.

Yosip (*silence*)   The reason the earth will be lost to us is
that every day fewer and fewer of us know it, know the
earth on which they walk and work and sleep. (*Of the bath.*)
How much life is in there? Oh, but you are an expert on
the earth. Forgive me. I have a bad habit. I tell everyone
who comes here more or less the same thing. Sometimes I
am caught out. (*He laughs.*)

Daniel   Tell me the truth. Was it my fault?

Yosip   Yes. Was what your fault? Don't answer. It was.
Especially the fighting. But for the dam there would have
been no fighting. But for you there would have been no
dam.

Daniel No. If I hadn't done the work someone else would have.

Yosip But it was you! Today! Hundreds of years ago! So it is your fault! It was quite right what you told me the first time we met. The world would be a better place if you were never born. Did you say that? I can't remember now. Was that you?

Dusja *comes in with a tray: tea pot, cake tin, bottle of jam. She puts it down, sets out the cups and plates, sits next to* **Yosip**, *pours tea.*

Yosip How long since you had food?

Daniel A week.

Yosip That's long enough. You take everything much too far. Eat. It's only tea. What good can it do?

Dusja *speaks.* **Yosip** *laughs.*

Yosip I don't know why but she won't change her mind. She doesn't like you and that's that.

Dusja *takes a cup to* **Daniel**. *She sticks out her tongue at him, goes back to* **Yosip**. **Daniel** *drinks.*

Yosip My word, you can drink it so hot? Won't you scald your tongue? (*He laughs.*) I'm glad you were here long enough to see the first signs of spring. The wind is cold but you get an impression of how lush it will be in summer.

Daniel Let me stay and see it.

Yosip (*angry*) You were told to go. You must leave in (*Checks his watch.*) half an hour. Is this a social visit? Am I your friend?

Daniel You are my friend.

Yosip You see? Why stay longer? You have learnt nothing. I am your enemy. (*Silence.*) This is the first day for weeks she hasn't wept for her father. Isn't that good? If she had a slice of cake it would be even better. (*He opens the tin.*) Oh, my goodness. (*He cuts slices.*) It's a little dry. But we have jam. Not much. Never mind. Rosa will bring more.

Yosip *and* **Dusja** *eat.* **Daniel** *is still smoking.*

Daniel   If I stay I can help you. I can try to do for you what her father did.

Yosip   You help me? I asked you to do one thing: give up smoking. (*He sighs deeply. He looks at his watch.*) Shall we try a different way? (*He has two pieces of cake on a plate. He holds up one.*) Do you know what this is? Hold out your hand. (*He puts it on* **Daniel**'s *hand.*) It is all created being. It is everything that has ever been created. It is in your hand. Do you believe me?

Daniel   I do.

Yosip   Oh wait, I've made a mistake. (*He changes the pieces of cake.*) That's it. Now you have the right one. Good.

He watches **Daniel** *for a moment, then gathers together papers and books. He starts to go.*

Daniel   But what must I do?

Yosip   Are you cold?

Daniel   Yes.

Yosip   Then put on your coat. (*He goes.*)

Daniel *stands for a moment, then he laughs. Laughing he goes to the coat, starts to put it on. Then he understands. He stops, takes off the coat, folds it carefully over his arm. He starts to go, turns, sees* **Dusja**, *goes towards her, holding out his hand.*
Before he reaches her, **Rosa** *calls, off.* **Dusja** *shouts excitedly.*
Rosa *comes on holding a basket. She kisses* **Dusja**, *then, chatting with her, she lays a rug on the ground. She and* **Dusja** *sit on it.* **Rosa** *takes out bottles of jam, puts them down.*
Daniel *watches as* **Rosa** *takes a brightly wrapped box from her basket, gives it to* **Dusja**. **Dusja** *takes off the wrapping, removes the lid, starts to take out pieces of tissue paper.*
Feeling the cold, **Daniel** *puts on his coat.*

Appendix

*The dialogue below should be translated into whatever language —
real, invented, or a combination of the two — is used to represent the
language of the part of 'the Balkans' where the play takes place.*

pg 221.

Nico *speaks harshly to* **Takic**:

Nico   What are you looking for here? There's nothing for
you. Go back where you belong.

pg 223.

Takic *speaks.* **Nico** *argues with him:*

Takic   His heart is hurting. I can see it.

Nico   He's here. Then he goes. That's it.

Takic   His heart is crying. Can't you hear it?

Nico   Go away! You always cause trouble. This is nothing
to do with you.

Nico *translates:*

Nico   He himself doesn't know how he feels. He thinks
his pain belongs to someone else.

Takic *speaks:*

Takic   Tell him not to worry. I'll take care of him.

Takic *speaks:*

Takic   You can persuade him better than me. Tell him
to trust me.

Takic *speaks:*

Takic   Tell him if he doesn't come with me he'll die of
sorrow.

pg 235.

Takic *speaks to* **Dusja:**

Takic   Do it. Now. Don't be frightened.

pg 237.

Nico *speaks to* **Rosa:**

Nico   Get him something to cover himself.

pg 241.

Pintilje *shouts at him* (**the Old Man**):

Pintilje   What are you crying for? It doesn't hurt you. I'm the dentist. I'll tell you if it hurts you.

pg 242.

He (**Pintilje**) *calls* **Rosa:**

Pintilje   Put his suitcases in my car. Make sure you lock it properly.

Nico *calls to* **Takic** ... *They talk:*

Nico   Did you do what we arranged? Tell the truth.

Takic   They never do what they say they'll do. I waited for him, he didn't come.

Nico   He says you robbed him. You took his shirt, his money.

Takic   This is the first time I've seen him since we saw him together right here.

pg 243.

Takic *speaks:*

Takic   Every word he speaks is a lie.

Nico *speaks.* **Takic** *answers:*

Nico   Did you take him up the mountain or not?

Takic   I swear on my child's life.

Nico   Then how does he know you have a child?

Takic (*laughs*)   Who doesn't? Every man has got one.

The men shout out as they watch:

Men   Give him one! Look, he can fight! Hit him! Hit him!

Takic *speaks. Everyone bursts out laughing:*

Takic   He accuses me of robbing him. But it wasn't me who stole his cock, that I promise you.

Takic *speaks. Everyone laughs again:*

Takic   His wife carries it in her handbag. That's why he's so keen to find her again.

Yosip *speaks. Everyone laughs:*

Yosip   Few men know what they are looking for. But if you are right, he knows.

pg 244.

Pintilje *speaks:*
Pintilje   A goat walks into the kitchen. What does he do? He shits on the floor. Never mind. There's plenty of room in the oven. (*They laugh.*) I'm taking him off to the oven. (*They laugh.*)

pg 245.

He (**Yosip**) *shouts to the men:*

Yosip   See if you can catch up with them. Bring them back. Try.

pg 260.

Nico *asks. The man answers:*

Nico   He asks when the snow will fall.

Man   Can't you hear the wind? Tomorrow.

pg 261.

Nico *laughs, tells the men:*

Nico   He's heard it. He's not a fool, this one.

Some of the men shout at the **Guard***:*

Men   You've got to put us somewhere safer. Or let us go! Let us go!

Guard   They're your people. You tell them to stop! You tell them!

pg 262.

Men   Let us go and we'll tell them! Let us go!

Three men dash forward shouting:

Men   Don't hurt him! Be gentle with them! Why are you hurting them? They are your brothers! They are your brothers!

The **Guard** *points his rifle at the men and shouts at them:*

Guard   Shut up! Hands behind your heads!

The **Guard** *shouts at them:*

Guard   Shut up! Shut up! Keep quiet!

pg 263.

Soldiers *run into the room. They shout:*

Soldiers   Stand up! Stand up! Put your hands behind your heads!

*He (***Pintilje***) speaks to the* **Soldiers***:*

Pintilje   They need you outside. Go.

*He (***Pintilje***) speaks to the* **Guard***:*

Pintilje   This isn't mine. Bring me mine.

He barks orders:

Pintilje   No! Let them stay where they are! Do as I told you! Fool!

He ... shouts at the **Guard***:*

Pintilje   Fetch me my coat! Get it wrong again, I'll shoot you.

pg 264.

Pintilje ... *speaks* (*into the phone*)*:*

Pintilje   Yes. Yes. Yes. Good. Do it.

pg 266.

He speaks to the **Guard** *who answers:*

Pintilje   Have they eaten?

Guard   There's no food for them.

He speaks to the **Guard** *who answers:*

Pintilje   You have plenty of coffee.

Guard   We were given none.

pg 267.

*He (***Pintilje***) speaks to the* **Guard** *who ...*

Pintilje   You have cigarettes? Give them to me.

He speaks to a man who answers:

Pintilje   How many do you smoke a day?

Man   Eighty.

pg 268.

*He (***Pintilje***) speaks to the* **Guard** *who ...*

Pintilje   Give him one.

pg 269.

He speaks to the **Guard** *who goes out:*

Pintilje   Bring one of those shits in here.

Appendix 281

Pintilje *shouts at the* **Prisoner**, *shouts again:*

Pintilje Take off your shirt! Bastard! Do what I tell you!

The **Guard** . . . *shouts at him:*

Guard Do what you're told, pig's turd!

Pintilje *speaks:*

Pintilje Take it off!

Pintilje *speaks, then shouts:*

Pintilje And your trousers. Do it or I'll kill you!

He speaks:

Pintilje Put a cigarette in his mouth. Light it.

pg 270.

He speaks to the **Guard***:*

Pintilje Pull that sack off him.

Pintilje *speaks to the* **Guard** *who ignites . . .*

Pintilje Light the cigarette.

He (the **Guard***) speaks to* **Pintilje***.*

Guard They say they can't hold them back.

pg 272.

The **Soldiers** *jeer at him:*

Soldiers He needs something to put in his mouth to keep him quiet. Who's got something for him? Something big. Something soft. Something sharp. I've got it. I've got something for him here.

pg 273.

*He (***Yosip***) speaks to* **Dusja**. *She replies:*

Yosip I'm ready for tea as soon as you are.

Dusja I'll fetch it, uncle.

pg 274.

Dusja *speaks:*

Dusja   Why is he so ugly and stupid? Are all his people as ugly as he is?

pg 275.

Rosa *calls, off:*

Rosa   Dusja! Dusja! Where are you? I'm coming.

Dusja *shouts excitedly:*

Dusja   She's coming! She's coming! Hurry! Hurry! I want to see you!

They play and chatter together:

Dusja   Did you bring my present?

Rosa   Yes, I've got it, don't worry.

Dusja   What is it? Let me see, let me see.

Rosa   I'll show you. Let me get my breath. I'm tired from climbing so far.

Dusja   I didn't cry. I've been good. So let me see it.

Rosa   You didn't cry. Good girl.

Dusja   Is it big or is it small?

Rosa   Wait.

Dusja   Hurry!

Rosa   Here it is.

Dusja   Oh. Oh.

Rosa   Open it. Go on.

Methuen Modern Plays
include work by

Methuen Student Editions

John Arden	*Serjeant Musgrave's Dance*
Alan Ayckbourn	*Confusions*
Aphra Behn	*The Rover*
Edward Bond	*Lear*
Bertolt Brecht	*The Caucasian Chalk Circle*
	Life of Galileo
	Mother Courage and her Children
Anton Chekhov	*The Cherry Orchard*
Caryl Churchill	*Top Girls*
Shelagh Delaney	*A Taste of Honey*
John Galsworthy	*Strife*
Robert Holman	*Across Oka*
Henrik Ibsen	*A Doll's House*
Charlotte Keatley	*My Mother Said I Never Should*
Bernard Kops	*Dreams of Anne Frank*
Federico García Lorca	*Blood Wedding*
John Marston	*The Malcontent*
Willy Russell	*Blood Brothers*
Wole Soyinka	*Death and the King's Horseman*
August Strindberg	*The Father*
J. M. Synge	*The Playboy of the Western World*
Oscar Wilde	*The Importance of Being Earnest*
Tennessee Williams	*A Streetcar Named Desire*
Timberlake Wertenbaker	*Our Country's Good*